Creative Approaches in Foreign Language Teaching

Selected Papers from the 1992 Central States Conference

Edited by

William N. Hatfield
Purdue University, West Lafayette, Indiana

Coeditors

Mary Carr
Lawrence North High School, Indianapolis, Indiana

Michael Oates
University of Northern Iowa, Cedar Falls

National Textbook Company
a division of *NTC Publishing Group* • Lincolnwood, Illinois USA

Published by National Textbook Company, a division of NTC Publishing Group.
©1992 by NTC Publishing Group, 4255 West Touhy Avenue,
Lincolnwood (Chicago), Illinois 60646-1975 U.S.A.
All rights reserved. No part of this book may be reproduced, stored
in a retrieval system, or transmitted in any form or by any means,
electronic, mechanical, photocopying, recording or otherwise, without
the prior permission of NTC Publishing Group.
Manufactured in the United States of America.

2 3 4 5 6 7 8 9 0 VP 9 8 7 6 5 4 3 2 1

**CENTRAL STATES CONFERENCE ON THE
TEACHING OF FOREIGN LANGUAGES**

Board of Directors, 1991-92

Gale Crouse, Chair, Board of Directors (FY93)
Diane Ging, Vice-Chair, Board of Directors (FY93)
Jody Thrush, Executive Director (FY92)
Luz Berd, Recording Secretary (FY92)
Emily Spinelli, Program Chair (FY92)
Donald Spinelli, Assistant Program Chair (FY92)
Anne Nerenz, Local Chair (FY92)
William N. Hatfield, Editor, *CSC Reports* (FY92)
Valorie Babb, JNCL/NCLIS Delegate (FY92)
Philip J. Campana, ACTFL Executive Council Delegate (CY91-94)
Leslie Caye, Director (FY92)
Leon Book, Director (FY92)
Toni Theisen, Director (FY93)
Emily Spinelli, Director (FY93)
Dave McAlpine, Director (FY93)
Marilyn Gordon, Director (FY94)
Alan Garfinkel, Director (FY94)
Dorothea Bruschke, Director (FY94)
Paul Hoekstra, Director (FY95)

Preface

By most indications, 1992 will be remembered as a benchmark year. Two events in particular provided the impetus for reflection on our changing world and the approaching twenty-first century and third millennium: the 500th anniversary of the encounter of the civilizations of Europe and the Americas and the beginnings of a Europe united within an economic community. These events helped shape the theme and focus for the twenty-fourth annual Central States Conference held in Dearborn, Michigan, in conjunction with the Michigan Foreign Language Association.

The conference theme "Unity through Diversity" provided the organizing principle for the conference program. That theme stressed the idea that differences in language, culture, and ethnicity are not barriers to the achievement of harmony, solidarity, and global understanding. It is hoped that the theme "Unity through Diversity" will remain even after the conference has ended and will become a goal of all foreign language education.

The challenge of obtaining unity through diversity was explored in a number of theme-related sessions, workshops, and panels at the 1992 Conference. Articulation, nontraditional students, nontraditional teaching locations and methods, diversity of students and course content, and less commonly taught languages were some of the major topics explored in 137 sessions, 29 workshops, and 2 panels. Both the keynote speaker, Harold L. Hodgkinson, and the Conference Luncheon speaker, John DeMado, spoke to the issue of meeting the educational needs of our increasingly diverse student populations.

It is believed that the 1992 Central States Conference offered a variety of interesting topics for a broad range of foreign language professionals. The conference also continued in its tradition of providing a forum for the investigation and discussion of major issues facing our profession and furnished ideas for the implementation of solutions to the problems that challenge us.

Emily Spinelli
1992 Program Chair

Contents

Introduction   William N. Hatfield   ix

1. **Flesh Out Your FLES Program: Developmental Sequencing in Teaching Units**   1
   Zoe Louton, Robert Louton

2. **Lights! Camera! Action! . . . Using the Camcorder as a Tool, Not a Toy**   11
   John Liontas

3. **The Yorktown High School Foreign Language Interactive Videodisc Project**   25
   Barbara Underwood, Karen Brammer, Rocco Fuschetto, Sigrid Koehler, Jack Jorden, James Mervilde

4. **Literature: A Rich Resource for Teaching Language and Culture in Context**   32
   Aleidine Moeller

5. **A Case for Cooperative Learning in the Foreign Language Classroom**   50
   Susan Colville-Hall

6. **Exploring Cross-Cultural Reading Processes: Beyond Literal Comprehension**   64
   Naomi Ono, Martha Nyikos

7. **Motivating Unenthusiastic Foreign Language Students: Meeting the Challenge**   81
   Christine Campbell

8. **Teaching the Working Adult and Retiree: Considerations for the Nontraditional Classroom** 92
Jennifer L. Knerr

9. **Learner-Initiated and Learner-Friendly: Questions to Get Them Talking** 110
Gregory K. Armstrong

10. **High School, College, and University Articulation: The Renewed Crisis in Foreign Language Instruction** 115
Barbara Gonzalez Pino

11. **The Impact of Site-Based Management and School-Based Teacher Training on Foreign Language Education** 129
Audrey Heining-Boynton

12. **The Cooperative Curriculum Development Project** 120
David McAlpine, Gayle Yeska

13. **Evaluating Communicative Risks and Achievements for Students Abroad** 156
Philippa B. Yin

14. **The Popular Song: An Authentic Tool for Enriching the Foreign Language Classroom** 168
Jayne Abrate

Introduction:
Creative Approaches in Foreign Language Teaching

William N. Hatfield
Purdue University

The 1992 CSC theme, "Unity through Diversity," and the title of this volume, *Creative Approaches in Foreign Language Teaching*, bear a clear family resemblance. Just as a perusal of the session titles in the conference program demonstrates a broader range of professional foci than ever, likewise does a glance at the table of contents of this volume illustrate the attention paid to divergent polestars in foreign language teaching. The search for truth continues and is perhaps partially revealed in the fourteen articles that were selected for publication this year. The 1992 *Report* is, on purpose, a collection designed to appeal to a broad readership. The scope of topics includes basic language teaching in elementary school as well as unusual configurations in adult and retiree instruction; controlled research as well as almost conversational-style presentations on how to motivate students to participate; the new technology of videodiscs and camcorders as well as very practical advice on how to hold students responsible for specific learning tasks in study-abroad programs.

Zoe and Robert Louton draw from Piaget's theories of learning to lay the groundwork for developmentally appropriate FLES teaching. Foreign language instruction parallels the regular classroom content and focuses on involving the pupil physically, cognitively, and emotionally. A sample lesson plan is included to illustrate the process.

John Liontas talks about the exciting success achieved with the camcorder when students themselves are actively involved in the planning and carrying out of instructional units. Participation and learning are enhanced when their tasks grow out of concrete and immediate communication needs. The author provides many video activities that add a large measure of variety to the activity.

In their article about the videodisc project in the Yorktown (Indiana) High School, Barbara Underwood, Karen Brammer, Rocco Fuschetto, Sigrid Koehler, Jack Jorden, and James Mervilde detail the events that involved their faculty with IVD, the planning and implementation of their program, and the benefits that have accrued to the students. Often a frustrating but always a rewarding experience for these foreign language teachers, their model may serve as an inspiration for others.

Drawing from reading theory and current research, Aleidine Moeller presents arguments for including literary texts in all levels of foreign language instruction and offers interactive teaching strategies based on discovery techniques that encourage students to encode their own personal meanings derived from the texts studied. Through literature, students become aware of cultural information that is essential for full participation in a literate community.

In her article on cooperative learning, Susan Colville-Hall presents a rationale for the approach in foreign language classes. Looking to the future and the skills our youth will need to be productive members of society, she argues for classroom techniques based on group efforts that will help to build interdependent relationships among students and eventually among nations and societies. She offers some suggestions for specific classroom techniques.

Drawing on principles from psycholinguistic and transactional theories of reading comprehension, Martha Nyikos and Naomi Ono describe a research project with Japanese students to determine learners' reading strategies and ways of using their cultural background knowledge for comprehension. Reading selections were American short stories written in English with varying degrees of cultural proximity to the Japanese culture, which permitted the researchers to explore how cultural schemata influence students' reading comprehension.

Christine Campbell reviews the research in motivation of foreign language students beginning with the work of Gardner and Lambert in the late 1950s and concluding with the work of Macnamara in more recent times. She elaborates thirteen techniques that have proved successful in involving students actively in the foreign language learning process.

Teaching adult students and retirees presents particular challenges in methodology, goal setting, and meeting the learning needs of these special students. Jennifer L. Knerr offers practical techniques to deal with problems such as hearing, vision, memory, motivation, purpose, age, and fatigue, among others, that are often found in the advanced-age student.

Gregory K. Armstrong shares techniques that are designed to allow students to take more control of their learning in a foreign language class by focusing on the skills needed to raise a student from a novice to intermediate level speaker on the ACTFL Guidelines. Drawing from his personal experience, he describes ways to move from a teacher-centered to a student-centered classroom and reports improved student motivation and achievement.

The never-ending problem of articulation between high school and university foreign language programs is examined carefully by Barbara Gonzalez Pino. Using questionnaires to gather information from recent high school graduates enrolled in foreign language classes in universities in Texas, and foreign language supervisors at both levels, she identified specific problems of transition between those levels of instruction. Results show that placement practices vary widely and are magnified by the 1000 school districts and more than 200 colleges and universities in the state of Texas.

Audrey Heining-Boynton discusses site-based management and school-based teacher training, focusing in detail on the Wake County, North Carolina, teacher-training project. She points to significant advantages and disadvantages and the implications these concepts may have on foreign language education in the United States.

David McAlpine and Gayle Yeska describe a cooperative curriculum development project carried out in Iowa. Mandated by the Iowa legislature in 1988, all school districts were required to establish an ongoing needs assessment and five-year plan to achieve their identified educational goals. The authors detail the many steps and procedures required to carry out the project.

In order to benefit from study abroad, students need to be prepared properly by their program director before departure. Philippa B. Yin proposes that their social behavior, language competence, and general communication patterns be evaluated and appropriate activities planned to help students improve their communicative competence. To this end, she presents varied task lists to guide them and to provide the basis for subsequent assessment of their skill development.

Jayne Abrate discusses the role of popular music in the classroom. She points out the rich and diverse sources of cultural information contained in this medium in addition to the obvious benefits to language skill development. She suggests how to select and prepare song texts, how to organize listening comprehension and pronunciation exercises, and how to deal with grammar, vocabulary, reading, and speaking tasks growing out of the cultural context of the song.

These articles, while representative of the overall tone and content of the 1992 Central States Conference, are but samples of the many outstanding sessions given by dedicated professionals on many different topics of current concern. Achieving unity through diversity is a difficult task, but this conference has accepted the challenge.

Acknowledgments

The work of compiling this volume was made easier by the contributions of the following, who read and evaluated the papers submitted for inclusion. My sincere thanks go to Linda Albertson, Eagan High School, Eagan, Minnesota; Marge Artzer, Northern Kentucky University; James Becker, University of Northern Iowa; Leslie Caye, Anoka-Henentin School, Coon Rapids, Minnesota; Lynn Haire, Ferndale Public Schools, Plymouth, Minnesota; Mary Ann Kollros, Sacred Heart Academy, Louisville, KY; Andi Laidlaw, Community High School, Ann Arbor, Michigan; Moira McCluny, Wartburg College, Waverly, Iowa; Sandy Nyhus, Clear Lake High School, Clear Lake, Iowa; Cathy Olson, St. Paul Academy and Summit School, St. Paul, Minnesota; John Sheridan, Waukegan High School, Waukegan, Illinois; Ron Walker, Colorado State University.

I want to express my special and warm thanks to my coeditors, Mary Carr, Lawrence North High School, Indianapolis, Indiana, and Michael Oates, University of Northern Iowa. They were responsible for obtaining their teams of readers and making sure that deadlines were met. Their excellent and timely reading and critiquing of all the manuscripts was most helpful in the selection and final editing of the articles for this volume. Their professionalism is worthy of note and the frank but gentle advice they offered made this task easier and considerably more enjoyable than it might otherwise have been.

1
Flesh Out Your FLES Program:
Developmental Sequencing in Teaching Units

Zoe E. Louton
Filley Schools, Filley, Nebraska
Robert E. Louton
Blue Valley Mental Health Center, Beatrice, Nebraska
University of Nebraska, Lincoln

FLES specialists, chronically in need of curriculum material, turn increasingly to the academic content of the core curriculum (Crandall and Tucker 1990). At any grade level the core curriculum provides a rich and varied source of meaningful material and a touchstone to validate that material. In order to increase both the consistency and the scope of the curriculum, the classroom teacher and the foreign language specialist should integrate the foreign language instruction into the classroom content so as to achieve some degree of parallel instruction. Such a partnership is ideal for achieving the maximum potential in a foreign language program. It helps provide "real" subject matter and materials to aid the pupils' advance to higher levels of reading, writing, and general application of the foreign language. It encourages pupils to see broader applications of the foreign language instruction to their daily lives. It facilitates articulating the foreign language curriculum with the regular classes. Some caution is required, however, when developing lesson plans for materials taken from a content area.

One risk that is apparent is the tendency to water down the instruction in the foreign language. This can be avoided if the classroom teacher first presents the subject at the appropriate grade level in English. The foreign language teacher may then focus on selected parts of the unit to review and reinforce in the target language. A second concern is to maintain the integrity of the instructional goals of the unit. For example, "Simplifying the vocabulary . . . should not result in concept simplification" (Curtain and Martinez 1990, p. 208). These concerns should not discourage the foreign language specialist from developing content units. Material can indeed be watered down and superficial when the foreign language teacher is attempting merely to add on the language rather than internalize the language.

2   Creative Approaches in Foreign Language Teaching

There is a lag in foreign language acquisition between learning the words and getting the music; a clue to the solution may lie in the developmental origins of language itself. In language instruction this means that if there is no depth of feeling for and understanding of the subject, the words are essentially meaningless and hollow. A way to flesh out the FLES program is to acknowledge this acquisition lag through cooperative development of teaching units by the classroom teacher and the foreign language teacher.

The rationale used to develop foreign language teaching units must take into account the natural whole context in which language is acquired as well as the apparent lag in getting the "music" with the "words." The procedures described here sketch out a bare-bones theoretical orientation based on the work of Piaget, then focus on one element of foreign language instruction that we call the Language Acquisition Gap (LAG), and suggest the type and timing of teaching unit applications.

Theoretical Orientation

For anyone attempting to read the works of Piaget there is a nearly overwhelming awareness that his descriptions often do not fall into neat categories nor do his terms lend themselves easily to definition. Piaget's elegant theory basically states that we assimilate bits of information, compile and sort them, and then place the clustered information into a new or different organization (Flavell 1963). One product of accommodation, the "schema," is basically an operational term related to an action and is independent of the various stages of development. Examples include "sucking" and "throwing." The development of these schemata is not dependent upon any particular stage of development, which means that they can be just as easily defined or developed during the formal operational stage as during the sensory-motor stage of learning. A label such as "speaking" or "dancing" attached to a schema is the short-cut symbol for a whole set of discrete actions.

During the initial stage of sensory-motor activity the child's entire system is engaged in symbolic play, creative imagination, reproductive imagination, representative imitation, and intuition. These translate into operational activities through constructional games and reflective imitation. External and internal activities also contribute to language symbols representing a thing or action. Piaget (1962) describes the process in which the external activity of "imitation is linked with that of representation" (p. 5), which is internal. The logical extension of the internalized representation of objects and operations is that of accumulated symbols that make up language. And, not surprisingly, language is the symbolic representation of objects, schemata, and operations. Piaget powerfully describes the dynamics of images by noting that an image "is the result of a construction akin to that which produces the schemata of intelligence" (p. 70). We are led to the next logical step, in which the images and symbols of language are not merely add-ons but are an integrated and inseparable property of the whole person. The process of language acquisition begins during the earliest stages of the sensori-motor development and expands through formal operational thinking. Since each image, symbol, and schema is the result of the accommodative process, however, each has a considerable set of actions, perceptions, and other elements that have gone into its creation. This raises a particularly difficult question: What is the process of symbol substitution? How might this affect foreign language acquisition?

Language Acquisition Gap

The hypothesis is that, without exploring symbolic denotation and symbolic connotation, rote memory function can easily allow for symbol substitution. To this extent "hund," "hound," and "chien" are denotatively interchangeable. On the other hand, when dealing with connotative elements in which multiple clusters of meanings, emotional experiences, and physical associations are knotted together, the connections shift to internalized symbols and away from rote memory. During the classroom instruction the teacher, working toward concept development in the native language, calls upon the full range of the students' experiences and comprehension. In the foreign language class, however, the language symbols are "new" to the nervous system, which provides little on which the students can hang these symbols. This results in acquisition of the foreign language with its meaning and concepts lagging behind those of the native or primary language and concept development—a language acquisition gap (LAG).

While developmental lag refers to a slowness in the development of some physical or functional aspect of a child, LAG suggests a rather unique view of foreign language acquisition. There appears to be a significant difference between the "native" and "foreign" language acquisition. The development of the "native" language during the sensorimotor stage progresses from action to accumulated language symbols; the "foreign" language has traditionally been acquired by learning one set of language symbols that are then substituted for the native language symbols in such a way that the basic sensorimotor elements and basic images are not touched. More recent developments in foreign language teaching methods have focused on relating action to language symbols with a great deal of success, but a fundamental gap between first and second language development remains. This gap must be addressed when developing teaching units since the underlying schemata, images, symbols, experiences, and concepts that are available in the native language have not yet been developed in the foreign language.

Teaching Unit Applications

Foreign language is learned best when it is not the purpose of the instruction but rather incidental to the expression of the energies, or drives, the pupil already has. Each unit should be designed to focus on acquiring new learning in the various subject areas and thus capitalize on the innate curiosity that originates from the pupil's sensorimotor stage. The energy of the pupil's drive to learn is like a moving train on which the new foreign language can be loaded and the train and the cargo become one. In addition, the teaching design should maintain motivation, involve the student physically and emotionally, and offer opportunities for challenge, success, discovery, and creativity. Each unit should utilize more than one of the senses and more than one of the acquired skills. Touching and moving at younger ages, and singing and interacting at older ages, are particularly powerful when associated with the language.

Ideally, each teaching unit should be developed in conjunction with the classroom teacher so that the parallel content is maintained. This creates opportunities to generalize not only the language but also the concepts. With the teachers working together, the material remains more or less continuous and self-reinforcing. Since the level of abstraction of the classroom material is already age-appropriate, we may assume that the concepts will not generally present barriers to the pupils' learning in the foreign language. We have learned, however, from Piaget and others, that language symbols get "meaty" only when they have some basic supporting images, schemata, and other elements. How does the teacher then develop the content concept when these language supports have not been acquired at the corresponding level in the foreign language?

The unit in which the concepts are developed in the native language should be presented in a manner or context consistent with the preceding developmental level in the foreign language. Even though the unit is introduced at a preceding developmental level, the concomitant activities practice the concept at the pupils' present age level. For example, a story to illustrate a science concept consistent with the concrete operational stage can be created to appeal to the pre-operational stage. The classroom activities, however, are consistent with the age level. (See Appendix 1A, Sample Lesson Plans.) The concept development is not weakened, but viewed from another perspective. While normal concept development proceeds in the regular classroom, the foreign language instruction uses that development to enhance the new language symbols. This will facilitate connections with materials and experiences already part of the student's internalized and accommodated information.

In order to increase the efficiency of the curriculum, it is reasonable to design teaching units and instructional plans that take advantage of the process of transfer of training. This means that skills acquired in one set of activities can be transferred in whole or in part to other, similar activities. Thus, the art teacher may be instructing the principles of perspective, a skill useful to the science teacher trying to teach notions of planetary retrograde. In a foreign language class, shopping skills or concepts learned in home economics can be applied to similar skills and vocabulary in the foreign language. Another example for the third-grade child might be classroom work with map skills and directionality, which in the FLES class could be transferred to locating places and compass points in the foreign language. In any event, the foreign language teaching unit is most effective when using age-appropriate content presented at a level that induces understanding.

In the FLES program at Filley, Nebraska, original materials and teaching units that appeal to appropriate acquisitional levels and that address the LAG have been developed. For example, in a science unit referred to above, the story appeals to the domain of magical thinking, which would approach more closely the pupils' level of foreign language acquisition skills. The classroom teacher has already taught to the concrete operational level. Many of the units, furthermore, are structured to reflect a whole language perspective, an approach that places language elements in whole contexts. Whole language operates from the view that language has meaning when it is used to accomplish a purpose (Altwerger et al. 1987), and as such will always occur in a situation with a perceived valid purpose. The language itself is not the purpose; it is incidental to the purpose. This view adapts well to the content-based FLES program, where the purpose of the foreign language session is to serve as an extension of the regular subject matter from another perspective. The instruction just happens to be in another language (Cutting 1989). This approach is especially appropriate for foreign language instruction, because it parallels the way children learn their first language.

Second, since whole language develops content themes from whole contexts that range across the curriculum, the child is able to internalize the language in ways approximating schema development. For example, in the science unit the pupil colors the rainbow through a set of physical movements that parallels the movement of light through the prism to produce a rainbow. While the physical actions are occurring, the colors are being labeled in the foreign language, integrating the process as a whole. This is consistent with the process of schema development, where objects are assimilated to the activity as a whole. A further reason for using some features of whole language theory is that it provides a common ground for cooperation among elementary teachers in the system.

For each unit a story is created in the target language around a theme identified by the classroom teacher, and a big book for the text and illustrations is constructed. Individual lesson plans are developed for each page (or two), which are designed to be completed in one or two class sessions, and according to the following structure:

1. Concept: The teacher determines the vocabulary area or content-related skill to be learned from the page.
2. Introduction: The teacher demonstrates the lesson, relates it to the concept, and reads to the pupils from the big book the relevant part of the story.
3. Activities: The pupils apply the concept to appropriate activities that provide "whole contexts" for the new words or skill. Each pupil receives a copy of the page to read and color.
4. Shared language: As a culminating process, the teacher and children sum up and generalize the concept.

At this point in each unit a brief assessment of teacher and student performance is done according to the following four criteria:

1. Acquisition of new vocabulary and increased comprehension: Are the pupils able to understand and discuss in the target language topics covered in the unit?
2. Enhanced performance in other disciplines: How do the pupils' experiences in the foreign language class carry over into other disciplines?
3. Demonstration of newly acquired skills: Are the pupils able to read aloud and individually their copies of the story?
4. Teachers' subjective assessment of the pupils' motivation: Do the pupils maintain a strong interest in the foreign language class sessions?

This ongoing evaluation is an important element in planning and presenting future units, as well as in modifying present instruction (Eggleton 1990). Assessment procedures at this stage of unfolding FLES systems require flexibility and a forgiving structure. As more programs are developed and tested, better questions are expected to emerge. There is an ongoing effort to develop instruments to assess proficiency at the elementary level (Met 1991), but at this time much research is still needed to evaluate pupils' progress in FLES programs.

In addition to assessing teacher/student performances, the FLES program itself and its relationship to the school curriculum needs to be evaluated in such a way as to provide documentation for accountability purposes. It will also serve as a basis for change, continuation, and growth of the program. This need has been addressed by the development of the FLES Program Evaluation Inventory (FPEI). This inventory seeks input from teachers, students, administrators, and parents and results in a global community program rating instrument (Heining Boynton 1990).

Conclusion

A FLES instructional system has been developed in which the core curriculum is a source of material and a touchstone to validate that material. The foreign language specialist and classroom teacher form an ideal partnership for maximizing FLES instruction. This approach may facilitate internalizing the material rather than adding to general native language skills and may overcome the lag between surface elements and internalizing whole meaning.

The theoretical support derives basically from an extension of the work of Piaget and draws on his recognition of how language symbols are developed. Language symbols, which have developed from the process of internal representation of objects and operations, both are sustained by and are frequently labeled as schemata. Thus, the skeleton for language includes actions leading to internalization of symbolic representations, which, in turn, play a major role in forming the whole person. In developing teaching units, the instructor should take advantage of the internalizing process by involving the pupil as a whole: physically, cognitively, and emotionally. The language skeleton is thus fleshed out when the units take advantage of the pupils' innate curiosity and energies, and when the purpose of the instruction becomes language expression rather than language instruction. The instructional mission is achieved when the teaching units appeal to appropriate acquisitional levels and internalize the essential qualities of the foreign language.

References

Altwerger, Bess, Carole Edelsky, and Barbara M. Flores. 1987. "Whole Language: What's New?" *The Reading Teacher* 41: 144–54.

Crandall, Joann, and G. Richard Tucker. 1990. "Content-Based Instruction in Second and Foreign Languages," pp. 187–200 in Amado M. Padilla, Halford H. Fairchild, and Concepcion M. Valadez, eds., *Foreign Language Education: Issues and Strategies*. Newbury Park, CA: Sage.

Curtain, Helena A., and Linda S. Martinez. 1990. "Elementary School, Content-Based Foreign Language Instruction," pp. 201–22 in Amado M. Padilla, Halford H. Fairchild, and Concepcion M. Valadez, eds., *Foreign Language Education: Issues and Strategies*. Newbury Park, CA: Sage.

Cutting, Brian. 1989. *Getting Started in Whole Language*. Bothell, WA: The Wright Group.

Eggleton, Jill. 1990. *Whole Language Evaluation*. Bothell, WA: The Wright Group.

Flavell, John H. 1963. *The Developmental Psychology of Jean Piaget*. New York: Van Nostrand Reinhold.

Heining-Boynton, Audrey L. 1990. "The Development and Testing of the FLES Program Evaluation Inventory." *Modern Language Journal* 74: 432–39.

Met, Myriam. 1991. "Elementary School Foreign Languages: What Research Can and Cannot Tell Us," p. 65 in Ellen S. Silber, ed., *Critical Issues in Foreign Language Instruction*. New York: Garland.

Piaget, Jean. 1962. *Play, Dreams and Imitation in Childhood*, trans. C. Gattegno and F. M. Hodgson. New York: Norton.

8   Creative Approaches in Foreign Language Teaching

Appendix 1A
Sample Lesson Plans

The general design of each instructional unit given in the target language consists of a story and supporting lesson plans. The story communicates the instructional concept. Lesson plans designed for each session include activities, the accumulation of story pages and vocabulary word cards, and shared language. The teacher works from a big book version of the story, presenting it in increments of a page or two for each session. The pupils discuss the text and then move to activities that provide contexts for the new words and content-related concepts. After the activity, each pupil receives a copy of the story page to read and color. (At the end of the unit the accumulated story pages are gathered into a book that is bound and given to the child to keep.) Each lesson closes with shared language, related culminating activities in which the pupils share what they have learned. One activity scheduled for every other lesson involves receiving materials for a "word ring," a set of 1" by 4" cards with a hole punched at the left margin for the insertion of a holding ring. On each card is printed one word of the newly acquired vocabulary. These cards are color coded for parts of speech and gender, if nouns. By the end of the unit the pupils have accumulated word cards they can manipulate in order to practice the new vocabulary.

The following lesson plans are representative pages from a teaching unit in science that presumes a level of language skills beyond the first year or two. The story, *Color, Where Are You?*, is 15 pages in length, each page containing a large illustration and one or two lines of text. The original text is in the target language but is presented in English for the purposes of this paper. The story was devised in response to the classroom teacher's request for reinforcement of the concept of light refraction. It is targeted for fourth and fifth grades, in which the pupils are expected to be well into concrete operational thinking. Recognizing the language acquisitional gap, the story has been designed in such a way as to appeal to preoperational thinking, even magical thinking. The activities, however, reinforce the science concept at the appropriate concrete operational level, touching as well on other areas of the curriculum.

The story line deals simply with light bulb characters of different sizes and shapes symbolizing wavelengths of the color spectrum. One by one the colored bulbs step forward on a stage and are presented to the readers as unique characters. After the presentation the color characters are tossed together in a box (prism), where they lose their individual differences and become white light. Workers try various means to help the individual colors exit the box, succeeding only when they make windows that conform to the size (wavelength) of each color character. As the colors exit, they form a rainbow arc. At the end of the story, children learn that each small water drop can be a color box (prism). Sample lesson plans follow.

Lesson VI Theme: Rainbow Colors

The color characters have been introduced individually on a stage and now stand together receiving applause.

Concept: Self-concept development, accepting differences (social studies)

Flesh Out Your FLES Program 9

Introduction: Teacher models own eye color. Asks for eye colors of various pupils.
Teacher models own hair color. Asks for hair colors of pupils.
Teacher models own skin color and asks for that of pupils.
Teacher asks for pupils' favorite color.
Teacher asks for colors of their favorite foods.
Teacher reads to pupils aloud unit story *Color, Where Are You?*, this time adding the latest pages referred to above where color characters receive applause.

Activity: Pupils make individual rainbows. (The empty sections of the picture of a rainbow are each labeled and colored appropriately, such as eye color, skin color, favorite color, etc.)
Pupils receive and color new story pages covered in this lesson.

Shared Language: Each pupil reports on his/her eye color/hair color/skin color to class or cooperative learning group. Others respond "You are so beautiful" and "I like you." Pupils receive latest cards for word ring (manipulative vocabulary).

Lesson VIII Theme: Rainbow Colors

The color characters have been mixed together in the box (prism). Workers using various tools are trying to get them out.

Concept: Science of mechanics and work (social studies)

Introduction: Discuss and demonstrate tools and what work they do.
Ask what sounds each makes (loud/quiet).
Ask "Where are the colors?" Hold up sack of crayons. Say "There they are. Take out the red crayon." Teacher takes out red crayon. "Take out the blue." Teacher takes out blue crayon.
Teacher reads to pupils aloud unit story *Color, Where Are You?*, this time adding the latest pages referred to above where the workers are trying to get the colors out of the box.

Activity: Hold up sack of crayons again. Call on various pupils. Say "Take out red/blue." Pupil takes out appropriate crayon.
Pupils receive and color new story pages covered in this lesson.

Shared Language: Pupils pass bag to each other, asking the next person to take out a certain color.
Make rainbow name: Pupils write each letter of their names with the colors of the rainbow in sequence. Keep in packet.

Lesson X Theme: Rainbow Colors

Workers make windows of the appropriate size for each color. The color characters exit at the same time, and in so doing create a rainbow.

Concept: Demonstrate the spectrum (science)

Introduction: Review weather vocabulary.
Shine a beam of light on the prism to create a rainbow (use flashlight or filmstrip projector). Say "The colors are coming through their windows from the white light. We are making a rainbow."

10   Creative Approaches in Foreign Language Teaching

                Teacher reads to pupils aloud unit story *Color, Where Are You?*, this time adding the latest pages in this lesson where the characters exit the prism, creating a rainbow.

Activity: Set up activity centers:
1. Hold prism to eyes to see rainbow colors outlining objects in the room.
2. Place a small mirror in a glass of water with mirror tilted against the glass.
3. Observe how a drop of oil on water produces colors.
4. Blow bubbles from commercial preparation. See colors on bubbles.

                Pupils receive and color new story pages covered in this lesson.

Shared Language: Receive word cards for word ring (manipulative vocabulary).
Write in journals what activity worked and what didn't.

2
Lights! Camera! . . . and Action!
Using the Camcorder as a Tool, Not as a Toy

John I. Liontas
Richmond Senior High School

Given today's emphasis on video technology and the fact that camcorders are becoming commonplace in almost every household, it makes educational sense to use them as a methodological tool for drilling, measuring, developing, and building students' communicative competencies. Many researchers have already argued very strongly for the use of the video camcorder in improving the skills of teaching assistants and students in method courses (Goodman 1985), while others stress its potential in providing preservice and inservice training for teachers (Frager 1985; Cook et al. 1988; Skeel 1989).

Yet the potential use of the video camcorder in the language classroom, a device that records images and sound directly onto videotape with the push of a button, has received only minimal attention. This article offers a pedagogical justification with specific and concrete guidelines for its use and outlines, in detailed steps, how activities, projects, and testing procedures can become user-friendly experiences for both teachers and students at all levels of instruction.

Making the Case for Video Camcorders

Helping students use the language with and for a purpose is a priority for foreign and second language teachers. To this end, many approaches, techniques, and strategies have been suggested in the professional literature that make use of a variety of technological (Smith 1987; Lambert and Sallis 1987; Goode 1990; Liontas 1991) and nontechnological (Birckbichler 1982; Omaggio 1986; Rogers and Medley 1988) media.

While audio, video, computers, and print media afford students unprecedented opportunities to encounter and practice language as it occurs in the target culture, they all lack, to a certain degree, one basic element: the active participation of the students in creating, reviewing, and analyzing their linguicultural proficiency in a variety of natural settings. This is perhaps the most profound impact the video camcorder can have in the language classroom. Other compelling reasons for integrating the video camcorder into the language curriculum are

1. It allows teachers to generate excitement in their classes by making language use real, contextualized, and aimed at the specific needs and interests of the students.
2. It invites—if planned properly and used wisely—active participation by all students of all ability levels and ages without labeling any of them as weak or strong in their attempt to be creative with the target language and culture.
3. It creates a fitting environment for cooperative learning in which outgoing students can delegate responsibilities among the group participants before, during, and after the video production, while others assume responsibility for less challenging tasks.
4. It offers tangible rewards and immediate feedback not only on students' verbal behavior but also on their nonverbal behavior.
5. It helps transform the conventional language classroom from one of passive to one of active interaction by resuscitating materials that are "buried" between the covers of a language textbook.
6. It stimulates creativity and imagination during planning, improves performance during production, creates awareness of strengths and weaknesses, facilitates a greater learning potential within well-defined, realistic, and natural contexts, and, finally, challenges participants to reach for higher levels of proficiency.
7. It helps teachers view their own teaching strategies, analyze their techniques, critique their verbal and nonverbal behavior during instruction, evaluate students' reactions, and make conscious decisions about any changes.
8. It promotes opportunities for risk taking at all learning levels.
9. It encourages the exploration of new options other than those that are predictable and safe.

Planning for Video Camcorder Use

Little will be gained if the video camcorder is used as a toy that fills the Friday afternoon with fun and laughter. To achieve optimal results, five issues become pertinent:

1. What is the real purpose of using the video camcorder? For whom is it intended and who is the target audience?
2. Are students emotionally and cognitively ready to view their verbal and nonverbal behaviors on tape?
3. When are videotaped activities most effective? Are structured activities better suited from videotaping than spontaneous ones?
4. With whom is videotaping most successful? Is it equally beneficial for students of all abilities in all age groups?
5. Are certain in-class or out-of-class productions better suited for videotaping than others? How much videotaping is advisable?

Answering these concerns is as important as knowing what skills and techniques are necessary for successful videotape production. Because a number of published guides have already addressed this issue (Utz 1980; Lancien 1987), the guidelines offered below focus primarily on classroom implications.

Twenty Guidelines for Video Camera Productions

Ideally, the video camera as a vehicle for self-motivation should be used in the language classroom from the very beginning of instruction. Why? Because students neither will wonder as much if the video camcorder becomes an integral part of their daily language experience from day one, nor will they feel intimidated by its presence and use. In fact, students tend to be more alert and attentive during the presentation of material and seem to take their on-camera performance more seriously when they know they are being videotaped (Korb and DeMeritt 1990).

The following guidelines depict accepted practices and techniques supported by research and classroom experience (see also Geddes and Sturtridge 1982; Lonergan 1984):

1. *Place the video camera* in an area that does not block anyone's view or hinder work during class. At best, the camera should be hanging from the ceiling at an angle or placed on top of a piece of furniture for long shots.
2. *Do not distract the students* by walking around the class with the video camcorder, which at times may be intimidating and counterproductive to what you are trying to achieve.
3. *Use a variety of shots.* Mix static shots with different angles, zooms, pans, fades.
4. *Make sure students understand* that what they say on camera is as important as how they behave in front of it.
5. *Point out the things students do "right"* when reviewing videotapes. Remember that constructive criticism can work wonders in promoting active interaction and future participation.
6. *Help students accept* the camcorder as their personal language tutor and friend that mirrors their true performances. Use yourself as a role model and do not shy away from pointing out the areas that need improvement.
7. *Make your goals and objectives known* to your students (and, if necessary, to their parents and other colleagues). Students appreciate knowing the real purpose so that they do not feel like "lab animals under observation."
8. *Experiment with a smile!* Take risks and do not be afraid to try new things and procedures during taping. Not everything will meet with your approval.
9. *Provide students with concrete,* easy-to-understand assignments and clearly establish the activity's parameters such as language functions, vocabulary, structures, length, setting, types of shots, and degree and amount of detail.
10. *Encourage creativity and imagination,* both in language performance as well as in video production. Point out to students that sometimes *less is more.*
11. *Combine videotaped activities and projects* with material already discussed in class and *capitalize* on what students know and can handle with a high rate of success.

12. *Anticipate and predict possible problems* (linguistic, cultural, technical) before giving students their assignments.
13. *Increase students' assignments* in range and level of difficulty as they become more aware of their capabilities and gain more experience in working with the video camera and the finished video productions.
14. *Choose authentic contents and natural contexts* that are sociolinguistically and socioculturally relevant and immediate to the students' environment and everyday tasks.
15. *Know your final objectives and select* video-directed productions that complement and challenge the abilities, needs, interests, and styles of learning of all age groups of students.
16. *Provide students with rough scripts and practice sessions* before the actual videotaping can take place. Base your decision on their age and ability level, not on the number of scripts already available.
17. *Make provisions for assignments, activities, or projects* that are either cultural, grammatical, communicative, and functional or that integrate and correlate skills across areas.
18. *Hold students accountable* for their actions, reactions, and interactions from the beginning to the end of taping. Evaluation guides and in-class feedback sessions need to reflect these purposes as well.
19. *Encourage students to strive for higher levels* of language without losing sight of their present operational level.
20. *Break down the walls of insecurity and intimidation* by ensuring continually and consistently high levels of success that build communicative self-assurance.

Getting Started

To get the most out of planning for and using video productions in the language classroom, teachers should include in their approach the following four phases:

Phase One: Video Preparation

In this phase, students cooperatively discuss pertinent information regarding the theme and the sociocultural setting of the taping session; review and practice essential grammar points, vocabulary, pronunciation, and nonlinguistic features such as physical gestures and facial expressions conveying emotional states and nuances with the teacher monitoring their accuracy; write scripts or storyboards, make corrections where necessary, decide upon the tape format and script breakdown for shooting, and rehearse in class singly or in groups; and, finally, consult with a technician from the language lab or the audiovisual department about last-minute technical questions such as lighting, sound track, musical background, editing, titles, and credits.

Phase Two: Video Production

Whether taping is done in class or out of it, the exclusive language during production remains the target language. In addition, no retakes should be allowed during taping and time limits need to be followed rigidly to be fair to all students.

Exceptions could be made in extraordinary situations, e.g., unforeseen technical difficulties.

Phase Three: Video Evaluation

During playback sessions, students identify, analyze, and correct both the linguistic and the nonlinguistic features of the videotape and, upon completion, using a weighted evaluation form, judge the overall *quality* of the video (see Appendix 2A). Prizes may be awarded (in addition to grades!) at the end of this session. Problem areas in vocabulary, grammar, pronunciation, or culture should be used as a basis for further discussions that reinforce correct verbal and nonverbal behavior.

Phase Four: Going for the Oscar!

If appropriate to students' ages, abilities, and levels of sophistication, students should be encouraged to produce a movie, a documentary, or a soap opera in the target language that could reveal current teenage issues explaining contemporary conflicts, among other things. Community-oriented programs that are cultural in scope, informative in nature, and entertaining could be supplied with English subtitles and aired on the local cablevision channel. Such video productions could then easily become the catalyst of an entire language course if students know well in advance that their "Oscar performance" will be featured on the public airways. Obviously, these kinds of production need to exemplify the best of sound, music, and performance before they are advertised in the local newspaper and on the community cable channel. The end of the school year also provides a most welcome opportunity for inviting the school community to come and witness firsthand *Oscar Night* at your school. "Oscars" could be given in the categories of best actor/actress; best film; special effects, sound, editing; best script; best director; best supporting actor/actress and so on, thus making the premiere both an unforgettable experience for all participants and an annual event in the school calendar.

Video Activities and Projects

A number of activities and projects could be videotaped. While virtually everything that takes place in a language classroom may be suited for diagnostic taping, only a few well-defined and carefully selected activities and projects need be videotaped and used, if necessary, as a testing instrument. If students are to perceive the video camera as more than a toy, it must be linked to the topics that are discussed in their textbook and that are relevant and immediate to their everyday environment.

The literature on producing and using video productions with success answers this concern with a variety of suggestions and examples (Phillips 1982; Korb and DeMeritt 1990; Pelletier 1990). The classroom-tested video activities and projects described below add to that list of examples and are offered as additional suggestions in the hope that they will generate greater discussion among language professionals without limiting the boundaries of other plausible and unconventional video productions.

16   Creative Approaches in Foreign Language Teaching

Video Activities

The Hot Seat.   Place a swivel chair in the middle of your classroom with students' desks around it. One student sits in the chair while the others ask him or her, in turn, all possible *Wh*-questions they can think of within a five-minute limit. This type of activity permits every student (weak and strong) to be an active participant in the learning, prompts spontaneity and instant recall, makes students more attentive to what has already been asked, and promotes the direct use of previously learned knowledge and material.

News at Eleven.   Using current stories and headlines, students report on news, entertainment, sports, and weather in a fashion similar to that of the news on television. Naturally, the four students responsible for each section of the news show need to be told a day in advance about their assignment. Collaborative work ethics, individual ability levels, and amicable relationships among the four selected students are important in the smooth operation and success of the activity. Authentic print-media materials add additional opportunities to this activity as a valuable reading process.

Time to Cook!   Using a recipe from the target country, a student demonstrates with words and actions the preparation of a dish using, wherever and whenever possible, the appropriate cultural references such as kilo, gram, liter, and so on. Materials, ingredients, preparation, and heating instructions need not be complex, but there must be a set time limit to allow ample time for reviewing and discussing the videotape.

The Neverending Story.   Have five students select one card from a stack. Each card should contain a topic that may or may not have been discussed previously in class. Each student in turn talks for a minute without stopping. When time is called, he or she must stop the narration with an "and," upon which another student continues the story and finishes with another "and" until the whole story has been told or until a predetermined time is up.

To Tell the Truth.   Three students sit in front of the class. Each student relates an experience, but only one tells a real experience. The rest of the class has to decide which of the three given "experiences" is true by first asking questions of the storytellers and, based on the answers given, argue for the "true" experience.

1-800-Dial-a-Date.   Bring two phones to the class and have two students, sitting back to back, role-play caller and dating-service operator. The caller must make the purpose of the call very clear while the operator, using a profile dating questionnaire, must ask the kind of questions that will elicit the complete profile of the caller. Information regarding age, height and weight, color of hair and eyes, educational background, and interests become the line of questioning. Higher-level students should also describe in greater detail the person they are seeking, contact that person, and, if agreed, make plans to meet. This type of phone-based activity could be expanded to include other topics such as making reservations or appointments, calling train stations or airports for information, placing classified ads for cars, pets, furniture, lost-and-found items, and virtually every relevant real-life situation that makes use of a phone.

Love Connection. Have one student act as the host of the show and another student make a choice based on the answers he or she receives from the three or four students who assume the roles of the dating candidates. Separated by a screen, the candidate seeking the "perfect" mate asks a number of questions that will enable him or her to make the right choice. At best, dating candidates should come from another language class so that voice familiarity cannot be a factor in the selection. Once the perfect match has been found and after the dating couple has returned from their date, they must share their date experience with the host of the show and audience in the next show. This way, students who meet only during club meetings can meet the other language students and work together to improve their language skills while having fun. For the next dating show, selected students could prepare a two-minute description of themselves and argue why they are the "perfect" candidates. Based on the appeal of their descriptions, candidates are selected by a ballet or popular vote.

"Shag" the Dance. One student demonstrates the basic steps and moves of the Shag while the others follow his or her directions to the letter. Other dances, such as the "Electric Slide," the "Cha-Cha," the "Two-Step," and so on could be used equally well by the students who are already familiar with them. Dances from the target country should be performed by the teacher first before expecting students to perform in front of a video camera.

Siskel and Ebert. Have two students watch a movie on television or at the theater and prepare themselves for a debate that is to take place in front of the entire class. The two students need not agree or disagree on every point about the film, but classroom experience with this activity has indicated that heated debates are the result of defending one's opinion in a give-and-take argument. Ideally, a target language movie should be shown in class. Use that encounter as a springboard to additional cultural and communicative activities. In either instance, the two students (whose names were drawn from a hat) must justify their position using every available language skill. If available, authentic reviews are extremely helpful.

The Oprah/Donahue Show. A topic that lends itself easily to a panel discussion and that invites questions and comments from the audience is the best candidate for a talk show. Topics such as teen pregnancy, child abuse, drugs and alcohol, guns in school, sports vs. academics, and the like are themes that students are aware of, that are part of their daily school or family life, and most importantly, that generate strong opinions in everyone. A student, assuming the role of Oprah or Donahue, introduces the guest or guests of the show, asks questions pertinent to the topic, and allows the audience to interact with him or her and the panel. In addition, the arrangement of the chairs in front of the audience, the microphone, and the camera all contribute to the authenticity of this activity. Above all, such activities enable students at all ability levels to be active participants in a fun-filled natural and challenging learning atmosphere.

The Performer. Have a number of students memorize short poems, songs, parts of a play, or famous quotes from the target literature and have them perform in class. Materials that have already been discussed in class offer excellent opportunities for review and for improving listening comprehension. While a student is performing, the rest of the class has to guess the title, author, and any relevant information that could be derived from it. After the correct guessing, the teacher should quickly brainstorm with the students about important background knowledge that can help connect each performance to the literature of the target country.

Video Projects

To facilitate proficiency in the target language it is necessary to go beyond the textbook. World events and international issues, news headlines and local news, for instance, can serve as an excellent basis for increasing the range and level of difficulty of the videotape productions. Recognizing and emphasizing the value of planning, producing, and evaluating unconventional productions will, in turn, encourage students to seek projects other than those that are predictable and safe.

One Day in School. The school environment, regardless of level, offers a large amount of language material with which students are already familiar. The classroom, the cafeteria, the library, the gym, the bookstore, the offices, and the football stadium are excellent settings for reporting related information *in situ*. Each location breakdown for shooting could be done by a different student, who individually or collectively decides upon the amount and detail of the script. Special events add an additional flavor to school life. Following the successful completion of the video evaluation phase, the videotape production, furnished with music, titles, and credits, could be sent to a language class in another school, city, or country. Such pen-pal video exchanges could easily become the vehicle for disseminating cultural information on a regular basis that can lead to long-lasting friendships and partnerships among different language classes from around the world. Before setting up such production exchanges, it is strongly suggested that the entire class and the teacher undertaking this project introduce themselves either singly or as a group to their new "friends" and state the purpose and benefits of such a cooperative effort (see also Cummins 1989; Altman 1989).

The Championship Game. This and other suitable events offer higher-level students excellent opportunities to practice using their translation skills in a setting where translation of one's comments is both necessary and authentic. Students could interview the players and their coaches about the game, strengths and weaknesses, winning chances, predictions of final score; introduce the players and their coaches; provide background information on certain players or referees; offer statistical or personal comments; compare and contrast the two teams; or narrate the action of the play. At half time or at the end of the game, students could conduct follow-up interviews with coaches, players, fans, and "famous" people and summarize the event with a few concluding remarks. On other occasions, have students create a video about how to play football, soccer, basketball, baseball, tennis, or volleyball; what the responsibilities of each player, referee, linesman are; or have one student demonstrate and perform a skill or technique pertaining to the sport of their choice while another student could be reporting, narrating, describing, or summarizing what the player is doing.

Safari Tales. While taking a day trip to the zoo as a class or individually, a number of students tell tales or riddles about an animal by offering enough information without naming the animal in question. Another approach to this

Lights! Camera! . . . and Action! 19

production could be to have students play a kind of scavenger hunt where students, using a zoo map, have to find their way to the next meeting point without ever revealing where they are in the zoo grounds. When the tape is viewed in class, the other students, using the same zoo maps, have to locate their positions and, based on the information provided, anticipate their next meeting point. Points may be awarded to groups for each correct guess during the viewing session.

The Berlin Wall. Every year, on November 9, millions of people remember the downfall of the wall that symbolized an entire country's silence for more than twenty-eight years. While the Berlin Wall is directly linked with the German people and their language, students of other languages could just as easily produce a video on the history of the building or downfall of the wall, its profound impact upon the lives of the people of Germany and its neighbors, and its significance to everyone's life today. Recent political, economic, cultural, and social changes in Europe provide an additional platform for exploring this topic to the fullest. Any school or German Club activities commemorating the event offer a pragmatic purpose for conducting a series of interviews and reporting upon these events. A class visit to a museum that exhibits a block of the Berlin Wall authenticates the importance of the video report.

Oktoberfest. With celebrating taking place in more than 3000 cities around the world, the likelihood of this festival taking place in your hometown or a nearby city is very high. While generally most people gladly associate the biggest festival in the world, Oktoberfest, with drinking the so-called water substitute "beer," the tradition and history of this event remains unspoken, and, sadly enough, *unknown* to the larger school population. Students could review the history and traditions of the Oktoberfest, including the marriage of the late Bavarian king Ludwig I to Princess Therese von Sachsen-Hildburghausen on October 12, 1810, and the annual 12-gun salute at exactly 12 noon with the traditional slogan *"O 'Zapft es."* In addition, students could explore the significance of the traditional costume parades, the cultural exhibits and dances, or the impact this 182-year-old festival has in our lives today. Similar projects could expand into the areas of culture or state fairs, art exhibitions, car shows, and virtually every plausible event for which students would be intrinsically motivated and interested to attend and report on specific details. On-location interviews and reports are, of course, the most powerful devices for lending greater authenticity to these projects.

Two Special Projects for 1992

Europe 1992 and Beyond. With economic, political, and social changes never before seen in Europe, the year 1992 marks the beginning of a new united Europe and an unprecedented opportunity for all teachers to bring alive historical events. Students could report on the economic, political, geographical, industrial, and cultural changes in Europe, interview students and faculty at their school (and translate their comments into the target language) or administer oral questionnaires in their community. Since this topic is closely connected with information from abroad, collaboration and cooperation between and among teachers, librarians, and students is of paramount importance. All in all, time, dedication, and availability of materials coupled with students' knowledge on the topic and levels of proficiency will help ensure the success of this project.

The Columbian Quincentenary. The five hundredth anniversary of Christopher Columbus's voyage of "discovery" to the New World has set in motion a plethora of festivities, lecture series, films, conferences, and discussions on the meanings of and differing attitudes toward the encounter, conquest, and colonization of America. Exploring this topic from the viewpoints of history, philosophy, language, linguistics, literature, religion, and social sciences should offer a welcome opportunity for students to produce a video program to that end. Students could produce a photo series in a chronological order followed by narrations and descriptive comments, interview students on the importance of Columbus's momentous voyage, organize activities commemorating the event that are then videotaped in the form of a report, or even write and perform their own play. Hence, not only will students keep abreast of events taking place here and abroad, but more importantly, they will engage themselves in an event that has changed the course of history like no other event.

Conclusion

The implications for camcorder use in the language classroom are myriad, but to begin to take advantage of it we need to insist that it be used as a vital teaching tool in the development of proficiency. Video technology can have an enormous impact on language teaching and learning if it is made an integral part of the curriculum and if it is offered as an extension to viewing and using culturally authentic videos. The greatest advantage of them all, however, remains the fact that students can exercise *shared control* over their own videotape productions.

Past experiences with successful video productions have repeatedly shown that whenever students are given opportunities to control the linguistic features, the thematic areas, and the sociocultural settings of their learning, they also seem to control very skillfully their own rate of success, which is perhaps the most important asset any instructional technology can offer. Much to our satisfaction and approval, students tend to become more excited and eager to learn with video productions when they can see their artistic and creative achievements, contributions, and participation turn into positive learning rewards and when their assignments grow out of concrete and immediate communication needs.

Because the use of the video camcorder in the language classroom is so crucial for the development of functional proficiency, and it is flexible enough to be adapted for any approach, method, or teaching strategy, it is safe to state that *no goal is out of reach and no amount of success unattainable* as long as we do not impose any limits upon the boundaries of the language process or the risks students are willing to take beyond the acquisition of factual knowledge.

Video technology is here to stay. Whether we take full advantage of this medium or we decide to combine it with other instructional technology will depend upon our personal conviction of its potential and the amount of time, energy, and dedication we are ready to invest.

References

Altman, Rick. 1989. *The Video Connection: Integrating Video into Language Teaching.* Boston: Houghton Mifflin.

Birckbichler, Diane W. 1982. *Creative Activities for the Second-Language Classroom.* Language in Education: Theory and Practice Series, no. 48. Washington: Center for Applied Linguistics.

Cook, Dayton G., David F. Stout, and Rex C. Dahl. 1988. "Using Video to Increase Oral Proficiency: A Model for *Lehrerfortbildung."* *Die Unterrichtspraxis* 21: 97–101.

Cummins, Patricia W. 1989. "Video and the French Teacher." *The French Review* 62,3: 411–26.

Frager, Alan M. 1985. "Video Technology and Teacher Training: A Research Perspective." *Educational Technology* 25: 20–22.

Geddes, Marion, and Gill Sturtridge, eds. 1982. *Video in the Language Classroom.* London, Eng.: Heinemann Educational Books.

Goode, Stephen. 1990. "Classes in the Country via Satellite." *Insight on the News,* January 8.

Goodman, Pearl. 1985. "Video in Second Language Teacher Training." *Video and Second Language Learning.* Special issue of *Studies in Language Learning* (Junetta B. Gillespie, ed.) 5,1: 77–82.

Korb, Richard A., and Linda C. DeMeritt. 1990. "Lights! Camera! Action! Videotaping in the Conversational Class." *Die Unterrichtspraxis* 23: 112–17.

Lambert, Steve, and Jane Sallis, eds. 1987. *CD–I and Interactive Videodisc Technology.* Indianapolis: Sams.

Lancien, Thierry. 1987. *Le Document video.* Paris: CLE International.

Liontas, John I. 1991. "Authentic Videos in the Foreign Language Classroom," pp. 85–99 in Lorraine A. Strasheim, ed., *Focus on the Foreign Language Learner: Priorities and Strategies.* Proceedings of the Central States Conference on the Teaching of Foreign Languages. Lincolnwood, IL: National Textbook Company.

Lonergan, Jack. 1984. *Video in Language Teaching.* Cambridge, Eng.: Cambridge Univ. Press.

Omaggio, Alice C. 1986. *Teaching Language in Context: Proficiency-Oriented Instruction.* Boston: Heinle and Heinle.

Pelletier, Raymond J. 1990. "Prompting Spontaneity by Means of the Video Camera in the Beginning Foreign Language Class." *Foreign Language Annals* 23: 227–33.

Phillips, Elayne. 1982. "Student Video Production," pp. 86–100 in Marion Geddes and Gill Sturtridge, eds., *Video in the Language Classroom.* London, Eng.: Heinemann Educational Books.

Rogers, Carmen Villegas, and Frank W. Medley, Jr. 1988. "Language with a Purpose: Using Authentic Materials in the Foreign Language Classroom." *Foreign Language Annals* 21: 467–78.

Skeel, Dorothy J. 1989. "Using Technology to Build Teacher Decision-Making Skills." *Foreign Language Annals* 22: 149–55.

Smith, William Flint. 1987. "Modern Media in Foreign Language Education: A Synopsis," pp. 1–12 in William Flint Smith, ed., *Modern Media in Foreign Language Education: Theory and Implementation.* The ACTFL Foreign Language Education Series, vol. 18. Lincolnwood, IL: National Textbook Company.

Utz, Peter. 1980. *Video User's Handbook.* Englewood Cliffs, NJ: Prentice Hall.

22 Creative Approaches in Foreign Language Teaching

Appendix 2A
Video Production Evaluation Form

Name(s): Class:
Date: Total Score:

I. BASIC DATA

Title: Content:

Subject: Context:

Length: Functions:

II. GENERAL CHARACTERISTICS (Maximum 5 points)

			POINTS
Category:			1
○ History	○ Civilization	○ Language	
○ Philosophy	○ Social Studies	○ Linguistics	
○ Religion	○ Culture	○ Literature	
○ Other			
Purpose of video project:			1
○ To inform	○ To instruct		
○ To entertain	○ To persuade		
Intended audience:			1 2 3
○ Language students only	○ School population	○ Community	
		Subtotal:	_____

III. TECHNICAL CHARACTERISTICS (Maximum 30 points)

Images:			1 3 5
○ Fuzzy/Blurred	○ Clear	○ Sharp	
Sound track:			1 3 5
○ Inaudible	○ Audible	○ Lucid	
Script breakdown (sequence of scenes):			1 3 5
○ Unrelated	○ Related, but inconsistent	○ Logical	
Scenery:			1 3 5
○ Inappropriate to the topic	○ Acceptable	○ Appropriate	
Music and sound effects:			1 3 5
○ Distract	○ Complement	○ Enhance	
Editing of video:			1 3 5
○ Amateurish	○ Acceptable	○ Professional	
		Subtotal:	_____

Lights! Camera! ... and Action!

IV. LINGUISTIC/PARALINGUISTIC CHARACTERISTICS
(Maximum 50 points)

Verbal and nonverbal behavior (gestures, facial and body expressions, emotions and nuances) **complement one another:**			1	3	5
○ Never	○ Sometimes	○ All the time			
Rate of delivery:			1	3	5
○ Slow	○ Rapid, but not natural	○ Near native			
Quality of articulation:			1	3	5
○ Incomprehensible	○ Comprehensible	○ Articulated			
Voiceover (off-screen) narration (not applicable to all videos):			0	0	0
○ Not needed	○ Complementary	○ Required			
Message:			1	3	5
○ Confusing	○ Misleading	○ Very clear			
Communication:			1	3	5
○ Hindered	○ Sufficient	○ Successful			
Grammar use:			1	3	5
○ Limited	○ Basic/concrete	○ Extensive			
Vocabulary use:			1	3	5
○ Limited	○ Basic/concrete	○ Creative			
Accuracy:			1	3	5
○ Frequent errors	○ Some errors	○ No errors			
Fluency:			1	3	5
○ Low	○ Medium	○ High			
Portrayal of culture:			1	3	5
○ Stereotypical/ generalized	○ Outmoded	○ Up to date			

Subtotal: _____

V. CREATIVE CHARACTERISTICS (Maximum 15 points)

Level of creativity and imagination:			1	3	5
○ Limited	○ Medium	○ Very high			
Props, costumes, and chromakey (fake backgrounds done with small photos or pictures):			1	3	5
○ Amateurish	○ Mediocre	○ Innovative			
Acting performances:			1	3	5
○ Amateurish	○ Convincing	○ Worth an Oscar			

Subtotal: _____

Commentary (Please make constructive comments and confine your remarks to strong or weak aspects of the video production):

II. ____
III. ____
IV. ____
V. ____
Total ____

VI. "The envelope, please . . . !

(Check all nominations to be made for this video.)
____ Best actor/actress
____ Best supporting actor/actress
____ Best director
____ Best picture/documentary
____ Best script
____ Best musical score
____ Best special effects/sound/editing

____ Other (specify) _____

VII. RECOMMENDATION

Submit video to *Cablevision*
____ As is (excellent project: strongly recommended)
____ After adding titles and credits (good project: recommended)
____ After considerable work (project has some merit: recommended with reservations)
____ Do not submit (project is not recommended)

3
Yorktown High School Foreign Language Interactive Videodisc Project

Barbara Underwood
Mt. Pleasant Township (Indiana) Community School Corporation
Karen Brammer
Rocco Fuschetto
Sigrid Koehler
Jack Jorden
James Mervilde
Yorktown High School

The Foreign Language Learning Center at Yorktown High School places language learning within the environment of interactive videodisc (IVD) technology. The basis of this medium is a laser videodisc interfaced with a computer. IVD brings authentic language to the learner in an interactive learning environment that is responsive to the learner's interest, ability, performance, and pace.

In the spring of 1990, the foreign language staff at Yorktown (Indiana) High School undertook the challenge of integrating this multimedia technology into the foreign language program. Since the onset of this project, foreign language instruction at Yorktown High School has progressed from a traditional teacher-centered instructional approach to a student-centered, interactive instructional model. The purposes of this article are to (1) relate the events that led to the school's involvement with IVD, (2) describe the process of planning and implementing the Yorktown IVD project, and (3) discuss the benefits of IVD for language learning.

The staff's interest in the use of IVD technology for teaching foreign language was stimulated by the interaction of several factors. Since 1986, the number of students enrolling in foreign language classes at Yorktown High School has increased from 25 percent to 54 percent of the high school population. This positive increase in enrollment has been tempered by a fairly high attrition rate (over 40 percent) between levels 1 and 2. Finding ways to develop more positive attitudes toward language learning, to stimulate students' interest in continued language study, and to increase students' competence and proficiency have been ongoing challenges. A second factor that led to the exploration of IVD was an interest in restructuring the foreign language curriculum to include more student interaction and involvement in the instructional process. A third goal was to design and implement a curriculum that reflected more of a proficiency-based approach.

The *Indiana Foreign Language Proficiency Guide* (Indiana Department of Education 1987) and the *ACTFL Proficiency Guidelines* (ACTFL 1986) published by the American Council on the Teaching of Foreign Languages stress that the focus of the foreign language curriculum should be to help students use language for meaningful purposes (proficiency-based). These guidelines indicate that students should have proficiency in speaking, understanding, reading, and writing, as well as knowledge of the foreign culture and the ability to behave in ways appropriate to it.

> Increasingly clear is the fact that learning languages is not a simple matter of learning content; being able to recite grammar rules and perform well on vocabulary tests does not ensure the ability to understand language in context. (Bush 1991, p. 111)

Research on the use of interactive video as a tool for teaching foreign language has supported the concept that authentic video is motivational and teaches students real language. Authentic video exhibits a linguistic and cultural richness that is not found in written text materials (Fletcher 1988). Relating interactive video lessons to the regular curriculum helps students to understand how the language principles they are learning function in the target culture, and the long-term goal of building proficiency is enhanced.

Project Planning and Implementation

Yorktown High School's involvement with IVD resulted from a fortunate series of events. During the 1989-90 school year, the Yorktown High School foreign language staff was evaluating and revising the foreign language curriculum. At the same time, the high school received a request for proposals for innovative technology projects from the Indiana Department of Education. The staff already knew how to use interactive videodisc technology for the science curriculum. The questions of if and how this technology might be used to improve the foreign language program was discussed. The consensus was that there was reason to expect a place for IVD technology in the foreign language program, and that IVD might significantly improve the teaching/learning process.

Within a few days of the initial discussions, the staff started to review professional journals and to place phone calls to foreign language professors at universities within the state, consultants at the state department, and commercial distributors of videodiscs. Initial contacts were discouraging. No one contacted had any direct experience and little helpful information on how the effort should proceed. The general feedback was that there were few institutions using IVD for foreign language instruction and that implementing such a program could be a difficult undertaking. Underlying the pessimism were hints of optimism that IVD could have a positive effect on the teaching of foreign language.

Through further research and good fortune, a short article appeared in the *School Board News* (Mecklenburger 1989) about the Language Learning Center at the United States Air Force Academy. This was the turning point! After a phone call to Major Miguel Verano at the Air Force Academy, the Yorktown High School IVD project was launched.

After much more reading, consulting, and researching, the staff submitted a grant proposal to the Indiana Department of Education in February 1990, and the proposal was approved for funding in April 1990. What has been accomplished since that time has been phenomenal. To imply, however, that the route has been a smooth one would be misleading.

While conducting further research into the uses of interactive videodisc technology in the teaching of foreign languages, it became apparent that the staff of the Department of Foreign Languages at the United States Air Force Academy were pioneers in the technology. In May 1990, the Yorktown High School project staff traveled to Colorado to consult with Major Miguel Verano, Director of the U.S. Air Force Academy's Language Learning Laboratory.

The visit to the Language Learning Center at the Air Force Academy was informative and enlightening. The Yorktown High School delegation had an opportunity to gain much background information from the Academy staff, to talk with students, and to try out the IVD lessons and hardware. It became obvious that the Academy's well-researched and well-designed software, which is based on the ACTFL's proficiency guidelines, could be used effectively by high school foreign language students.

The challenges faced in launching this project were many. After visiting the Air Force Academy, it became clear that it was impractical, if not impossible, to expect Yorktown High School teachers to have the time or the expertise to design and develop IVD instructional programs. It was also discovered that commercial interactive programs were virtually nonexistent. Several foreign language laser videodiscs were available commercially; few, however, were accompanied by computer software programs that provided the computer-based interactivity.

Being novices, the project team expected to purchase computers and videodiscs, secure the Air Force Academy's software programs, and be ready for teachers to begin training and curriculum development work in the summer of 1990. What really happened was a six-month saga of hardware and software problems that made it impossible for the foreign language teachers even to work at the computer stations.

The software problems were a result of incompatibility between the Academy's software and the authoring software. Only after numerous phone calls from the high school's computer coordinator to the Air Force Academy and after sending one of the computers to the Academy in December 1990 were these problems resolved. The Academy's staff reconfigured their software to run with our authoring software. In February 1991, the Yorktown High School Foreign Language Department finally possessed a functional Sony VIW 5000 foreign language interactive videodisc laboratory.

During the fall of 1990, while waiting for the hardware and software problems to be resolved, the foreign language instructors reviewed the written scripts for the laser videodiscs and wrote curriculums for beginning Spanish and German classes that integrated the interactive videodisc programs. This document provided a framework for beginning and trying out the interactive videodisc technology.

In January 1991, the Yorktown High School computer coordinator conducted training sessions for the foreign language teachers in the use of the IVD laboratory. The integration of the IVD lessons into the beginning Spanish and German classes began in February 1991.

Description of Hardware and Software

The Foreign Language Interactive Videodisc Laboratory at Yorktown High School consists of ten freestanding student workstations, each equipped with a Sony VIW 5000 Interactive Delivery System. The system integrates a color monitor, computer, videodisc player, keyboard, mouse, and a lightweight stereo headset connected to the videodisc player. An authoring workstation consists of the same hardware as a student workstation with the addition of 2 MB extended memory. IconAuthor software is used to author the computer lessons that accompany and control the videodiscs. Currently the videodiscs *The Random House Spanish Video Program for Beginning Spanish* and the *Velvet Series* are being utilized.

The lessons authored by the U.S. Air Force Academy begin with a situational video segment that is viewed by the learner. Language lessons are drawn from everyday life situations. Most of the segments are very short, running 2 to 5 minutes. The students can watch each segment as many times as needed. Each dialog can be broken down into individual parts, giving students easy access to individual words and phrases, as well as to the entire conversation. The program has an easy-to-use menu system that allows students to retrieve any dialog or to repeat passages. During the overview, the students may display the text of the video or select any word in the text and obtain a definition.

After the overview, the students proceed through a series of activities, including scrambled words, scrambled sentences, and a mastery check. Students may at any point return to the video or to any of the activities. The activities are keyed to the video segment. If a student makes an incorrect response in the scrambled word or sentence activities, the associated video segment is replayed.

After the 20- to 30-minute IVD lessons, instructors follow up with classroom activities, including question-and-answer sessions about the segment, written and oral exercises, and role-playing situations using the content of the video lesson.

Benefits of IVD for Foreign Language Instruction

The initial experiences with IVD support the literature on the potential benefits for language learning:

1. *Authentic video:* Through the use of IVD, students experience authentic language within a cultural context. IVD allows students to see, hear, and

read the language simultaneously. This is a reflection of the use of language in real-life situations. The combination of verbal and visual elements enhances language acquisition.

2. *Active learning:* Effective learning requires dynamic interaction between the learner and the material. IVD technology requires that the student function as an active participant in the instructional process. Students experience and interact with the lesson as they watch, listen, and respond to the programs.
3. *Self-pacing and sequencing:* The design of the IVD lessons enables students to proceed through the instructional sequence at a pace and sequence that are determined by their own needs and abilities. The learner may repeat any of the activities as needed to improve comprehension of the lesson. Students are able to control the learning process and have opportunities to pursue their own learning strategies.
4. *Learning styles and modalities:* IVD enhances the teacher's ability to accommodate individual learning styles and modalities. IVD provides an opportunity for students to see, hear, and do. Varied audiovisual activities and teaching methods address personal learning-style preferences.
5. *Development of complex skills:* "The language learner must acquire a degree of proficiency in vocabulary, grammar, pronunciation, speaking, listening comprehension, spelling, writing, reading, non-verbal gestures, comprehension and culture" (Slaton 1991, p. 27). The interactive videodisc system has the capability to include all of these processes.
6. *Cooperative learning:* Cooperative learning has been found to increase achievement and to foster positive attitudes toward learning (Johnson et al. 1981). Students work at the computer stations in pairs. The design of the lessons requires that the students consult and interact with one another as they progress through the lesson.

Evaluation

During the implementation stages of the project, teachers observed and documented the use of the interactive video instruction. The teachers developed a brief questionnaire for students to complete at the end of each lesson. The instructors also monitored and documented difficulties and successes experienced by the students.

The use of hardware and software was easily mastered by students and teachers. Very little time was needed to train teachers to utilize the programs or to orient students to use the IVD lab.

Students responded very positively to the authentic interactive video format. Attitudinal assessments have documented the students' positive attitudes toward the use of IVD. Students indicated that the ability to listen and watch video segments as many times as needed was very beneficial. They also responded positively to the capability of progressing through the lessons at a pace appropriate to their learning needs. Students appreciated being able to control the instructional process. This has the potential to help students become more self-directed, independent learners.

Students also responded that the lessons were interesting. Hearing native speakers in authentic situations was identified as a positive attribute of the IVD programs. Students expressed, often with a sense of surprise, that the conversations could actually be understood, and that the IVD programs made learning the dialog much easier.

Because of the cutting-edge status of IVD technology for foreign language teaching, there are problems yet to be resolved. As stated previously, it is impractical to expect that high school teachers will, to any great extent, design and develop instructional programs. High schools will be the consumers of the work done by university and commercial developers. The platform compatibility problems (the ability to run a software program on different types of computers) are also discouraging. There is a hope that as demand increases, the cost of hardware and software will be less prohibitive to the high school market and that an adequate supply of high-quality materials will be available.

At the beginning of this project, the focus seemed to be more on the technology than on the teaching/learning process. This may well be a problem inherent in the implementation of new technologies. As the project progressed, more emphasis was placed on the pedagogical issues and less on the tools.

Full-scale implementation of interactive videodisc technology for foreign language instruction is very expensive. Nevertheless, the benefits of the technology can be realized with only minimal hardware and software. There are high school teachers utilizing this technology with only one or two computer stations. Options for working in this environment include using the programs for whole-class instruction, having students rotate through learning-center activities with the IVD lessons as one activity, and having students schedule time outside of class to complete the activities as homework assignments.

The Next Phase

Much more work is needed to fully realize the potential of IVD technology for improving foreign language teaching and learning at Yorktown High School. Some of this work will be accomplished by the project team. Other improvements will have to await the work of the researchers, developers, and technicians.

During the 1991–92 school year, the project staff is concentrating on improving the instructional process. Deigning introductory activities for each IVD lesson and designing effective followup activities will help focus more clearly on the pedagogy than on the technology. The ultimate goal is to exploit the potential of the technology to bring about more effective learning.

"For interactive video to effect significant improvements it must find its place in an appropriate model or paradigm of language study" (Rowe 1991, p. 73). The teaching and learning process must be reconceptualized. The success of the learning environment depends upon finding the most effective roles for the teacher, the learner, and the technology. The challenge is to coordinate the work of the theorist, researcher, developer, and consumer.

Yorktown High School language instructors will also attempt to author IVD lessons. Time constraints preclude a large-scale development effort. It is hoped that a generic template concept will allow teachers to develop lessons efficiently and effectively.

Conclusion

The project staff has had many opportunities to meet and interact with other professionals across the nation who are pioneering the use of IVD technology for foreign language instruction. This project has been professionally challenging and rewarding to the participating educators.

For the project team this has been a challenging, frustrating, exciting, and motivational undertaking. The enthusiasm has not waned. The team discovered that this is more than a cutting-edge project. It can be more accurately described as a "bleeding edge" project. This realization has made it easier to accept the frustration and more rewarding to celebrate the successes.

The efforts being undertaken at various sites across the country to develop foreign language instructional materials for IVD are encouraging. Many excellent videodiscs are currently available, and we hope the development of computer-based interactive lessons will begin to keep pace.

The Yorktown High School project team is even more convinced that interactive videodisc technology has the potential to transform the teaching of foreign language.

References

ACTFL. 1986. *Proficiency Guidelines*. Hastings-on-Hudson, NY: ACTFL.

Bush, Michael. 1991. "From Interactive Videodisc to CD–XXX: The Future," pp. 111–17 in Michael D. Bush, Alice Slaton, Miguel Verano, and Martha E. Slayden, eds., *Interactive Videodisc: The "Why" and the "How."* CALICO Monograph Series. Provo, UT: Brigham Young University.

Fletcher, William H. 1988. "Authentic Video in the Foreign Language Curriculum: The Annapolis Interactive Video Project." Unpublished handout. Proceedings of Interactive '88, The Hague Conference.

Indiana Department of Education. 1987. *Indiana Curriculum Proficiency Guidelines*.

Johnson, D. W., G. Maruyama, R. Johnson, D. Nelson, and L. Skon. 1981. "Effects of Cooperative, Competitive and Individualistic Goal Structures on Achievement: A Meta-analysis." *Psychological Bulletin* 89: 47–62.

Mecklenburger, James. 1989. "Air Force on Cutting Edge of Educational Technology." *School Board News*, August 30.

Rowe, A. Allen. 1991. "Language Discovery Environments," pp. 73–88 in Michael D. Bush, Alice Slaton, Miguel Verano, and Martha E. Slayden, eds., *Interactive Videodisc: The "Why" and the "How."* CALICO Monograph Series. Provo, UT: Brigham Young University.

Slaton, Alice. 1991. "How to Get Started in Interactive Videodisc: A User's Perspective," pp. 25–35 in Michael D. Bush, Alice Slaton, Miguel Verano, and Martha E. Slayden, eds., *Interactive Videodisc: The "Why" and the "How."* CALICO Monograph Series. Provo, UT: Brigham Young University.

4
Literature:
A Rich Resource for Teaching Language and Culture in Context

Aleidine J. Moeller[1]
University of Nebraska–Lincoln

> To want to teach a cultural language as a second language, without teaching its literature, is a form of barbarism. (Weinrich 1983, p. 11)[2]

Proficiency and Literature

The proficiency emphasis in the teaching of foreign languages has brought with it a realistic and real-world application of language. The goal of a proficiency-oriented classroom is to talk *in* the language and not *about* the language. The curriculum, therefore, is no longer driven solely by grammar, but rather by communicative functions. Students are prepared to communicate on a variety of topics and learn to negotiate meaning in contexts "motivated by real communicative needs" (Littlewood 1985, p. 70). The learner becomes an active participant in the language-learning process and becomes a skill-user, not merely a skill-getter (Rivers 1972). Language teaching theorists and experts (Birckbichler and Muyskens 1980; Carrell 1984; Kramsch 1983; Swaffar 1984; Swaffar et al. 1991) have underscored classroom interactions based on functional settings. As a result of this focus, the role of reading has been stressed, "particularly the reading of literature in language acquisition" (Rankin 1990, p. 24). In light of these developments, the role of literature in the foreign language classroom has been reevaluated.

Traditional Approaches to Literature

Traditional approaches to the teaching of foreign literatures have historically been characterized by a teacher-centered classroom, consisting largely of biographical and historical lectures or a New Critical approach. Technical discussions of style and literary concepts were stressed and "literature" referred exclusively to the great classics. Such a teacher-dominated classroom focused on the "magical unlocking of the meaning of the text" (Bretz 1990, p. 336). The learner was regarded as the receiver of information, an empty vessel if you will, who would be provided "the true" interpretation by the instructor. The reader/

learner was the passive recipient of knowledge, not an active participant who was required to think, comprehend, apply, analyze, synthesize, and evaluate.[3] As a result, the learner/reader felt helpless without the aid of an instructor when reading a piece of literature and became "disempowered," often resulting in the cessation of attempts to read on his or her own.

It is perhaps for this reason that Omaggio (1986, p. 163) relegated the role of literature to the advanced level on the proficiency scale. To understand lectures on technical literary style or the New Critical approach, and to express opinions and interpretations would require an advanced proficiency. Content questions might help to make the plot clearer, but at the same time these questions underscore the "one answer only" approach. Such content questions do not provide sufficient interaction to promote any real degree of proficiency.

Literature in the Beginning Language Classroom

As a result of numerous scholarly studies on discourse analysis (Kramsch 1985) and the dynamic processes of reading (Carrell 1984), teaching methods and strategies were explored that promoted a student-centered, interactive approach to the teaching of literature. Bredella (1987), Kast (1984), Krusche and Krechel (1984), and Morewedge (1987) have provided numerous creative and innovative techniques and strategies that allowed the reader to become intimately involved with the literary text. Such pedagogical approaches to the study of literature and literary texts emphasized that "skill development and content-processing should go hand in hand, and the higher-level cognitive operations that are associated with content-processing should be part of each student's earliest language experiences" (Jurasek and Jurasek 1991, p. 93).

Littlewood (1985) has pointed out that foreign language learning does not occur in a "step-by-step progression through the separate parts of the system" (p. 96). He promotes teaching communication strategies that encourage learners to use language as a system "which is elaborated globally and increases gradually in communicative potential" (p. 92). This is in keeping with Krashen's (1982) theory that advocates authentic, natural, comprehensible input that is "roughly tuned" and is pegged slightly above the level of the student. Krashen's "input + 1" supports the incorporation of activities to build communicative competence through well-designed activities that build comprehension and proficiency.

Hans Hunfeld (1990) promotes the use of literature in the very beginning stages of language instruction so that language students learn the connotative use of language from the onset and build from there. He feels that the language textbook should be supplemented with literary texts that are linguistically and culturally rewarding for the language learner. He points out that the inherent danger of a textbook is to underestimate the ability of the learner. Since the cognitive development of learners far exceeds their ability to express themselves in the target language, the result can lead to boredom and disinterest. Hunfeld suggests finding a connection between the textbook and literary texts that would "express the multiplicity of the texts in foreign language teaching"[4] (p. 33).

Hunfeld recommends the inclusion of lyric poetry into the foreign language classroom. He argues that lyric poetry is designed to initiate a reaction from the reader. When this reaction moves language learners to speak, the practical language goals of the classroom have been achieved. If language learners are motivated to express their opinions, then poetry takes on the hermeneutic dimension. Hunfeld argues that lyric poetry speaks differently to foreign learners than to native speakers. This provides fertile ground for the classroom teacher to discuss similarities and differences in the language and culture, a task that is difficult to achieve in the textbook (Moeller 1991).

Learning Theory and Learning in Context

Recent research in education has clearly proven that optimum learning is achieved through discovery, rather than information-giving (Hyde and Bizar 1989). Strategies such as cooperative learning, pair work and small-group activities, and hands-on activities accomplish long-term retention and understanding of concepts, rather than mere memorization of facts. Holistic approaches to reading, listening, speaking (whole language), and writing (portfolio assessment) have redefined the curriculum for elementary education. Upon close analysis of these curricular movements in education, it becomes clear that there are numerous parallels in the field of second language learning. The emphasis is on "authentic texts," "learning in context," and functional use of language.

Another matter of concern in the area of education is teaching across the curriculum. Teaching subjects in isolation fails to provide students with the necessary context to fully comprehend the interconnectedness between the disciplines, thus no allowance is made for higher-level skills such as synthesis and analysis. By linking language and subject matter from other areas of the curriculum (e.g., social studies, history, art), the isolation of the language class can be countered. It is the contention of this paper that all of the objectives ranging from oral proficiency to connotative language understanding to cultural literacy can be achieved through the use of literary texts in the foreign language classroom.

Reader Response: A Context-Based Approach

As discussed earlier in this paper, literature has traditionally been viewed exclusively as the "great classics," and has been taught in an objective, formal, text-centered manner (New Criticism). Reader-response theorists have promoted a holistic, reader-centered, context-based approach that views the text as a dynamic, allowing for a variety of interpretations based on the past experiences and knowledge of the reader. According to Stanley Fish (1980), the emphasis should not be placed on the text as the object, but rather on the responses of the reader. "Response," according to Fish, incorporates much more than feelings and the affective domain, but includes "any and all of the activities provoked by a string of words: the projection of syntactical and/or lexical probabilities—their subsequent occurrence or nonoccurrence; attitudes towards persons, or things, or ideas referred to, the reversal or questioning of these attitudes and much more" (p. 2). According to this view of literature, the reader is treated as a coauthor who brings to the text a set of experiences and knowledge that will determine the interpretation of the text. According to Reader Response Criticism, a text "scarcely exists until somebody reads it" (Holeman and Harmon 1986, p. 412).

The reader's experiences and imagination will determine how the *Leerstellen/ Umbestimmtheitsstellen* ("holes"; unclear spots) that occur in a text will be filled (Bredella 1984). If reference is made to a dog in a text, each reader envisions a dog unique to his or her knowledge and personal experiences. By allowing the reader the opportunity to articulate, or describe, what he or she is imagining or visualizing, the reader becomes actively involved in the text and classroom. According to Hunfeld (1990), then, literature takes on the hermeneutic dimension, in that the reader is motivated to express an opinion.

Literature: A New Definition

The narrow definition of "literature" as the "great classics" has recently been revised and expanded to include a variety of literary texts that include "popular theater, television dramatizations, cartoons, advertisements, political discourses, and film" (Schofer 1990, p. 327). Schofer contends that the "aim is not to call all written texts 'literature' but rather to show our students how literary devices permeate every part of our lives" (p. 327).

This expanded definition of literary texts allows the classroom teacher to incorporate a wide variety of texts, including the classics.

Criteria for Selection of Literary Texts

The most important considerations in choosing appropriate literary texts for the foreign language classroom include the following criteria:

1. appropriate linguistic level
2. appropriate length of the text
3. age of the student
4. whether the content awakens interest and motivates the reader
5. whether the text expands cognitive, esthetic, and emotional development
6. whether the text promotes cultural understanding (deeper understanding/ communication with the culture through common literacy)
7. whether the text expands vocabulary skills and acquisition of vocabulary

In summary, the literary texts should prove culturally and linguistically rewarding to the readers and should be personalized to meet the needs of the individual classrooms and students. Motivational considerations should outweigh "a desire to introduce representative authors and themes" (Wells 1984, p. 197) in the choice of texts. It is generally accepted that a text should be no longer than 400–600 words at the third-year level if it is a nonliterary text. Literary texts can be 800–1000 words in length because the plot provides a context to remember the facts outlined in the text (Wells 1984, p. 199).

Theory in Practice

Keeping in mind all the theoretical considerations discussed at length in this paper, an analysis of these premises from a practice-oriented approach is in order. How do these theoretical studies and insights actually work in the practice of teaching a literary text?

Bremen Town Musicians: *A Concrete Example*

In order to illustrate how a literary text might be used to incorporate the above-mentioned strategies, it is necessary to select a single text that will serve as a frame of reference for illustrating possible activities and strategies to achieve the goals stated in the first half of this paper. A Grimm's fairy tale entitled *The Bremen Town Musicians* will serve as the literary text in the foreign language classroom. The example presented here is in English in order to cross language lines. The reader can easily transfer these strategies onto any literary text in his or her foreign language.

Emphasized will be the integration of culture, art, history, literary genres, pair work/small-group activities, reading, writing, speaking and listening activities appropriate for the novice- or intermediate-level foreign language classroom. Cooperative learning and interactive activities that lead to a student-centered, proficiency-centered classroom will be highlighted and concretely illustrated and described.

Prereading Strategies

The teacher places a transparency depicting the four animals from *The Bremen Town Musicians* on the overhead machine (see figure 4-1). Students are asked to identify the four animals they see pictured. The teacher can then quickly introduce the prepositions *under, between,* and *on top of* by describing the positions of the animals. Have students walk to the screen and point out the animal the teacher describes in words such as "This animal is located between the cat and the donkey." The animal sounds can be added to the description. A discussion could ensue on the different sounds animals make in different languages. An American rooster says "cock-a-doodle-doo" and a German rooster says "kikeriki." This is an excellent global activity that can lead to insightful discussions and comments. A quick comprehension check of prepositions and animal vocabulary can be carried out by having students raise their left hand for false and right hand for true statements, such as "the donkey is under the dog" or "the rooster is on top of the dog."

Students could be divided into groups of three for a maximum of 5 minutes to create a story about these four animals. This is done in English at the novice level. The purpose of this activity is threefold: (1) it is one way to motivate students to want to read what really happens, (2) the students become personally involved with the text before actually reading it, and (3) it kindles the imagination of students and lowers the affective filter as students become better acquainted with each other and work together to create a story.

Another approach is to begin with an associogram. The teacher writes the words "Grimm Brothers" on a transparency and asks the class to respond with the first thing that comes to their minds (see figure 4-2). As students begin to respond, the teacher records the answers on the transparency. Each answer will trigger responses from other students. These responses can serve as a springboard for a discussion on the Grimm brothers and the fairy tale.

An interactive activity that ensures a combination of reading, listening, and speaking skills is the following pair-work activity. Students are divided into pairs

Literature for Teaching Language and Culture in Context   37

Figure 4-1. The four animals.
Used by permission of HIGHLIGHTS FOR CHILDREN, INC., Columbus, OH
Copyright © 1980.

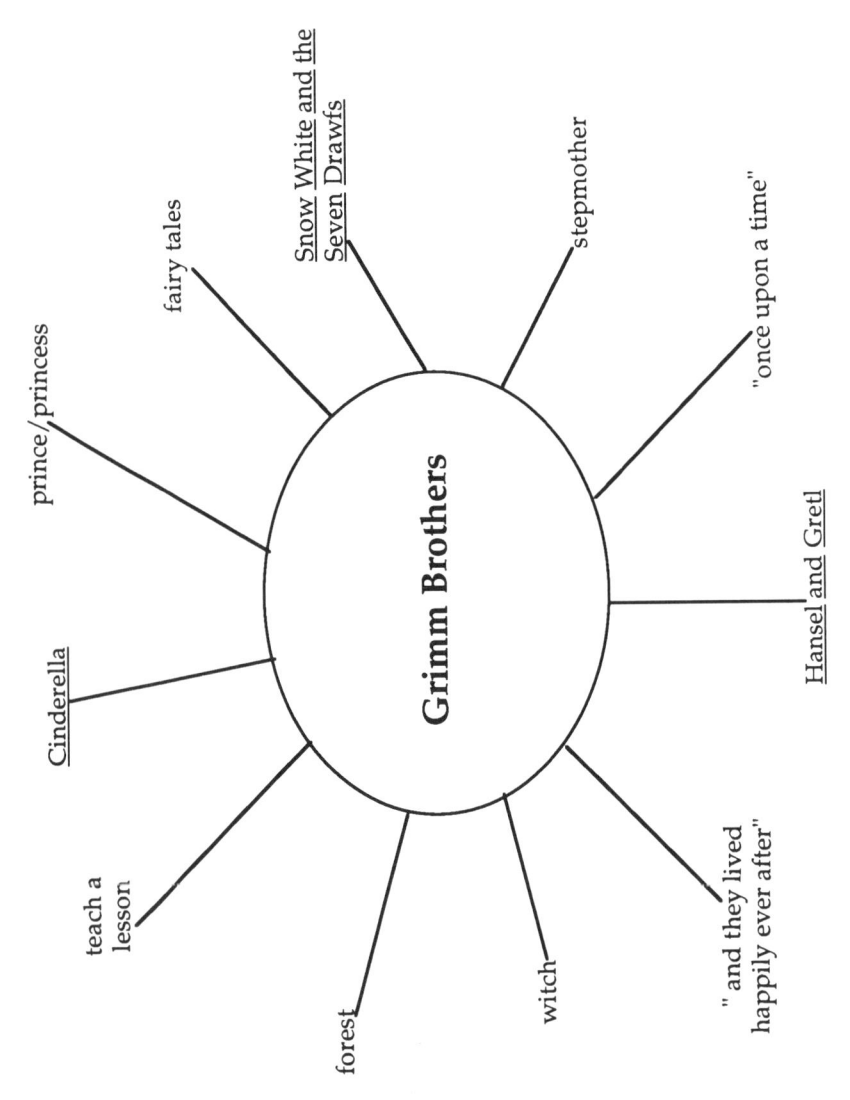

38   Creative Approaches in Foreign Language Teaching

Figure 4-2. An associogram of Grimm brothers for novice-level learners.

(*A* and *B*). *A* is given a reading text containing a picture of the Grimm brothers and a text containing biographical and historical information about the two brothers (in the target language). *B* is given a text containing information about Grimms' fairy tales and the elements that make up a fairy tale. On the bottoms of both *A* and *B*'s papers is a series of questions (true/false; fill in dates; sentence completions) that must be answered by the student (see figure 4-3). The students are required to elicit information from one another in order to answer these questions. This activity involves active reading, posing questions, listening for responses, and recording the required information. In addition to all this, the students are learning about two important German figures, a literary genre, and a historical period and are provided with what is a part of every German's cultural literacy—Grimms' fairy tales. This provides the vital link of a "shared frame of reference" to the target culture that is not readily achieved through a textbook.

First Reading Activities

The students are handed a one-page text without a title (see figure 4-4). They are asked to keep it turned over until told to do otherwise. The teacher instructs the students to read the first paragraph only and, once finished with the paragraph, to turn the page over again. The teacher then gathers the answers to the following questions on an overhead transparency: who, what, when, where why. This is all conducted in the target language. Students are able to respond in single words and short phrases to answer these questions. The resulting answers already provide the student with a framework for the story (who: donkey; what: master who wants to get rid of him; when: don't know; where: Bremen; why: he's old and can't carry the sacks). It is a good idea always to number the lines of all the lines of all texts so in case of dispute, the students can easily identify the line of text upon which they are basing their answer. This allows for a variety of legitimate answers, as long as they can be validated in the text itself. This is an excellent strategy for getting the students to do a more detailed reading of the text a second and third time to find confirmation for an answer.

An excellent listening activity aimed at increasing vocabulary is possible by providing the students with a cloze text of the fairy tale. A recording of the fairy tale (either commercial or self-produced) is played and students fill in the blanks as they listen to it. It is a good idea to do such an activity in short segments of text and to allow the students to work in pairs. This lowers the anxiety and encourages a cooperative atmosphere. The teacher follows up this activity by placing an overhead transparency containing the cloze text and calls upon the students to read the sentences with the correctly filled-in blank. The students can walk up to the transparency projector and fill in the blanks as the teacher circulates to assist those with questions. As a homework assignment, students are given ten true-false statements they must either correct to make true, or designate as already being true. In doing so they must record the line of the text that confirms their answer.

Small-Group Activities

Another effective approach is to divide the text into six or seven segments. In teams of three, each team must underline unfamiliar words and attempt to guess at the meaning of these words from the context. This promotes contextual guessing skills, an important skill for problem solving. It is recommended that at least two teams have the same segments so that they can then join the team with the same paragraph and compare answers and revise according to the consensus of the larger group. Dictionaries are not allowed in this exercise. The idea behind the activity is to train students to read larger segments of text without looking up

Partner A: Grimms' Fairy Tales

Fairy tales were stories people told to each other by word of mouth for many centuries. In the 19th century two brothers in Germany, Jakob and Wilhelm Grimm, became interested in these stories. They wrote these oral tales down and published them. Some of the most well known fairy tales are *Cinderella, Hansel and Gretl, Rumpelstiltskin,* and *Snow White and the Seven Dwarfs.* Fairy tales often begin with the phrase "Once upon a time" and end with "and then they lived happily ever after." The place a fairy tale happens is never really made clear in the tale. The people in the story don't always have names, or they have simple names like Jack or Tim. They never have a last name. The fairy tales usually describe how a human being meets a fairy—as in *Cinderella,* when she meets her fairy godmother. The plot usually consists of three parts: (1) the hero/heroine is being treated badly at the beginning of the story, (2) the hero/heroine must survive danger, (3) the solution to the problem in which the hero/heroine uses a magical means, fights, and conquers. The bad person is punished.

The characters in a fairy tale do not possess the characteristics of a real human being. They are bad or good and remain superficial, one-dimensional figures. Animals have the ability to speak in fairy tales. Numbers play a significant role in fairy tales. The numbers 3, 7, and 12 are the most common. A hero must accomplish three deeds, or has three wishes. There are seven dwarfs and seven years in most tales. The numbers 7 and 12 are sacred numbers: the Catholic Church has seven sacraments; there are seven days of the week; there are seven colors; the Old Testament speaks of twelve tribes of Israel and there are twelve apostles. Fairy tales serve to entertain and take the reader into a world of make-believe, away from the real world. Many of the fairy tales teach a moral lesson, making them especially popular with children.

Pose the following questions to your partner (B) and record your answers.

1. In what years were Jakob and Wilhelm Grimm born?
2. Which countries were in power during their lifetimes?
3. From whom did they hear many of the tales included in their collection of fairy tales?

True or false? If false, make the statement correct.
 _____ Wilhelm Grimm is famous for his book on German grammar.
 _____ Wilhelm and Jakob Grimm collected books on fairy tales.

Figure 4-3a. Pair-work activity: Partner A's sheet.

Literature for Teaching Language and Culture in Context   41

Partner B: The Grimm Brothers

Jakob Grimm was born January 4, 1785, at Hanau in Hesse-Kassel. Wilhelm was born on February 24, 1786. They grew up when Germany was a loosely organized federation of states. Prussia and Austria were the leading kingdoms. They studied law at the University of Marburg. Jakob came into contact with a famous law professor and scholar named Savigny, who interested him in the legends of the Middle Ages and in the songs of the minnesingers, the German poet-singers of the 12th, 13th, and 14th centuries. Jakob and Wilhelm became librarians at the University of Göttingen. Both brothers were given professorships at the University of Berlin and were elected to the Academy of Science. Jakob wrote a book on German grammar that is still considered a great work in language study. Both worked on a dictionary of the German language and on the collection of folktales. They spent fourteen years collecting stories that were included in their three volumes of fairy tales. The first volume, *Kinder und Hausmärchen*, was published in 1812. Among those they interviewed regarding these folktales was a Margarethe Viehmännin, a peasant woman who lived near Kassel. She had an amazing memory and served as a rich source of tales for the Grimm brothers. A second volume was published in 1815, and a third in 1822.

Pose the following questions to your partner (A) and record the answers.

1. What are the three common elements of a plot in a fairy tale?
2. Describe a typical fairy-tale character. Give a minimum of three traits.
3. Why are fairy tales still popular?

True or false? If false, make the statement correct.

_____ Fairy tales were collected and recorded for the first time in the 12th century.

_____ The numbers 3, 7, and 12 were used in fairy tales because they are magical and sacred.

_____ *Hansel and Gretl* is a fairy tale collected and recorded by Hans Christian Andersen.

Figure 4-3b. Pair-work activity: Partner B's sheet.

The Bremen Town Musicians

Once there was a donkey who had carried his master's sacks to the mill for years. Now that the donkey was old, his master wanted to get rid of him. The donkey sensed that something bad was in the wind and set out for Bremen, where he thought he might become town musician.

Walking a short way, he came upon a hound panting by the side of the road. The donkey asked, "Hound, why are you out of breath?"

The hound answered, "I am old. I can no longer keep up with the hunt. My master wants to kill me. I ran away. What can I do?"

"I am off the Bremen to become town musician. Why not join me?"

The hound agreed and they walked together. Shortly, they came to a cat with a face like three rainy days. "What's wrong?" they asked.

"I am old and would rather sit by the oven than hunt mice. My mistress wants to drown me. Where can I go?" asked the cat.

"Cats are full of night music. Come and be a musician in Bremen."

The cat joined them. Walking on, they came to a cock crowing wildly.

"You cries shiver my spine," said the donkey. "What's wrong?"

"My mistress wants to cook me when company comes for Sunday dinner. So I am crowing with all my might while I still can."

"Come with us and call out your morning music in Bremen." The cock agreed and the four walked on together.

But Bremen was too far off to be reached in a day. At dusk they came upon a wood where they decided to spend the night. Seeing a light in the distance, they headed for it. The light came from a house. The donkey, being the biggest, went and looked in the window. "What do you see?" asked the hound.

"I see good things to eat and drink all laid upon a table," responded the donkey. "And I see robbers making themselves very comfortable."

"I wish we could trade places with them," said the cock.

The others agreed. So they huddled together, and at last they hit upon a plan to drive the robbers from the house.

Hound upon donkey, cat upon hound, and cock atop, they perched by the window. Then came music—the donkey brayed, the hound barked, the cat yowled, and the cock crowed. The frightened robbers ran for the forest.

The four companions made free with the food on the table, eating it all. Afterwards each sought a sleeping place befitting his nature. The donkey lay upon the dunghill in the yard, the hound behind the door, the cat on the hearth, and the cock on a roof beam.

At midnight, when the house had been quiet for some time, the robber captain ordered one of the robbers to scout the house.

Finding everything still, the robber went in. Thinking the cat's glowing eyes were glowing embers, he held a match to them to get light. The cat flew at him, spitting and scratching. Terrified, the robber ran out the door, and the hound bit his leg. In the yard the donkey kicked him sharply. The hubbub woke the cock, who cried "Cock-a-doodle-do!"

Returning to the captain, the robber gasped, "A horrible witch came at me and scratched my face. By the door a guard stabbed me in the leg. In the yard a monster beat me with a club. From above, a judge called, 'Cook him in the stew!' So I got away as fast as I could."

Well, the robbers would have nothing to do with the house. But it suited the four musicians just fine, and there they stayed.

Figure 4-4. *The Bremen Town Musicians (Highlights)*
Used by permission of *Highlights for Children, Inc.*, Columbus, OH, Copyright © 1980.

every word. This encourages skimming and scanning for meaning in preference to a word-for-word translation. This builds the students' self-esteem and confidence in their ability to comprehend the gist of a lengthier text and motivates them to continue reading.

In groups of three students, reread the text and pick out the fifteen key words in the story. Again, this can be performed with shorter text segments, in which case each team is limited to three key words. A variation of this activity is to have students pick out word pairs such as donkey–miller; Bremen–town musicians; hound–hunt; cat–mice; cock–crowing; robbers–house. This forces the student to read the text very closely to determine logical pair matches. The next day the teacher hands each student a sheet of paper with one word in large letters written on it. When the bell rings, the teacher asks the students to find their partners and line up in front of the classroom. After the students have had time to consult, the students are asked to explain the context of the word pair from the story. Once this is completed, the teacher asks the students to line up chronologically according to the order of the story line. They may get help from their peers and teacher if they ask in the target language. Once lined up chronologically, each student makes up a sentence with the word he or she is holding and the next student builds upon that sentence to eventually retell the story in its entirety. The students have now worked with the text using a variety of skills: they have read the text numerous times, picked out the key words, retold the story, and listened to the text in a variety of settings.

As a homework assignment, students are asked to paraphrase the story in ten short sentences. The next day, the teacher collects these sentences and places them in random order on a sheet of paper, and students must put them in the correct chronological order (this can serve as a comprehension check or a quiz). The activity can be simplified by assigning a letter to each of the ten sentences. In a box numbered one through ten, the students are asked to place the correct letter in chronological order. For example: (a) The robber captain orders one of the robbers to scout the house. (b) The donkey decides to go to Bremen. (c) The donkey meets a hound on the road. (d) The animals rest in the forest. The properly filled in box would look like this: 1. b, 2. c, 3. d, 4. a. This is easy to grade and tests the way the text was taught.

A variation of the comprehension check is to cut up the story into several logical parts and place them in an envelope. Each team, consisting of three members, must place the text segments into the correct order. The first team to finish can be rewarded with extra-credit points for all the team members. This can be done by matching pictures or scenes from the story with the text as well. The Goethe Institute has produced a cartoon version of *The Bremen Town Musicians* with the text that can easily be used for such an activity (Schweckendiek 1987). Beautifully illustrated Grimms' fairy tales are readily available in children's bookstores. Copies can be made of the illustrations and used for retelling and text-matching activities.

Strategies for Building Vocabulary

One of the major advantages of using literature in the classroom is that vocabulary is learned in the context of a plot or story. Research has revealed that learning is facilitated and vocabulary comprehension and acquisition is enhanced when presented in context (Omaggio 1986). An effective way to expand vocabulary skills is through contextual clusters, in which students are required to list all associations that have to do with one concept or character. In *The Bremen Town Musicians,* for example, the students might be asked to find and list all associations with the donkey. The result might look like this: donkey: miller, town musician, old, carried sacks, Bremen, master, makes friends, brayed, robbers, forest. Such contextual clusters could be limited to verbs or adjectives describing each animal.

An alternative way of building vocabulary skills is to pin up the names of the main characters from the text on the bulletin board. The teacher passes out a series of facts recorded on index cards to the students. The students must place the fact under the appropriate character. Examples of such facts from *The Bremen Town Musicians* might be: (1) he could no longer carry sacks, (2) they are the bad guys, (3) she can no longer catch mice, (4) he's afraid of becoming Sunday's supper. The teacher reads them aloud to determine if they have been placed under the appropriate character. The entire story is thereby reviewed and discussed in detail.

An outstanding interactive oral activity for the classroom is a game that is a version of the television show "$20,000 Pyramid." The teacher prepares an overhead transparency that contains numerous lists consisting of six words that were taken from the text of *The Bremen Town Musicians*. The transparency might look like this:

I	II	III	IV
donkey	hound	cat	midnight
window	light	drown	cock-a-doodle-doo
forest	captain	bark	crowed
robbers	house	sacks	Sunday
miller	table	old	light
musician	Bremen	roof	mice

The class is divided into teams consisting of four to six players. Team A comes to the front of the class and they are seated as follows: the captain of the team sits facing the overhead screen and the remaining team members have their backs to the screen and cannot see the words on the transparency. The entire class and the captain of Team A can see the words on the transparency. It is the task of the captain to get his or her teammates to say the six words under rubric one within sixty seconds. The captain is required to keep his or her hands behind his or her back while giving the clues. The clues cannot make use of any part of the word (e.g., classroom—it's a room), and only the target language must be spoken. The captain may pass a word, proceed to the next word, and return to the skipped word if there is time remaining. The teacher reveals one word at a time and will say "correct" if the team provides the correct answer. The total number of correct responses is the number of points earned. The members of each team sit in separate rows. After sixty seconds Team B is up and they follow the same procedures with List II. Usually in one class period one can get through two preliminary rounds and one final bonus round. The bonus round is worth 2 points per correct answer. This is an excellent review activity the day before a unit

Literature for Teaching Language and Culture in Context 45

test. The team members on the winning team are entitled to 10 bonus points each on the unit test. This activity is ideal for building proficiency skills. The first few times this game is played it is slow, but the students very quickly learn tricks to elicit responses from their teammates by using expressions like "plural form," opposites, and the like. The students often resort to the context of the story to describe the word they want to elicit from their teammates. This is a truly interactive oral strategy and provides a lot of learning in a fun atmosphere.

The list of words for the pyramid game can also be restricted to specific subtopics such as (using *The Bremen Town Musicians* as an example): donkey: miller/sacks/Bremen/musician/old/mill. This provides the student with a specific context and narrows the number of options.

Simulations

The Bremen Town Musicians lends itself easily to a stage production or dramatization. The simple plot, the animal sounds, and the dialogs between the characters provide a rich basis for a story simulation. This should be videotaped and shown to the classes next year to illustrate to students (at the beginning of the academic year) how much they will learn and what they will be able to do before the year is over. Playing the videotape the following year to the same students who performed the play also provides a very humanizing and personalizing activity that tends to unify the class members and solidify them as a group.

In order to ensure that the students have an opportunity to create in the language, conversation cards can be created on index cards. An example from *The Bremen Town Musicians* might be as follow: Student A: You are the miller and are trying to convince the donkey to leave. You tell him he is useless and too old to work. He must leave or you will kill him, because you have no money to feed him. Student B: You are the donkey and try to convince the miller that you have been a faithful and loyal worker for twenty years. You can still carry the sacks to the mill, but it simply takes a little longer. Try to convince him that you should stay. The conversation cards must be adjusted to the linguistic competence of your students. Trying to convince someone is a higher-level skill on the proficiency scale, so you will need to adjust the function to the level desired (novice to advanced).

An advanced oral proficiency activity that works well with literature, and particularly with characters in a literary text, is the alter-ego activity. One student stands behind another student. The student in front represents the good side of the donkey, the student behind represents the bad side of the donkey. The good donkey makes a statement such as "I know I'm not as fast as I once was." The alter ego replies, "Well, neither is the miller, but no one is threatening to kill him." Donkey: "The miller is a good man, we have been friends for twenty years." Alter ego: "Friends, you say!! Would a friend kill you because you're old?"

Writing Strategies

Students are divided into groups of three and are asked to come up with an appropriate title for the literary text. This activity requires a thorough understanding of the text, since the title summarizes the main content of the story. This activity can be extended to having the students divide the text into logical segments and provide a title for each segment. Another departure from this type of activity is to omit the last paragraph of the reading text and have the students write the ending of the story. The titles provided by students are often better than the original titles themselves.

One of the most common writing assignments is to rewrite a paragraph in the present, past, or future tense. This is an effective homework assignment that provides the student with a guided practice opportunity in the area of grammar. Students are well acquainted with the text at this point and can concentrate on grammar specifically. Another grammar strategy is to have students paraphrase a particularly difficult sentence into simple language.

Creative writing activities in the classroom allow students who may not succeed in other aspects of the class to shine. The students are asked to write a poem in the shape of a diamond that consists of the following elements: the first line consists of one word that identifies the subject; the second line consists of two verbs that describe the subject; the third line consists of three adjectives that elaborate the subject further; the fourth line consists of a sentence made up of four words describing the subject; the fifth line is either a synonym for the subject or the same word. An example of this type of poem from *The Bremen Town Musicians* would look like this:

Donkey
carry, escape
musical, old, useless
seeking a new life
burro

Creating such poems requires a thorough understanding of the character and allows for individualization. The teacher may want to type poems on a ditto and distribute them to the class so that the poems can be analyzed and read by all members of the class. Such a poetry activity is especially effective with lengthier literary works in which the characters of a novel or short story are depicted in poem form. The cinquain, a five-line stanza, and haiku, an unrhymed verse form of three lines, offer other variations of such a poetry activity.

Concrete poems that illustrate the content of a story, or depict one of the scenes or characters in the text, also allow for individual creativity. The teacher can give a few examples of classic concrete poems and let students create their own concrete poems.

Rewriting *The Bremen Town Musicians* using four other animals is a challenging and creative writing assignment. Another variation might be to do a modern version of the fairy tale.

It is important to recycle aspects of the fairy-tale activity in the subsequent language levels. In the first year of language study, the illustration of *The Bremen Town Musicians* should be introduced as discussed above. In the second year the fairy tale should be introduced and taught while incorporating some of the strategies outlined in this paper. In the third year a more linguistically challenging fairy tale should be introduced. In the fourth year a good followup on the problem of aging depicted in *The Bremen Town Musicians* would, for German classes, be the short story by Bertolt Brecht entitled *An Unworthy Old Lady (Die unwürdige Greisin)*. This recycles vocabulary and themes and assures a gradual progression up the proficiency ladder.

The Cultural Link

The Bremen Town Musicians provides a wealth of opportunities to tap into aspects of German culture. The town of Bremen itself allows for a geography and history lesson. Located on the Weser River, it is the second-largest harbor in Germany. It was a prestigious member of the powerful Hanseatic League and still bears the honor of being the "Hansestadt Bremen." An innovative way to learn more about Bremen might be to distribute a variety of materials (authentic texts) about Bremen to the students, divided into teams of three. Two or three groups receive a brochure about Bremen and extract certain information from that brochure and report it to the class. Each team would be assigned to glean different information. A fourth team receives a novice-level reading text describing the history of Bremen, a fifth team receives several postcards and must list the most popular attractions in Bremen. The students become the experts on Bremen and report the information to the class, as the teacher records the information on an overhead transparency. This provides an ownership in the gathering of facts—learning through discovery, not mere fact-receiving from the teacher. The symbol of the city of Bremen is the statue of the four animals, which is located next to the city hall. After having read the Grimms' fairy tale, they are aware of the significance and meaning. This provides a "shared frame of reference" with the target culture.

The elements of a fairy tale might be discussed in the context of *The Bremen Town Musicians*. What is unique about a fairy tale, what is its purpose, and who collected them? Teaching across the curriculum can reinforce literary analysis and genre study (English). The historical times in which the fairy tales were popular and the historical context in which they were passed on by word of mouth and eventually collected and recorded provide a link to history. The Grimm brothers and their importance in literature, as well as in the history of the German language, can be highlighted in a variety of creative ways.

Testing

It is important to remember to test the way the text was taught. Providing key words/phrases and placing them in the correct chronological order; true-false statements in which the false statements must be made true; rewriting the paragraph in the past tense; creating a diamond poem about the robbers; finishing the retelling of the story; crossing out a phrase that does not fit with four other statements. Such test items will be an indication of what the students have learned by doing and results are bound to be positive.

Conclusion

An attempt has been made to provide theoretical and practical arguments for the inclusion of literary texts at all levels in the foreign language curriculum. Literary texts offer the opportunity to combine proficiency and literacy, denotative and connotative language learning, and learning in context. The reader/student takes center stage in that they become thinkers, position takers, and active learners. They are negotiators of meaning who have something to say and meanings to express. Interactive teaching strategies, such as those suggested here, allow the reader not "merely [to] decode fixed textual meanings, but also [to] encode meanings of their own" (Jurasek and Jurasek 1991, p. 91).

Literacy in its broadest meaning includes the process by which we make sense of the human experience and define ourselves. As knowledge is accumulated and literacy is expanded, the emphasis is increasingly shifted to the higher-level skills of analysis, synthesis, and evaluation (Bloom et al. 1956) in that connections must be made in terms of how the newly acquired knowledge connects, or fits in, with what is already known. E. D. Hirsch (1987) described his theory of education as "based on the anthropological observation that all human communities are founded upon specific shared information" (p. xv). He points out that each group (Japanese, Germans, Americans) has a specific different body of cultural knowledge. In the anthropological perspective, then, "the basic goal of education in a human community is acculturation, the transmission to children of the specific information shared by the adults of the group or polis" (p. xvi). Hirsch provides a list of "shared information" needed for Americans to communicate effectively with one another in their national community. According to Hirsch, "successful communication depends upon shared associations" (p. 59). When those shared associations are lacking, full participation in the literate national culture is not possible.

The foreign language classroom can and must provide a forum for exposing students to these "shared associations" of a specific culture within the context of the curriculum. Literature provides such an opportunity and forum. By utilizing and putting into practice activities such as those suggested in this paper, the goals of proficiency and literacy can be addressed and achieved.

Notes

1. For further information, contact Ali Moeller, University of Nebraska–Lincoln, 115 Henzlik Hall, Lincoln, NE 68588-0355, (402) 472-2024.
2. The original quote is as follows: "Eine Kultursprache als Fremdsprache lehren wollen, ohne gleichzeitig ihre Literatur mitzulehren, ist eine Form der Barberei."
3. Bloom's Taxonomy classifies six major levels into which cognitive objectives may be classified: knowledge, comprehension, application, analysis, synthesis, and evaluation.
4. Hunfeld states: "Das Beispiel fordert dazu auf, zwischen gängigen Lehrbuchtexten und literarischen Texten von Anfang an eine Verbindung zu suchen. Diese Verbindung muß die Verfältigkeit von Texten in der fremdsprachlichen Lehre zum Ausdruck bringen."

References

Birckbichler, Diane, and Judith A. Muyskens. 1980. "A Personalized Approach to the Teaching of Literature at the Elementary and Intermediate Levels of Instruction." *Foreign Language Annals* 13: 23–27.

Bloom, Benjamin, et al. 1956. *Taxonomy of Educational Objectives. Handbook I: Cognitive Domain.* New York: Longmans Green.

Bredella, K. 1984. "Literarische Texte im fremdsprachenunterricht: Gründe und Methoden," pp. 352–93 in M. Heid, ed., *Literarische Texte im Kommunikativen fremdsprachenunterricht.* Munich, Ger.: Goethe Institute.

―――. 1987. "Lesen als 'Gelenktes Schaffen': Literarische Texte in fremdsprachenunterricht." *Unterrichtspraxis* 20: 166–84.

Bretz, M. L. 1990. "Reaction: Literature and Communicative Competence: A Springboard for the Development of Critical Thinking and Aesthetic Appreciation." *Foreign Language Annals* 23: 335–38.

Carrell, Patricia L. 1984. "Schema Theory and ESL Reading: Classroom Implications and Applications." *Modern Language Journal* 68: 332–43.

Fish, Stanley. 1980. *Is There a Text in This Class?* Cambridge, MA: Harvard Univ. Press.

Hirsch, E. D. 1987. *Cultural Literacy.* Boston: Houghton Mifflin.

Holeman, C., and W. Harmon. 1986. *A Handbook to Literature.* New York: Macmillan.

Hunfeld, Hans. 1990. *Literatur als Sprachlehre: Ansätze eines hermeneutisch orientierten Fremdsprachenunterrichts.* Berlin, Ger.: Langenscheidt.

Hyde, A., and M. Bizar. 1989. *Thinking in Context.* New York: Longman.

Jurasek, B., and R. Jurasek. 1991. "Building Multiple Proficiencies in New Curricular Contexts," pp. 89–121 in June Phillips, ed., *Building Bridges and Making Connections.* Report of the Northeast Conference on the Teaching of Foreign Languages. Middlebury, VT: The Northeast Conference.

Kast, B. 1984. *Literatur im Unterricht: Methodisch-didaktische Vorschläge für den Lehrer.* Munich, Ger.: Goethe Institute.

Kramsch, Claire J. 1983. "Interaction in the Classroom: Learning How to Negotiate Roles and Meaning.: *Unterrichtspraxis* 16: 175–90.

―――. 1985. "Literacy Texts in the Classroom: A Discourse." *Modern Language Journal* 69: 356–66.

Krashen, S. 1982. *Principles and Practice in Second Language Acquisition.* New York: Pergamon.

Krusche, D., and Rüdiger Krechel. 1984. *Anspiel: Konkrete Poesie im Unterricht Deutsch als Fremdsprache.* Bonn, Ger.: Internationes.

Littlewood, William. 1985. *Foreign and Second Language Learning: Language Acquisition Research and Its Implications for the Classroom.* Cambridge, Eng.: Cambridge Univ. Press.

Moeller, Aleidine. 1991. Review of H. Hunfeld, *Literatur als Sprachlehre. Modern Language Journal* 75: 366–67.

Morewedge, R. 1987. "Literature in the Intermediate German Classroom: *Eine grössere Anschaffung.*" *Unterrichtspraxis* 20: 217–33.

Omaggio, Alice. 1986. *Teaching Language in Context.* Boston: Heinle and Heinle.

Rankin, J. 1990. "Re-Visiting *Der Besuch der alten Dame*: Strategies for Interpretation and Interaction at the Intermediate Level." *Unterrichtspraxis* 22: 24–34.

Rivers, Wilga. 1972. *Speaking with Many Tongues.* Cambridge, Eng.: Cambridge Univ. Press.

Schofer, P. 1990. "Literature and Communicative Competence: A Springboard for the Development of Critical Thinking and Aesthetic Appreciation of Literature in the Land of Language." *Foreign Language Annals* 23: 325–38.

Schweckendiek, J., et al. 1987. *Märchen als Schreib- und Sprechanlässe.* Munich, Ger.: Goethe Institute.

Swaffar, Janet K. 1984. "Reading in the Foreign Language Classroom: Focus on the Process." *Unterrichtspraxis* 17: 176–94.

―――, Katherine Arens, and Heidi Byrnes. 1991. *Reading for Meaning.* Englewood Cliffs, NJ: Prentice Hall.

Weinrich, Harald. 1983. "Die vernachlässigte 'Fertigkeit'—Literarische Lektüre im Fremdsprachenunterricht," p. 11 in K. Völker et al., eds., *Literarische Lektüre in der Unterrichtspraxis. I: Seminararbeit,* Munich, Ger.: Goethe Institute.

Wells, L. 1984. "Short Literary Prose Texts in Second-Year German Instruction," in M. Heid, ed., *Literarische Texte im Kommunikativen fremdsprachenunterricht.* Munich, Ger.: Goethe Institute.

5
A Case for Cooperative Learning in the Foreign Language Classroom

Susan G. Colville-Hall
University of Akron

The twenty-first century is less than a decade away. Reform is on the minds and the lips of educational institutions as they reexamine their mission, curricula, staffing, and effectiveness in educating the youth of America. Paralleling these concerns for reform, th foreign language profession is also involved in self-examination. Foreign language educators recognize the necessity of matching goals of language programs with the needs of students who will soon be functioning as part of a greater society. Incorporating the elements that will contribute to the preparation of individuals who can build satisfactory, interdependent relationships with other peoples, societies, and nations is essential to educational reform.

The purpose of this article is to examine closely two areas of study that are influencing how foreign language educators view language learning: (1) the study of language for the purpose of understanding, communicating, and negotiating meaning, and (2) cooperative learning for greater academic achievement and cooperation in group efforts. In addition, this report presents a rationale for using cooperative learning in the foreign language classroom and gives examples of some cooperative techniques found to be effective in the foreign language classroom. A partial listing of material sources for activities is also included.

Interactive Language for Purposes of Communication

Much of the reevaluation of language learning is due to research conducted in the last decade in second language acquisition. This research has transformed the focus of language study. Traditionally, the grammatical syllabus had guided language study. Studies in second language acquisition, however, have indicated that interaction through negotiation of the meaning of the message is essential in order for language acquisition to take place (Long 1985). A new focus, which Kramsch (1987) calls a "functionally-oriented, interactionally-based foreign language pedagogy," identifies what students can do through language rather than what students know about the language (Met 1990). Components other than grammar that are necessary for communication can no longer be ignored if, indeed, the goal of language study is to be able to interact with others in the language (Bejarano 1987).

A Case for Cooperative Learning in the FL Classroom

To be successful communicators in a foreign language, students not only need grammatical knowledge to create acceptable sentences, but also require discourse knowledge and skills (to effectively clarify and negotiate meaning, give and receive help, and initiate or extend interaction), sociolinguistic competence (to operate in the appropriate register for each given social situation), and strategic competence to use knowledge to guess what is being said when not all pieces of the message are known or make sense (Canale and Swain 1980). What a speaker can accomplish with language is illustrated in the following scenario. On a cold morning as two colleagues ride together to work, one colleague drives as the other asks, "Does your heater work?" This utterance tells that the speaker knows how to put a simple utterance together using the present tense (grammatical knowledge). It also indicates knowledge of how to ask questions and, thereby, initiate discourse by putting the tag "does" at the beginning of the sentence (grammatical and discourse knowledge). In addition, the speaker shows respect for the social position of a colleague by using a question instead of issuing the command "Turn on the heat" (sociolinguistic knowledge). If the utterance had not been completely heard, that is, if only "heater work" had been heard with a rising intonation, the listener could probably have guessed the meaning of the utterance (strategic knowledge).

This refocus on language study is forcing a change in the learning environment, in terms of instructional format. Traditionally, students' use of language in the classroom was largely in response to the teacher's questioning, the correction of activities, listening to the presentation of new concepts, and participating in drill practice. The teacher-centered environment has not provided students adequate opportunity to develop diverse linguistic capabilities. To acquire a second language successfully, many students need to experiment and practice in an open, nonthreatening environment (McGroarty 1989). Unfortunately, teacher-centered instruction has not been easy to change because teachers (and administrators) often prefer a learning environment that gives the appearance of students quietly learning and "under control." Even in immersion classes, the opportunity for contextualized exchanges in which peer learners test hypotheses about language is generally missing from the foreign language classroom (Swain 1985). In fact, foreign language learning environments often lack the criteria needed to facilitate learning language that produces a likeness to native speech: sufficient comprehensible input, interesting and relevant input, periods of absence from language production, integration of "tools" for conversational management, sufficient negotiated interaction, comprehensible output, and optimal affective factors (Schinke-Llano 1990).

Greater use of small-group interaction and pair work has increased student opportunities to use language in the foreign language classroom. Students working together are able to practice and appear to stay on task as long as the teacher holds them accountable for the activity. Through pair practice and small-group interaction, students are successful in making the meaningful communication that researchers acknowledge is important to the language-acquisition process (Long 1985; Long and Porter 1985). Studies conducted in immersion schools have suggested that peer exchanges in which meaning is negotiated provide the comprehensible output necessary to foreign language acquisition (Swain 1985).

In an investigation of interactions of students in a French class, college students, when assigned to small-group tasks, established discourse moves by initiating, eliciting, responding to, and extending interaction (Colville-Hall 1983). Transcripts produced evidence that students used social skills to create a supportive environment in which students assisted one another, agreed and disagreed with one another, made suggestions, and collaborated in a communicative effort.

Cooperative Learning

Cooperative learning, a method of instruction similar to small-group work but with a definite structure and specific criteria, is becoming a frequently used format in instruction in a variety of disciplines and at all educational levels. Cooperative learning consists of tasks requiring positive interdependence where students, who are accountable for their contributions, interact face-to-face to create a group product (Johnson, Johnson, and Holubec 1986). In completing these tasks, students use interpersonal and small-group skills. Groups are heterogeneous in nature, with all members considered as equal and sharing the responsibility for learning. There are two goals, the academic and the social:

1. Learning should be achieved to the maximum for each individual participating through total group efforts.
2. Students must maintain good working relationships that demonstrate amiability, mutual respect, and support while accomplishing assigned tasks.

It is important to teach social skills, such as leadership and the ability to communicate well, before the task is assigned. Also essential to group success in completing the assigned task is the role of the teacher as an observer and facilitator, one who intervenes only as a last resort.

Because of its inherent element of negotiation in the students' effort to accomplish a task, cooperative learning has certain benefits for language study. For the foreign language learner, cooperative learning instruction leads to greater frequency of linguistic practice, increased opportunity for more varied interaction, a positive feeling about language study, and a more active role as a learner (McGroarty 1989; Bejarano 1987). These advantages translate into increased growth in self-confidence for the foreign language learner. Improved self-confidence encourages students to participate in peer conversations in which they must attend to the discussion in order to (1) take their turns, (2) make guesses from the context if they do not fully comprehend the utterance, (3) agree or disagree, (4) support or contest, (5) focus on the main point, and (6) cooperate interactively to reach a mutual understanding.

The integration of cooperative learning tasks into foreign language instruction and the practice in negotiation inherent in peer interaction can bring about a more adequate preparation for language learners to meet the demands of communication in the interdependent world of the twenty-first century.

Rationale for Cooperative Learning

Results from numerous studies on cooperative learning are positive for both student achievement and students' attitudes toward learning. A significant number of empirical studies substantiate the effectiveness of cooperative learning methods in the achievement of higher academic skills. Students who work in groups to achieve group goals register greater improvement than students working in a traditional setting (Johnson et al 1981; Slavin 1983). In 1981 researchers reviewed 122 studies in a variety of academic areas and concluded that cooperation was considerably more effective than competition or individualist efforts (Johnson et al. 1981). A second analysis of a large group of studies supported cooperative learning methods as responsible for the successful interaction and achievement of minority and handicapped students (Johnson, Johnson, and Maruyama 1983).

One of the first studies on cooperative learning in a foreign language class found student attitudes to be positively affected by learning in cooperative groups (Gunderson and Johnson 1980). Peer support had a positive impact on the quality of the work of seventh graders studying French, how well they liked French, and how well they liked learning in peer groups.

In a study that focused on two different categories of learners, both minority ethnic students and majority ethnic students, in an eighth-grade English-as-a-foreign-language (EFL) class in Israel, minority and majority ethnic students alike derived greater academic benefit from small-group cooperative learning (Sharan et al. 1984). Minority students in a traditional setting participated less and earned lower scores on tests of achievement than the minority students who were in classes in which cooperative learning methods were used.

Later, Sharan and Shachar (1988) explored the effects of cooperative learning on higher-level thinking and informational knowledge (lower-level) in EFL classes. Results showed that students attained a superior level of academic achievement in activities requiring both low-level and high-level thinking. Cooperation tended to equalize the quantity of participatory remarks by both minority and majority ethnic group members, a situation normally dominated by the majority group in the traditional classroom format.

In addition to the positive affective factor and academic achievement, a third benefit of cooperative learning instruction, and perhaps one of the most important, is the socialization factor. Studies that reveal the success of the socialization process in students in cooperative learning settings in other fields are many. In foreign languages, one such study focused on handicapped and mainstreamed students in math and foreign language classes (Mesch et al. 1986). The cooperative learning experience in the foreign language class "promoted an enjoyment of the subject being studied, feelings of receiving all the help needed, a sense of improvement in competence, and perceptions of contributing to others' learning" (p. 332). It was concluded that integrating the socially withdrawn and isolated students into a typical social and academic setting is possible through cooperative networking.

Greater effectiveness of cooperative learning instruction in developing listening comprehension skills and in teaching and learning discrete point material such as vocabulary and grammar became apparent from the results of a study in EFL classes that linked communicative competence to cooperative learning instruction (Bejarano 1987). These results were attributed to the use of a communicative approach of deliberately assigning a learning task appropriate to the acquisition of language. Trained observers in classes reported that "students were actively involved in real communication rather than in using answers taken out of texts or manipulating given information or set linguistic structures" (p. 493). In comparing this class to what is often the case of language classes, observers saw that students were actively involved in clarifying their meaning by using a greater range of grammatical and syntactical patterns. This variety of practice is essential to helping students develop "extensive rather than minimal communicative skills" (McGroarty 1989, p. 131).

McGroarty (1989) categorized the advantages of the cooperative learning strategies for English as a second language (ESL) and bilingual instruction as follows:

1. Increased frequency and varied language practice
2. Greater cognitive development
3. Opportunity to integrate learning content with language instruction
4. Exposure to a more diverse variety of curricular materials
5. A gain in confidence as a resource for others
6. A more active role as a learner

Cooperative Learning Methods and Activities

The fundamental goal of cooperative learning is "to create a social environment for pupils conducive to mutual exchange of ideas and perspectives on academic subjects" (Sharan and Shachar 1988, p. 3). This can be achieved through the use of various methods and techniques created by proponents of cooperative learning, of which the most frequently used are (1) peer tutoring (STAD), (2) teams-games-tournaments (TGT), and (3) group investigation. "Quick cooperative starters" that can be readily used with teachers wishing to begin cooperative learning methods include (1) learning partners, (2) reading groups, (3) bookends (see Appendix 5A for a sample activity), (4) jigsaw, (5) drill partners, (6) reading buddies, (7) worksheet checkmates (see Appendix 5A for a sample activity), (8) homework checkers, and (9) test reviewers.*

In peer tutoring or STAD (Student Teams—Achievement Divisions), students work in a four-member, heterogeneous team. The teacher first presents new material, then students work together to ensure that all members know the lesson with complete mastery. A final quiz that evaluates all students individually allows for group as well as individual assessment. Teams' scores may reflect improvement by individual members. (See Appendix 5A for a sample activity.)

Group size and makeup for Teams-Games-Tournament (TGT) are the same as for STAD. Procedures are also the same, with the exception of the quizzes, which are replaced by weekly tournaments in which students compete for points with members from other teams who have a similar academic record at tournament tables. Students who win earn six points for their team, but are moved to tougher competition the following week.

In group investigation (GI) or discussion groups (DG), students in groups numbering 3–5 members carry out the assigned task following these six steps: (1) topic selection, (2) cooperative planning, (3) implementation, (4) analysis and synthesis, (5) presentation of the final product, and (6) evaluation. Participation in this task is approached democratically and requires equitable distribution of roles among group members. (See Appendix 5A for a sample activity.) The GI method is one of the most complex and ambitious of all cooperative learning methods (Sharan et al. 1984).

Conclusion

In looking toward the twenty-first century, Kagan (1989) states that the aim of educators is to prepare students with the skills they need for future success and to become happy, contributing members of society. This goal is further articulated in the statements on philosophy of education for secondary schools in many districts nationwide that contain objectives directed at the development of student responsibility, self-direction, ability to communicate and function effectively in a world community, and ability to adapt to change. These goals are often the focus of foreign language programs across the nation. Attainment of these goals, however, requires not only the study of the foreign language itself, but the practice of certain social and interaction skills that foster interdependence and cooperation.

Cooperative learning is vital because it can provide the opportunity for students to develop skills in cooperation and in communicative competence. Together with language study, cooperative learning in a foreign language class will allow students to explore new language structures and conversational patterns through peer interaction in an environment that does not inhibit or intimidate the learner. To become successful communicators, language students must have the opportunity to interact to acquire effectively discourse knowledge and skills, sociolinguistic knowledge, and strategic competence. Kagan (1989) views the cooperative experience as one in which "the heterogeneous team becomes a positive model of how society can cope with the demographic and economic shifts" (p. 2:2). Cooperative learning in the foreign language classroom can also provide a positive model of how individuals can manage conversation in a foreign tongue in an interactive environment. Citizens of tomorrow must possess skills to work in dynamic social structures that involve greater human diversity and require a sensitivity to interdependence. Teaching the functional uses of a foreign language in various social contexts will improve the learner's ability to interact and provide students with the opportunity to negotiate the meaning of a message. The development of these communication skills is essential to the preparation of American students for the global community of tomorrow.

Note

° For a more complete description of each quick starter, consult *Cooperation in the Classroom* by David W. Johnson and Roger T. Johnson (1990) or write to the publisher, Interaction Book Company, 7208 Cornelia Drive, Edina, MN 55435.

References

Bejarano, Yael. 1987. "A Cooperative Small-Group Methodology in the Language Classroom." *TESOL Quarterly* 16: 483–501.

Canale, Michael, and Merrill Swain. 1980. "Theoretical Bases of Communicative Approaches to Second Language Teaching and Testing." *Applied Linguistics* 1: 1–47.

Colville-Hall, Susan. 1983. "A Naturalistic Study of Student–Student Interaction in a French Class at the College Level." Ph.D. diss., Ohio State University.

Gunderson, Barbara, and David W. Johnson. 1980. "Building Positive Attitudes by Using Cooperative Learning Groups." *Foreign Language Annals* 13: 39–43.

Johnson, David W., Roger T. Johnson, and Edythe J. Holubec. 1986. *Circles of Learning: Cooperation in the Classroom*. Englewood Cliffs, NJ: Prentice-Hall.

Johnson, David W., Roger T. Johnson, and Geoffrey Maruyama. 1983. "Interdependence and Interpersonal Attraction among Heterogeneous and Homogeneous Individuals: A Theoretical Formulation and Meta-Analysis of the Research." *Review of Educational Research* 53: 5–54.

Johnson, David W., Geoffrey Maruyama, Roger T. Johnson, Deborah Nelson, and Linda Skon. 1981. "Effects of Cooperative, Competitive and Individualistic Goal Structures on Achievement: A Meta-Analysis." *Psychological Bulletin* 89: 47–62.

Kagan, Spencer. 1989. *Cooperative Learning Resources for Teachers*. San Juan Capistrano, CA: Resources for Teachers.

Kramsch, Claire. 1987. "Socialization and Literacy in a Foreign Language: Learning through Interaction." *Theory into Practice* 24,4: 243–48.

Long, Michael H. 1985. "Input and Second Language Acquisition Theory," pp. 377–93 in Susan Gass and Carolyn G. Madden, eds. *Input and Second Language Acquisition*. Rowley, MA: Newbury House.

—————, and Patricia Porter. 1985. "Group Work, Interlanguage Talk, and Second Language Acquisition." *TESOL Quarterly* 19,2: 207–28.

McGroarty, Mary. 1989. "The Benefits of Cooperative Learning Arrangements in Second Language Instruction." *Journal of the National Association for Bilingual Education* 13: 127–43.

Mesch, Debra, Marvin Lew, David W. Johnson, and Roger T. Johnson. 1986. "Isolated Teenagers, Cooperative Learning, and the Training of Social Skills." *Journal of Psychology Today* 120: 323–34.

Met, Myriam. 1990. "Proficiency Curriculums." *Educational Leadership* 48: 84–85.

Schinke-Llano, Linda. 1990. "Can Foreign Language Learning Be Like Second Language Acquisition? The Curious Case of Immersion," pp. 216–25 in Bill Van Patten and James F. Lee, eds., *Second Language Acquisition/Foreign Language Learning*. Philadelphia: Multilingual Matters.

Sharan, Shlomo, Yael Bejarano, Peter Kussel, and Rachel Peleg. 1984. "Achievement in English Language and Literature," pp. 46–72 in Shlomo Sharan, Peter Kussel, R. Hertz-Lazarowitz, Yael Bejarano, S. Raviv, and S. Sharan, eds., *Cooperative Learning in the Classroom: Research in Desegregated Schools*. Hillsdale, NJ: Erlbaum.

Sharan, Shlomo, and Hana Shachar. 1988. *Language and Learning in the Cooperative Classroom*. New York: Springer.

Slavin, Robert E. 1983. "When Does Cooperative Learning Increase Student Achievement?" *Psychological Bulletin* 94: 429–45.

Swain, Merrill. 1985. "Communicative Competence: Some Roles of Comprehensible Input and Comprehensible Output in Its Development," pp. 235–53 in Susan Gass and Carolyn G. Madden, eds., *Input and Second Language Acquisition*. Rowley, MA: Newbury House.

A Case for Cooperative Learning in the FL Classroom

Appendix 5A

I. Peer-Tutoring Activity

Activity: Abstract sculpture using pipe cleaners

Level: Intermediate

Group membership: 4

Materials: Colored pipe cleaners, vocabulary cards on shapes

Teacher roles: Presents vocabulary for the shapes, such as *square, oval, rectangular, round, cone, triangular,* etc., action words for making shapes with pipe cleaners such as *bend at an angle, attach to the end, wrap around, fold in half,* etc., and reviews colors. Students practice new vocabulary in groups with each member assuming one of the roles assigned. While students practice, teacher circulates and monitors progress. The group member assigned to the role of *pronunciation checker* should have immediate access to the teacher for model pronunciation.

Student roles:
Checker: Listens and checks pronunciation against model (teacher/tape).
Tester: Uses visuals and actions to test each member to make certain he/she knows words and can demonstrate meaning of vocabulary.
Observer: Checks list of vocabulary against each member's name to verify that all have participated in review of vocabulary and tallies number of times each member does not use target language.
Encourager: Uses foreign language expressions appropriate for motivating group members and for encouraging them to do well.

Performance test: Two members (A & B) are selected at random to demonstrate group achievement. Sitting back to back, one speaks (A) giving directives (while using pipe cleaners to demonstrate his/her wish), the other (B) listens and follows the instructions to create an abstract "objet d'art" from the pipe cleaners. There is a requirement for A to use at least five directives in the creation of his/her sculpture. B may ask as many questions as needed to clarify comprehension. Two members of another team who were not selected in the performance test sit as observers for A and B to check use of English during the performance test. There is a one-point deduction penalty for each use of English.

Final evaluation of sculpture:
25 points: B's sculpture is a mirror image of A's sculpture.
20 points: A's sculpture almost resembles B's sculpture.
15 points: A's sculpture somewhat resembles B's sculpture.
10 points: A's sculpture barely resembles B's sculpture.

10 points possible on self-evaluation of involvement and cooperation (self-evaluation sheet)

10 points possible on group processing (group evaluation sheet)

Maximum: 45 points per student

II. Discussion Groups (DG)

Activity: Planning a trip (adapted from *Du tac au tac* and *Imaginate*

Level: Intermediate or advanced

Group membership: 4 or 5

58   Creative Approaches in Foreign Language Teaching

Materials: Student activity worksheet, copies from travel guides and brochures (authentic materials)

Teacher role: Acts as facilitator, monitors group processing, and makes notes of groups' progress.

Students first review vocabulary useful for managing the conversation when planning a trip. The activity is carried out using the following six steps: (1) topic selection, (2) cooperative planning, (3) implementation, (4) analysis and synthesis, (5) presentation of final product, and (6) evaluation.

Student roles:
Leader:	Keeps the group focused on task assigned
Researcher:	Consults guides and other authentic materials
Agent:	Facilitates decision making about travel details
Checker:	Verifies that all members contribute and use new expressions
Recorder:	Writes group decisions about travel plans

Student Activity Worksheet: English Version
Listening Activity—How to Organize a Trip

Preparation: Listen to some friends who are talking about a future trip.

Presentation: Instructor's audiocassette from *Du tac au tac*, chapter 7, conversation 1. What expressions are used to (1) decide where to go, (2) show agreement and disagreement, and (3) resolve differences? Check your answers with those of others in your group.

1. _____

2. _____

3. _____

Discussion Activity: Where to Spend Your Vacation

1. Topic selection: Organize your travel buddies (group members). Imagine that you are going to spend two weeks in France: one week in Paris, one week in a province. It is up to you to organize the trip to the province. Use the Michelin travel guides and brochures (or information from copies of guides and brochures). You will also find useful expressions for organizing your trip (on the following page). Use these in your discussion.

2. Cooperative planning: What is of interest to you in each region?

La Bretagne:

Le Val de la Loire:

La Provence:

Les Alpes:

Les Pyrénées:

Which of the five regions will you (your group) visit? Don't forget to take care of the practical details of your trip. Who will assume this responsibility? What will these details be?

A. Transportation:

B. Lodging:

C. Money or budget allotment:

3. Implementation: Make an itinerary. Indicate what you will see in each place you stop.

A. Departure date and return:

B. Amount of time you will spend in each place:

C. What you will see at each stop:

4. Analysis and synthesis: Justify the selection of your itinerary based on the preferences of each group member. Why did you choose this region and this itinerary?

5. Presentation: Present your trip to the entire class. Each group member must contribute to the presentation.

6. Evaluation: 30 points for accomplishing the task according to specified criteria. 10 points for self-evaluation and 10 points for group evaluation of process.

60   Creative Approaches in Foreign Language Teaching

Useful Expressions (adapted from *Du tac au tac*)

to propose a trip:
What if we . . . ?
I would like to propose . . .
I have an idea.
Let's . . .
What would you say . . . ?
Would you like to . . . ?

to respond in the affirmative:
Yes, that's a good idea.
I like that.
I couldn't ask for a better . . .
Great!

to respond in the negative:
Absolutely not!
I don't like that.
I really hate that . . .
No, I would prefer . . .

to show indecisiveness:
It's possible, but . . .
I won't say no, but . . .
Well—I don't know.
I don't care.

to make a decision:
Well, are we going to . . . ?
It's for you to decide.
I vote for . . .
It's been decided.

to ask someone to do something:
Who is going to take care of . . . ?
Who is going to look after . . . ?
May I ask you to . . . ?

to accept doing something:
Sure, I'd like to . . .
I can do that.
Okay.
You can count on me.

to show appreciation:
That's fine with me.
That's really nice of you.
Thanks a lot.
With pleasure.

III. Bookends Activity (focusing on a book, film, or lecture)

Skill: Listening comprehension

Level: Advanced

Materials: Student worksheet, videocassette *L'Homme qui plantait des arbres*

Teacher roles: Presents pertinent vocabulary associated with trees and arid climates, then circulates and responds to questions students have raised in each group.

Student roles: After listing new vocabulary, students brainstorm what they already know about planting trees and living in an arid climate. They may raise some questions.
Recorder: Writes down ideas
Encourager: Encourages participation
Taskmaster: Makes certain each member has contributed one or two ideas

Performance activity: After watching the video, students work together to sequence the events in chronological order. Students discuss new information and formulate answers to questions.

Student Activity Sheet: French Version
L'Homme qui plantait des arbres *de Jean Giono*

Préparation:
   Que savez-vous sur comment planter des arbres?
   Que savez-vous sur les climats arides?
   Que savez-vous sur la géographie du sud de la France?

Présentation: Un récit en vidéo, animé. Écoutez d'abord. Dans votre groupe, mettez en ordre les phrases qui décrivent le déroulement de l'action du récit. Ensuite, lisez à tous votre narration du récit.

A Case for Cooperative Learning in the FL Classroom

A. Le narrateur a voulu aider le berger en triant les glands sur la table.
B. Cet homme simple mais généreux et tenace à son occupation est mort paisiblement dans un hospice.
C. Un jour un capitaine forestier, ami du narrateur, a appris le secret de cette forêt.
D. Le narrateur est resté chez ce bonhomme toute la journée car il était intrigué par le travail de cet homme.
E. En apercevant une silhouette noire dans le lointain, le narrateur a trouvé un berger avec ses trente moutons.
F. Puis, ils sont venus une délégation administrative, un deputé et des techniciens pour assurer la protection de cette forêt "naturelle."
G. En traversant ce pays de Provence dans un car, le narrateur a entendu le bruit de l'eau qui coulait dans un bassin.
H. Arrivée la guerre de 14, le narrateur était engagé comme soldat pendant 5 ans.
I. Le narrateur se promenait dans ce terrain désert où il n'y poussait que des lavandes sauvages.
L. Il y avait toute une forêt de chênes à admirer dans ce terrain anciennement désert.

Communication: À discuter:
1. Décrivez le paysage au début du récit.
2. Racontez l'histoire du berger.
3. Décrivez le travail de cet homme.
4. Décrivez le paysage vers la fin du récit.
5. Qu'est-ce que vous trouvez d'ironique dans ce récit?
6. Que trouvez-vous d'admirable dans l'histoire?
7. Connaissez-vous personnellement quelqu'un qui ressemble à ce berger? Comment?

IV. Worksheet Checkmates Activity (version a)

Skill: Translating

Level: Intermediate

Group membership: 2 or 3

Materials: Student worksheet and dictionaries

Teacher role: Facilitator and monitor of group progress

Student roles:
Reader: Reads items in French
Researcher: Consults dictionary if meaning not apparent
Recorder: Writes responses on one worksheet when all reach agreement

Student Activity Sheet: French Version

Connaissez-vous ces films? Quel est le titre anglais des films suivants? Travaillez dans votre groupe coopératif.

Titres français   *Titres anglais*

1. Les Jumeaux   _____

2. Qui veut la peau de Roger Rabbit? _____

3. La Petite Boutique des horreurs   _____

4. Un Poisson nommé Wanda   _____

5. Le Voyageur malgré lui   _____
6. Les Liaisons dangereuses   _____
7. Les Gorilles dans la brume   _____
8. La Couleur de l'argent   _____
9. Chambre avec vue   _____

IV. Worksheet Checkmates Activity (version b)

Skill: Writing narrative

Level: Intermediate

Group membership: 2

Materials: Dictionary and audiocassette of authentic sounds (1 minute)

Teacher role: Facilitator and monitor of group progress

Student roles:
Researcher: Consults dictionary if vocabulary is uncertain
Recorder: Writes narrative on one worksheet when both reach agreement

Procedure: Students listen to audiotape of noises. First they identify each sound. Then they write a short narrative about the actions of an individual based on the "sound narrative."

Appendix 5B
Resources for Cooperative Learning Activities

Article:
Coelho, Elizabeth
"Creating Jigsaw Units for the ESL Classroom"
TESL Talk 18,1 (1988): 69–81.

Books:

1. Brown, Guillermo
   ¡Que Tal Si Jugamos? (1987)
   IASCE
   136 Liberty Street
   Santa Cruz, CA 95060

2. *Finding Out/Descubrimiento*
   Contact: Dr. Edward A. De Avila
   Linguametrics Group
   P.O. Box 3495
   San Rafael, CA 94912

3. Cohen, Elizabeth G.
   Designing Groupwork (1986)
   Teachers College Press
   1234 Amsterdam Avenue
   New York, NY 10027

4. Christinson, Mary Ann, and Sharon Bassano
   Look Who's Talking! (1981)
   Alemany Press
   2501 Industrial Parkway West
   Hayward, CA 94545

5. Johnson, David, Roger Johnson, and Edythe Holubec
   Cooperation in the Classroom (1990)
   Interaction Book Company
   7208 Cornelia Drive
   Edina, MN 55435

6. Kagan, Spencer
   Cooperative Learning (1989)
   Resources for Teachers
   27134 Paseo Espada #202
   San Juan Capistrano, CA 92675

7. Villeneuve, Michel José
   Jouons ensemble (1980)
   Les Éditions de l'homme
   955 rue Amherst
   Montreal H2L 3K4, Canada

8. Villeneuve, Michel José
   Viens jouer (1983)
   Les Éditions de l'homme
   955 rue Amherst
   Montreal H2L 3K4, Canada

Audiocassettes and Texts:

1. Bragger, Jeannette, and Donald Rice
   Du tac au tac (1987)
   Heinle and Heinle Publishers, Inc.
   20 Park Plaza
   Boston, MA 02116

2. Chastain, Kenneth, and Gail Guntermann
   Imagínate (1987)
   Heinle and Heinle Publishers, Inc.
   20 Park Plaza
   Boston, MA 02116

6
Exploring Cross-Cultural Reading Processes:
Beyond Literal Comprehension

Naomi Ono
Martha Nyikos
Indiana University

Traditional reading instruction in foreign language places great emphasis on student comprehension. In order to decrease obstacles to understanding the information explicitly stated in the text, teachers tend to select reading materials on the basis of students' linguistic competence, vocabulary, and interests. It is assumed that students can read higher-level texts only after they acquire certain grammatical patterns and a given amount of vocabulary. Consequently, foreign language teachers evaluate students' reading comprehension ability chiefly by asking "factual" or noninterpretational questions about the reading material. Correct responses depend on understanding vocabulary and grammatical structures. When students cannot demonstrate this level of comprehension, they are regarded as poor readers.

Teachers who use such questioning techniques with texts controlled for vocabulary and syntax appear to believe that reading comprehension is an information-transfer process (see figure 6-1) in which the text is the reader's source of "factual" information and unambiguous meaning. Thus, they view reading as a process in which meaning is transferred from a text to the reader. This approach will hereafter be referred to as the traditional approach.

Theoretical Background

The traditional approach to reading comprehension has been criticized on the grounds that it regards reading as no more than a process of applying grammar rules in order to effect transfer of objective information contained in the text. Traditional reading instruction takes control away from students and discourages them from using a broader array of strategies to comprehend the text. The view of reading comprehension reflected in this mode of reading instruction is based on assumptions that stand in contradiction to positions shared by schema theory, the psycholinguistic perspective on reading, and the transactional view of reading comprehension.

A more recent conception of reading views it as a process through which meaning is produced from the text and from what readers bring to the reading act by way of their prior knowledge. In language comprehension, the critical role of background knowledge as an aid to comprehension has been formalized as schema theory (Bartlett 1932; Rumelhart 1980). According to schema theory, a text, either spoken or written, does not of itself carry meaning. Rather, a text only provides directions for listeners or readers about which relevant information from the reader's prior knowledge should be retrieved and how that meaning should be restructured in response to the text (Carrell and Eisterhold 1983). The structures of this previously acquired knowledge are called schemata and represent networks of previously acquired knowledge stored in relation to other things we know (Bartlett 1932; Adams and Collins 1979; Rumelhart 1980). Efficient comprehension requires the ability to relate the reading material to one's appropriate knowledge. Comprehending words, sentences, and entire texts involves more than readers' or listeners' linguistic knowledge. According to this theory, reading instruction should also take into account what knowledge and experiences readers bring to the reading act, since the readers' background affects their interpretation of the text (Carrell and Eisterhold 1983).

Research evidence supports the vital role of the readers' cultural background knowledge in comprehension. Indeed, cultural knowledge may be a factor of equal, if not greater, influence than vocabulary and grammar knowledge as two studies by Johnson show. For example, she compared the results of Iranian students' reading comprehension when reading Iranian folktales to these results when reading American folktales (Johnson 1981). In another study, Johnson (1982) compared ESL students' recall about Halloween tales before and after they participated in Halloween activities. In both studies Johnson concluded that the amount of cultural information acquired through participation in nonreading activities had a greater effect on comprehension than did syntactic and semantic level complexity. Steffensen et al. (1979) compared the recall scores of students from the United States and India who read letters about an Indian and an American wedding. According to these results, American students read the native or culturally familiar passage more rapidly, recalled a larger amount of information, and produced more culturally appropriate elaborations. This study underscored the critical role of cultural background knowledge in reading comprehension. All three studies illustrate that close cultural proximity (i.e., familiarity) of text to reader facilitates comprehension.

In the psycholinguist's view, the reader seeks meaning, makes tentative guesses, reads selectively, and constructs meaning based on his or her own understanding of the world. In this sense, the psycholinguistic approach implicitly recognizes that comprehension is filtered through one's cultural, religious, and emotional perspectives and that it is not completely individually determined. Goodman (1967) posited reading as an ongoing, cyclical process of sampling from the input text, predicting what will come next, testing and confirming or revising those predictions, and sampling further. In the psycholinguistic model of reading, the efficient reader does not use all the textual cues but skips over predictable or incomprehensible words, events, and discourse features. When the reader gains confidence in making correct predictions, less confirmation, via a close reading of the text, is necessary. Even in beginning levels of reading instruction, tasks such as reading for the gist, scanning for details about a specific event, and accessing relevant background knowledge encourage strategies used by effective readers. This view of comprehension refutes the traditional approach, which focuses on precise and complete understanding of each word's socially agreed-upon denotative meaning.

Smith, another psycholinguist in the field of reading, views reading comprehension as a process of reducing uncertainty, pointing out that "meaning does not reside in surface structure and that meaning that readers comprehend from text is always relative to what they know and to what they want to know" (Smith 1986, p. 155). In other words, Smith is saying that the meaning is not explicitly stated, but depends on individual readers' personal/cultural background knowledge and the expectations this knowledge builds while reading. He also asserts that "what readers see depends on what they are looking for, on their implicit questions or uncertainty" (p. 156). Goodman and Smith both emphasize the importance of inference and prediction in reading. Their arguments suggest that during the reading comprehension process, inferences drawn from textual information in combination with personal or background knowledge are more important than comprehension of explicitly stated information for making meaningful interpretations.

More recently, the psycholinguistic approach to reading is being superseded by the transactional view of comprehension. The transactional view of reading comprehension finds that readers perceive the text and transform the meaning into a new personal interpretation. One could say that readers create a "new text" that has a personally relevant meaning. In the transactional view, the reader is constructing a text parallel and closely related to the published text. The published text thus becomes a slightly different text for each reader. The reader's text is constructed through inferences, predictions, references, and coreferences that are reflective of the background knowledge or schemata that the reader brings to the text.

Reading comprehension is viewed as both a sociocultural process and a process of personal interpretation. In the transactional view of reading comprehension, meaning is always "a relationship between text—the document read—and context, and does not exist independently of someone's interpretation of that relationship" (Harste 1985, p. 12). That is, when students read the same text, the meaning of the document read is relative to each student's understanding of it. The meaning depends on readers' sociocultural backgrounds, which readers bring to the reading process. Good readers are able to use the text in order to explore their own beliefs and expand their mastery of the target language and their cultural literacy.

Having considered traditional views of reading comprehension, it becomes clear that teachers should attach more importance to the readers' meaning-seeking strategies that involve the use and further construction of students' background knowledge, particularly with respect to comprehension of texts from another culture. In order to understand this notion more clearly, this investigation sought answers to these questions:

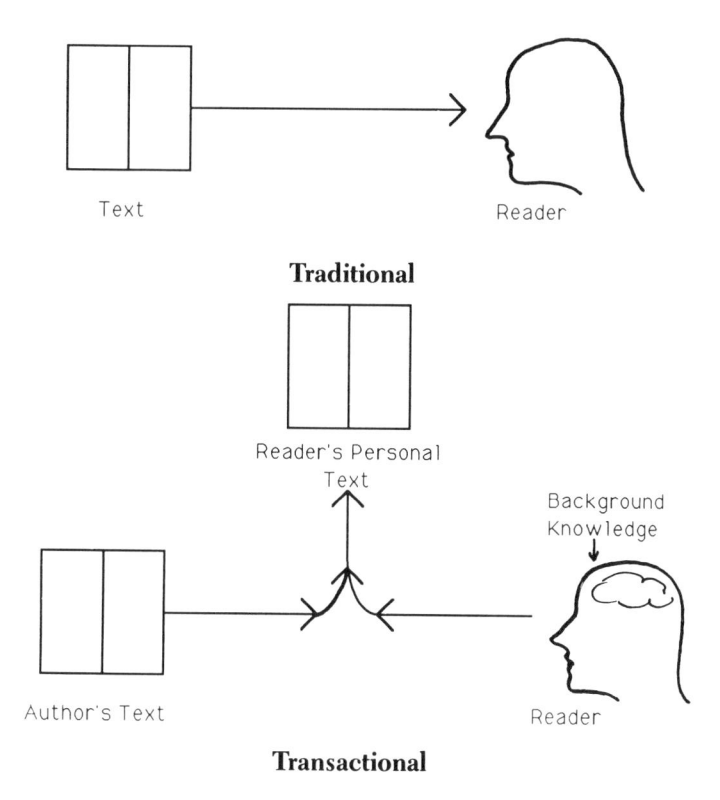

Exploring Cross-Cultural Reading Processes   67

Figure 6-1. Traditional and transactional reading models. (Adapted from Harste 1985.)

1. What strategies do foreign language students use to arrive at an understanding of a text?
2. Do reading strategies differ when students read texts that reflect various degrees of distance from the students' own background knowledge (i.e., reflect a close or distant cultural proximity)? In other words, when students read texts that use a familiar cultural background setting (close cultural proximity), what kinds of reading strategies do they use? Conversely, when students read texts that call on culturally unfamiliar background knowledge or schemata (distant cultural proximity), what kinds of reading strategies are used?
3. When foreign language learners read a culturally familiar short story, how do they use their background knowledge to comprehend the story? When they read a culturally unfamiliar short story, what background knowledge do they access to gain meaning for the story presented in unfamiliar cultural settings?

Research

The main purpose of this research is to document language learners' reading strategies and ways of using their cultural background knowledge for comprehension. In order to explore the questions above, research was conducted at Indiana University with Japanese learners of English as a second language.

A Think-Aloud procedure was used to analyze the patterns of the responses that emerged during the students' reading. According to Block (1986), Ericsson and Simon (1980) refer to Think-Aloud as a "concurrent introspective verbalization" (p. 218) in which respondents orally express their thoughts and reading strategies while reading a text. Originally developed by Newell and Simon (1972) to study cognitive problem-solving strategies, it has been applied to studying the reading process by Afflerback and Johnston (1984) and Olshavsky (1977). Think-Aloud allows researchers to assess subjects' thought processes during reading. The Think-Aloud procedure is therefore well suited to this study of the reading process and students' reading strategies when reading texts that are close or distant in proximity to the students' own culture.

The subjects were 9 Japanese students studying English as a second language (ESL) selected from beginning, intermediate, and advanced levels of the Indiana University Intensive English Program. There are two reasons that Japanese students were recruited for this research: first, the researcher was able to select texts whose cultural topics do or do not correspond with those students' cultural schemata, since one author is native Japanese, familiar with Japanese culture and thought. Second, the researcher's Japanese language ability allowed students to report their thoughts and reflections in Japanese during the Think-Alouds, making the study more reliable.

The students read three kinds of American short stories written in English. Short stories that are at different degrees of cultural proximity to students' backgrounds were chosen in order to explore how cultural schemata influence students' reading comprehension.

The first story was culturally close to the students, that is, a Japanese-American story. Short stories written by Japanese-American authors tend to retain some traditional eastern virtues such as patience, respect and politeness toward older people, uniformity, and sacrifice, even though the stories are set in America. "Shikata Ga Nai," written in English by a Japanese-American, Jeanne Wakatsuki (1984), was selected as the culturally familiar story. This story is about a Japanese-American girl's experience in an internment camp in the United States, where she and her family were forced to live during World War II.

The second was a culturally accessible story for Japanese readers, since the Japanese are familiar with notions about white, middle-class American culture, such as divorce, women's independence, and women's role in the family. Although they know theoretically that the American society is multicultural, Japanese are most familiar with mainstream American culture as it is depicted through the media in Japan. Selected for this category was "The Sock," written by a white American author, Lydia Davis (1985). The story is about a divorced woman who sets about giving a welcoming party for her ex-husband, his new wife, and his mother in order to make the family environment as harmonious as possible for her beloved son. In this story the sock, which the main character's ex-husband left behind, brings back some memories of her previous marriage to him.

The third selection was a culturally distant story or a culturally unfamiliar story for Japanese. Culturally distant topics would include stories about Hispanic-Americans and African-Americans. Through the media Japanese have gained familiarity with the general problems associated with minorities such as racial discrimination and low living standards, but not with those people's own perspectives and expressions. Therefore it might be hard for Japanese to understand how both minority and mainstream groups feel about such social pressures. "The Test," written in 1940 by an African-American author, Angelica Gibbs (1984), was selected as a culturally unfamiliar story. The story is about an African-American girl named Marian who tries to take her second test for her driver's license. She falls victim to the discrimination of the white inspector, who fails her again despite her white employer's encouragement.

Procedures were explained and the 9 students performed the Think-Aloud on their own. Students were asked to read silently, stop at asterisked places in the story, and verbalize their thoughts and strategies into a tape recorder while reading. They were allowed to stop at other places as well and to return to the previously read places and add comments. They were asked to audiotape all their comments. The students performed this procedure with all three stories. After the Think-Alouds, the students wrote answers to the following post-research questions to explore the influence of cultural proximity in the stories on the connections students made to their background knowledge and how this influenced their comprehension.

1. Which story was the easiest one for you to comprehend?
2. Why do you think so?
3. Which story was the most difficult one for you to comprehend?
4. Why do you think so?

The students were allowed to take as much time as necessary for both activities and they could use both English and Japanese to respond. In this way the constraint of language difficulty in expressing any thoughts was minimized, especially for the beginning- and intermediate-level students. Dictionaries were not permitted, since their use would discourage students from relying on their inferring ability and their personal background knowledge to make logical connections and create meaningful text while reading.

Data Analysis

The students' responses during the Think-Aloud protocol were in English, Japanese, or a combination. The responses that were made in Japanese were transcribed into English. All responses were then analyzed and categorized. In all, Think-Aloud responses fell into 14 response categories and were further subdivided into 2 groups. The first 6 categories reflect strategies that do *not* access culturally based knowledge (see Group A below). Responses analyzed as being directly affected by the readers' cultural background knowledge were categorized as *culturally sensitive* (see Group B below). Each category is followed by examples of Japanese students' oral responses in English, their target language. The title of the story is given in parenthesis.

70   Creative Approaches in Foreign Language Teaching

Response Categories

Group A.   Responses *not* directly related to cultural background knowledge (comprehension-based).

1. Asking about the meaning of words, phrases, or sentences.
   "I didn't understand this sentence." ("Shikata Ga Nai")
   "I don't understand this word 'Dog my cat.' I have never seen this word." ("The Test")
2. Expressing understanding.
   "I understand this part." ("Shikata Ga Nai")
3. Searching for connection between the title and theme.
   "When I read this paragraph, I found out the connection between the title 'The Sock' and the content." ("The Sock")
   "At this place I realized the meaning of the title 'Shikata Ga Nai.'" ("Shikata Ga Nai")
4. Summarizing or paraphrasing sentences.
   "After his father's leaving, uh, her mother decided to move to the island where there were used to be many Japanese there. For that child, for her, it was like a foreign countries because she has never been with other Japanese." ("Shikata Ga Nai")
   "Before taking the driver's test, uh, she found the road was crowded." ("The Test")
5. Grasping the gist or theme of the story.
   "This is a story about a divorced couple." ("The Sock")
   "The main character of this story is Marian." ("The Test")
6. Evaluating or reflecting on readers' own English ability.

   "After 'competent hands,' I cannot understand the meaning. I am poor at comprehending a long sentence." ("The Test")
   "There are still some words that I don't understand." ("The Test")

The following responses are grouped as *culturally sensitive responses,* since linguistic responses are directly affected by the readers' cultural background knowledge. Included in this subcategory is the reader's linguistic knowledge, because all comprehension in transactional reading is rooted in culture. In Group B below, however, culture is evident as the dominant perspective for interpretation and personal inferences.

Group B.   Responses directly related to cultural background knowledge (culturally sensitive).

7. Readers infer the meaning of words, phrases, or sentences on the basis of readers' linguistic and cultural knowledge.
   "In this part Mrs. Ericson is denying the discrimination, saying 'Oh, I don't think it's that,' so I think Mrs. Ericson is a white person." ("The Test")
   "I couldn't translate 'Do like [into Japanese].' I think that the subject is 'I' and probably I think that this 'do' [in English] is an emphasis and semantically it means 'like' [in Japanese]." ("The Test")

Exploring Cross-Cultural Reading Processes   71

8. Readers empathize with the characters in the story, making personal connections with certain events in the story.
"I'm from Kyushu. So I can imagine how she feels when she hears the Kyushu dialect. It reminds me that when I lived in Tokyo. My friend who is from Tokyo taught me the same thing." ("Shikata Ga Nai")
"I can really understand how the main character's mother feels in this situation. If I were her, I could feel so sad." ("Shikata Ga Nai")

9. Readers are talking to the character or asking what (s)he is thinking about or feeling at that time.
"At this time what is the child thinking?" ("The Sock")
"Why is this main character so nice to her ex-husband, his new wife, and ex-mother-in-law?" ("The Sock")

10. Readers project themselves into a character's position.
"If I were she, I would do the same thing." ("The Sock")
"This main character is too kind to her ex-husband and his new wife. If I were her, I wouldn't do that. She doesn't need to have such a party and a picnic for them because she wanted her son to feel happy. Anybody is exhausted if she/he will do this kind of thing." ("The Sock")

11. Readers change own interpretation.
"In the first part of this story I thought Marian had children and tried to get the car license in order to take her children to school. But I found out that the interpretation was wrong. Here I found out that Marian was going to get the license because she would take her employer's children to school." ("The Test")

12. Intertextuality—the readers connect the content to knowledge obtained from other reading experiences.
"I have read about this in Japan, that is, about the kind of poor ghetto for Japanese during World War II. This story reminds me of this." ("Shikata Ga Nai")

13. Readers' own emotional interpretations of incidents occurring in the story.
"Marian is miserable." ("The Test")
"This new wife is not a sensitive woman at all." ("The Sock")

14. Readers relate the story (theme, certain events, or the characters' behavior) to their own lives and dreams.
"I wish I could live in this house. My dream is to live by the beach." ("Shikata Ga Nai")
"I really want to take my car license." ("The Test")

Group B reflects culturally sensitive responses through a personal and thus necessarily cultural perspective that each reader brings to the text. Japanese readers relied on cultural background knowledge rather than on global message or theme in category 7 to interpret events and motives. Categories 8, 9, 10, and 13 make evident how feelings of empathy toward the characters and judgments about their actions are rooted in the readers' personal cultural perspective. Category 14 further narrows the readers' perspective to a more introspective filter

72   Creative Approaches in Foreign Language Teaching

through which personal hopes and experiences, seated in the home culture (although at times more universal) are projected into the creation of the new text. Table 6-1 illustrates the frequency with which each subject used these reading strategies during reading. Students A, B, and C are beginning students. Students D and E are intermediate students. Students F, G, H, and I are advanced students. The numbers 1 through 14 characterize each response according to the response categories given above.

With respect to learners' reading strategies, four main findings emerge from the response patterns in table 6-1. First of all, the beginning and intermediate students tended to use specific language-based questioning strategies (response category 1), such as asking for the meaning of each unknown word, phrase, or sentence (e.g., "I don't understand this word and that word"), while advanced students exhibit fewer such behaviors during reading. Second, advanced students summarize and paraphrase (response category 4) the content in order to comprehend the text while the beginning students tended not to do this, with one notable exception in each group (advanced student G and beginning student C). In no case was the most culturally distant story, "The Test," the most paraphrased. The most culturally familiar story, "Shikata Ga Nai," was the most paraphrased (47 times), while the culturally accessible story, "The Sock," was paraphrased 33 times, and the least culturally familiar story 31 times. These findings indicate that beginning and intermediate students lean toward word-oriented or bottom-up reading strategies while advanced students have meaning-oriented reading strategies.

The second major group of findings (Group B, response categories 7–14) illustrate the interpretations that result when readers use their cultural background knowledge when reading. The third finding was that learners' reading strategies do not differ according to cultural story type. The fourth finding revealed that the number of responses related to cultural background knowledge (response categories 7–14) does not differ according to the readers' general proficiency level nor with the degree of cultural proximity of the three stories. For example, comparing the number of culturally related responses for "Shikata Ga Nai" (culturally familiar story), beginning students (A, B, C) gave 26 responses, intermediate students (D, E) 24 responses, and advanced students (F, G, H, I) 35 responses. In "The Test" (culturally distant story), beginning students (A, B, C) gave 22 responses, intermediate students (D, E) gave 18 responses, and advanced students (F, G, H, I) gave 43 responses.

On the other hand, an important finding emerged from analysis of culturally sensitive responses. Cultural background knowledge is a clear influence on students' interpretation of both the cultural facts and making cultural inferences.

The following passages are excerpts from the three short stories used in this research followed by examples of students' interpretations of each excerpt.

"The Test" (culturally unfamiliar story)
On the afternoon Marian took her second driver's test, Mrs. Ericson went with her. "It's probably better to have someone a little older with you," Mrs. Ericson said as Marian slipped into the driver's seat beside her. "Perhaps the last time your Cousin Bill made you nervous, talking too much on the way."

Exploring Cross-Cultural Reading Processes 73

Table 6-1
The Response Chart for "Shikata Ga Nai," "The Sock," "The Test"†

Response Category	Students				
	A	B	C	D	E
1	3/6/7‡	0/4/6	3/9/6	2/1/2	1/0/1
2	4/0/4				
3				1/0/0	0/1/0
4	0/2/0		17/6/8		
5					1/1/1
6	0/0/1				
7	3/4/3	2/0/6	12/3/10	1/0/2	1/0/9
8				8/0/1	
9					1/1/0
10		1/0/0	1/7/0	2/13/3	1/2/0
11		0/0/1	0/0/1		
12			1/0/0		2/0/0
13		6/4/0	0/0/1	3/1/0	3/2/0
14				2/1/3	0/1/0

Response Category	Students			
	F	G	H	I
1		1/1/7	0/1/0	
2		1/0/1		
3		0/1/0		
4	12/7/11	1/1/1	4/7/4	13/10/7
5		0/0/1		
6		0/2/2		
7		1/3/1	1/0/0	0/2/4
8			3/1/2	
9			0/2/0	
10	0/1/1	14/10/18	12/13/16	
11				
12		2/0/0		
13			2/0/1	
14				

n = 9 students (A–I). A, B, and C are beginning level students; D and E are intermediate level; F through I are advanced level.

† Titles of three short stories.

‡ 3/6/7 in Response Category 1 (asking about meanings) indicate Student A asked about meanings *three* times for story 1, "Shikata Ga Nai," *six* times for story 2, "The Sock," and *seven* times for story 3, "The Test."

"Yes, Ma'am," Marian said in her soft unaccented voice. "They probably do like it better if a white person shows up with you."

Student C (beginning level): Mrs. Ericson and Marian are going to take the second-time driver's license test together. I guess that "a white person" means a Caucasian American. It suggests that Mrs. Ericson and Marian are a black mother and daughter.

Student E (intermediate level): I think Marian is the main character in this story.

Student G (advanced level): From this paragraph I find out that the racial discrimination between white Americans and black Americans is clearly addressed in this story.

Student H (advanced level): Marian knows that she is discriminated because she is black.

Student C thought that in the presence of a white person, a black person would not refer specifically to white people. Working on this assumption, the reader judged the relationship between Mrs. Ericson and Marian to be based on an intimate bond as would exist between mother and daughter, whereas Mrs. Ericson is actually her employer. Student E did not infer a racially unequal relationship, staying on a factual level. Student E's strategy was to identify the main character of this story from this paragraph, when she realized who Marian was. Student G and Student H strongly reacted to the words "a white person" when they read this paragraph. Both of them connected "a white person" with a social problem in an American society—racial discrimination. These personal inferences clearly stem from the Japanese students' knowledge and sensitivity to the American racial climate—which, as applied to this story, were overgeneralized.

"Shikata Ga Nai" (culturally familiar story)
["Shikata Ga Nai" (That is the way it is) is about a Japanese-American family before World War II.]

In December of 1941 Papa's disappearance didn't bother me nearly so much as the world I soon found myself in.

He had been a jack-of-all-trades. When I was born he was farming near Inglewood. Later, when he started fishing, we moved to Ocean Park, near Santa Monica, and until they picked him up, that's where we lived, in a big frame house with a brick fireplace, a block back from the beach. We were the only Japanese family in the neighborhood. Papa liked it that way. He didn't want to be labeled or grouped by anyone. But with him gone and no way of knowing what to expect, my mother moved all of us down to Terminal Island. Woody already lived there, and one of my older sisters had married a Terminal Island boy. Mama's first concern was to keep the family together; and once the war began, she felt safer there than isolated racially in Ocean Park. But for me at age seven, the island was a country as foreign as India or Arabia would have been. It was the first time I had lived among other Japanese, or gone to school with them, and I was terrified all the time.

Student A (beginning level): I guess that this family had a relatively rich life before the WWII.

Student B (beginning level): At this time the author was seven years old according to this story. I think it is amazing that a seven-year old girl can recall so much.

Student G (advanced level): This is very interesting because this father's attitude was just typical Japanese. He didn't want to live with other Japanese among Japanese.

Student H (advanced level): I don't understand that he doesn't want to live with other Japanese families but I think it doesn't necessarily mean that other members in his family think in the same way.

Student A inferred that these people are well-to-do from the statement that they lived "in a big frame house with a brick fireplace, a block back from the beach." In Japan, people who live in such a house are assumed to be rich, since such a big frame house is very expensive. On the other hand, Student B focused on the precise description of the story. Students G and H agree with the main character's (father's) attitude in this story only in the sense that his stubborn attitude reflects the typical Japanese spirit. However, both of the students (G and H) have different interpretations of the typical Japanese spirit (here: strong stubborn patriarch). Student H views the Japanese spirit as one where the father's will dominates over the family. In her opinion the family may not share his attitude. Student H interpreted the father's reactions as atypical, assuming a willingness to live in a predominantly Japanese community.

"The Sock" (culturally accessible story)
My husband is married to a different woman now, taller than I am, about six feet tall, very thin, and of course he looks shorter than he used to and his head looks a little smaller. She's not really what I had in mind for him. I had thought of someone shy and friendly and a little dumpy—wide hips, sandals. But who am I to choose?

Student A (beginning level): I didn't understand who this author means by "I had thought of." Probably the author is talking about herself. I think she had a complex about herself. By the phrase "I had in mind for him," the author expresses that she still loves her ex-husband.

Student E (intermediate level): This is a story about a divorced couple.

Student G (advanced level): From this first sentence, I assume that this writer is a European American.

Student H (advanced level): I think she feels jealousy to that woman because she doesn't think that the woman is more appropriate for him than she is. Also, she doesn't think that that woman is better than she is.

Students A and H have common opinions about the main character's feelings toward her ex-husband and herself. Student E's overriding reading strategy for all three stories was to try to grasp the gist of the story immediately at the beginning of the reading. On the other hand, Student G limited herself to the topic sentence. Here Student G seems to judge racial origin on the basis of the main character's way of thinking.

From these various modes of readers' interpretation, it is clear that very different images emerge in individual readers' minds as they encounter the language of the text and that readers access this language on the basis of personal perspectives, associations, and images while gaining a sense of the story's meaning. In "The Test," for example, Students G and H thought that the main theme of the story was racial discrimination based on the words "a white person." The students already had an image of racial discrimination connected with the words "a white person" appearing in an American context. On the other hand, Student C paid attention to the intimacy between Mrs. Ericson and Marian. For the student, the notion of "intimacy" is closely related to the relationship between a mother and daughter. The orientation to interpret interpersonal relations in this manner appears to stem from both the personal and cultural perspective of the reader and it is evident in the other two stories.

The kinds of interpretations or images that learners associate with words and phrases vary among individual readers even though these readers belong to the same culture. The readers produced these perspectives, images, and frames of reference throughout their intellectual and emotional development, which is rooted in a specific culture or cultures. Moreover, these perspectives or views seem to be *personally* based. The students in this study had different individual interpretations of the words, phrases, and events although all of them were raised in Japan.

Readers' cultural familiarity with the stories did not have any significant influence on how readily readers used their native cultural background knowledge for comprehension of a nonnative story. In both a psycholinguistic and transactional view of the reading process, students' chief meaning-making strategy is to rely heavily on this background knowledge to interpret the stories' events. This research underscores the importance of the culture-specific interpretation that is contributed through words and phrases to each reader's understanding of the native or the target culture framework.

Educational Implications

Based on the findings of this research we can recommend four possible activities for foreign language students that promote enhanced comprehension through personal reflection and logical thinking skills. These instructional activities include the use of pre- and post-reading essay questions, personal interpretation, and discussion based on an authentic text. These activities are designed to foster the types of processes suggested by a transactional view of the reading process. These include at least two general levels of processing per activity: cognitive and affective strategies (see table 6-2).

The questions are designed for one of the short stories ("The Test") used in this research project.

Exploring Cross-Cultural Reading Processes

Activity 1: Pre-Reading Question (Essay)
Before reading this story ("The Test"), ask students to write about a memorable incident associated with failure. Students could write in a journal that is only for themselves.

> Have you ever failed at something you really wanted to do? Write a paragraph about your reactions.

This activity calls on students' prior knowledge and experiences, allowing students to relate personal experiences to the theme to increase involvement and comprehension. The purpose of this activity is to lead students to connect their personal experiences with certain aspects of the text before reading, so that their background knowledge about the subject and culture will be activated to better comprehend the theme of the text. The topic should not be too specific or explicitly present the theme of the text. Rather, the purpose of this question is to allow students to become personally involved on an affective level and to increase their comprehension through schema activation on a cognitive level. By involving multiple approaches to processing information, students are allowed a greater range of access to a text without excluding certain learning styles.

Activity 2: Comprehension Questions (Stated/Implied)
Give students a series of statements both directly from the text and statements that are only implied in the text. Ask them to write down "stated" if the information is actually located in the text of the story, and "implied" if the statement is implied. If they choose "stated," ask them to indicate where the author stated the idea in the text. If they select "implied," they are instructed to indicate in a few sentences where they think that the author implied the idea.

1. Marian failed in her license test once before.
2. Marian liked the previous inspector.
3. Mrs. Ericson believes that because Marian is black, she became a victim of discrimination by the previous inspector.
4. Mrs. Ericson thinks that Marian will be able to get her driver's license this time.

In this activity, students are asked to distinguish the stated from the implied information and to provide the reason for both. This exercise will help foreign language students to realize whether they could comprehend factual information in the text. Furthermore, students will be able to practice writing their interpretations of the text in a logical and compact manner in order to let the others understand their interpretations. These questions challenge students to explain their thoughts in a communicative manner and are in line with the notion of creating one's own text in the transactional view of reading.

Activity 3: Making Personal Interpretations (Essay Questions)
Give students the following directions:

> Make your personal interpretations about the following statements. Write them down and explain them logically in a few paragraphs.

Table 6-2
Exploring Cross-Cultural Reading Processes: Beyond Literal Comprehension

Components	Activities			
	Activity One	**Activity Two**	**Activity Three**	**Activity Four**
Task Types	Pre-reading question (Essay)	Comprehension questions (Stated/implied)	Personal interpretations (Essay)	Discussion with peers (Essay+)
Cognitive Skills/ Strategies	Background knowledge • Schema activation • Multiple access	Critical thinking • Distinguish between stated and implied • Logical communication	• Create own text • Beyond literal "search and underline" approach to questions	• Synthesis • Integration of author's text and reader's text
Affective Skills/ Strategies	• Learning style • Empathy for characters' dilemma/situation • Multiple access	Own thoughts and connections	• Personal level of meaning creation • Reflect on own values • Encourages communication of personal reflections	• Interpersonal level of meaning (text) creation • Reflect on own values in relation to those of peer group

1. The inspector was fair to Marian the second time.
2. Mrs. Ericson agreed with the inspector's judgment about Marian's driving skills this time.
3. Marian could not drive well because she was so nervous.

This activity enables students to practice writing down their interpretations during and after reading the text and to explain their interpretations logically in essay form. Through activities 2 and 3, students are able to build up their ideas or reactions to the themes of the text.

Activity 4: Discussion
Discuss the following topic in class.

> Have you ever been discriminated against by somebody else in your society? If you have, how did you feel at that time? If not, how do you think those discriminated against based on their racial origin feel in that situation?

Here students will share their interpretations built up through the activities with other readers and they will be able to integrate their ideas with the ideas presented by other readers through discussion.

These activities will help foreign language teachers lead students to distinguish the explicitly stated information from students' personally oriented interpretations of the story, which are often unconscious, as illustrated by this study.

Foreign language teachers should provide students with not only comprehension questions for the explicitly stated information, but also essay questions so that students may react to the text on the basis of their own cultural and personal background knowledge. This allows students to present interpretations of the text beyond the literal level and explain logically the reasoning behind their interpretations. Asking students to reflect on the text also provides the teacher with a window on the types of personal associations students are making when they read a passage from another culture. The students' answers to questions on implied information can be read to monitor for total misinterpretations of explicitly stated facts as is conventionally done, but these questions, as advocated here, can also yield a rich source of data about the cultural and personal frame of reference students are using. In the process of reflecting on information that is not explicitly stated in the text, students' logical thinking skills are being developed as they decide which assumptions, judgments, and logical conclusions one can make within a given cultural or bicultural framework. Students begin to recognize, with guidance, which of the cultural frameworks are more appropriate for their logical inferring strategies, while continually building understanding of the target culture.

Furthermore, discussion will provide a good opportunity for students to express how they interpret the text, discuss what was learned, and analyze which reading strategies were useful. Discussion can help students to reflect on their reading comprehension, integrate insights for the theme of the text, and extend their interpretations of culture.

In selecting reading materials, foreign language teachers need not make a selection strictly on the basis of students' current linguistic level. Reading comprehension is not merely a grammar-rule application process. As indicated in this study, even beginning students can interpret the text by using their limited syntactic and semantic knowledge, together with their cultural background knowledge and specific strategies such as inferring from the title, personality of the characters, and logical chains of events. In light of these findings, foreign language teachers should consider the impact that the native culture has on students' interpretations of themes and characters presented and the events occurring in a story and how these contribute to their students' intellectual and affective development through teaching strategies that support multiple levels of interpretation.

References

Adams, M. J., and A. Collins. 1979. "A Schema-Theoretic View of Reading," pp. 1–22 in R. O. Freedle, ed., *New Directions in Discourse Processing*. Norwood, NJ: Ablex.

Afflerback, P., and P. Johnston. 1984. "The Use of Verbal Reports in Reading Research." *Journal of Reading Behavior* 16: 307–21.

Bartlett, Frederic C. 1932. *Remembering: A Study in Experimental and Social Psychology*. Cambridge, Eng.: Cambridge Univ. Press.

Block, Ellen. 1986. "The Comprehension Strategies of Second Language Readers." *TESOL Quarterly* 20,3: 463–96.

Carrell, Patricia, and Joan C. Eisterhold. 1983. "Schema Theory and ESL Reading Pedagogy." *TESOL Quarterly* 17,4: 553–73.

Davis, Lydia. 1985. "The Sock," in Anne Tylerm, ed., *The Available Press/Pen Short Story Collection*. New York: Ballantine.

Ericsson, K. Anders, and Herbert A. Simon. 1980. "Verbal Report as Data. *Psychological review* 87,3: 215–51.

Gibbs, Angelica. 1984. "The Test," in Jean S. Mullen, ed., *Outsiders*. Englewood Cliffs, NJ: Prentice-Hall.

Goodman, Kenneth. 1967. "Reading: A Psycholinguistic Guessing Game." *Journal of the Reading Specialist* 6: 126–35.

_____. 1984. "Transactional Psycholinguistic Model—Unity in Reading," in Harry Singer and Robert B. Ruddel, eds., *Theoretical Model and Processes of Reading*. 3rd ed. Delaware: International Reading Association.

Harste, Jerome C. 1985. "Portrait of New Paradigm: Reading Comprehension Research," in Avon Crismore, ed., *Landscapes: A STATE-OF-THE-ART Assessment of Reading Comprehension Research*. Bloomington, IN: Indiana University Language Education Dept.

Johnson, Patricia. 1981. "Effects on Reading Comprehension of Language Complexity and Cultural Background of a Text." *TESOL Quarterly* 15,2: 169–81.

_____. 1982. "Effects on Reading Comprehension of Building Background Knowledge." *TESOL Quarterly* 16,4: 503–16.

Newell, Allen, and Herbert A. Simon. 1972. *Human Problem Solving*. Englewood Cliffs, NJ: Prentice-Hall.

Olshavsky, Jill Edwards. 1977. "Reading as Problem-Solving: An Investigation of Strategies." *Reading Research Quarterly* 12: 654–74.

Rumelhart, David E. 1980. "Schemata: The Building Blocks of Cognition," pp. 35–58 in R. J. Spiro, B. C. Bruce, and W. E. Brewer, eds., *Theoretical Issues in Reading Comprehension*. Hillsdale, NJ: Erlbaum.

Smith, Frank. 1986. *Understanding Reading: A Psycholinguistic Analysis of Reading and Learning to Read*. Hillsdale, NJ: Erlbaum.

Steffensen, Margaret S., Chitra Joag-Dev, and Richard C. Anderson. 1979. "A Cross-Cultural Perspective on Reading Comprehension." *Reading Research Quarterly* 15: 10–29.

Wakatsuki, Jeanne. 1984. "Shikata Ga Nai," pp. 55–60 in Sandra McKay and Dorothy Petitt, eds., *At the Door: Selected Literature for ESL Students*. New York: Viking Penguin.

7
Motivating Unenthusiastic Foreign Language Students:
Meeting the Challenge

Christine M. Campbell
The Defense Language Institute

> "I don't know how I can get my students to become interested in French. It seems as if they have no intellectual curiosity at all."
>
> "I don't understand it. I'm a conscientious teacher who prepares class lessons that I think are good. But when my students come into my classroom, they are obviously not excited to be there."
>
> "I love Spanish art! Unfortunately, my students don't share that feeling. As a rule, they show little interest in things cultural."
>
> "A Spanish 101 student who didn't know that I was a teaching assistant in Spanish said to me the other day, with surprising bitterness, "Why do I have to take Spanish? I have no plans to visit some poor Third World country on vacation!"

The author heard foreign language teachers make these comments during a workshop the author gave on student motivation at a college in the Midwest in the fall of 1991. All the comments refer to an apparent lack of motivation or interest among students.[1] Why are some students unenthusiastic about learning a foreign language?

In the author's opinion, some of our foreign language students display a lack of motivation for reasons unrelated to the discipline itself, such as personal problems. These students usually exhibit the same behavior in their other classes. Other students, specifically those in high school and college, are particularly unmotivated in the foreign language classroom because they resent being forced by the "Establishment" to take foreign language either to get into or to graduate from college. Others believe that the study of a foreign language is a waste of time because they do not envision ever using it once out of high school of college. Some junior high and high school students, as they search for their own identities as young adults, have the view that what is different is somehow bad; as a result, they have a negative attitude toward the study of a language and culture other than their own. Others, though idealistic teachers may not want to admit it, actually do have little or no intellectual curiosity.

How can teachers deal with the resentment and lack of motivation encountered in some students? The resentment can partially be curbed and motivation can be enhanced by consciously adopting strategies to motivate students. Before describing thirteen strategies teachers can use to enhance student motivation, this paper will present an overview of the research on motivation in foreign language learning.

Motivation Research in Foreign Language Learning

Until the late 1950s when Gardner and Lambert (1959) began doing research in motivation, relatively few researchers in the field of foreign language learning had focused on the role of learner motivation in the foreign language classroom. In 1939, Lorge reported that adult learners of Russian who were paid to study learned equally well whether or not they were interested in the particular learning task. In 1948, Dunkel studied the effect of reward in foreign language learning. He found that students who were promised a monetary reward for academic achievement did not perform significantly better. In 1950, Mowrer theorized that an infant begins to learn a first language because of the infant's desire to imitate its parents. The infant associates its parents and the sounds they emit as speech with the satisfaction of basic biological and social needs. Because of this association, the infant wants to imitate the parents' speech. Mowrer called this process of imitation "identification."

Gardner and Lambert (1959) read Mowrer's work and hypothesized that the motivation needed to become proficient at a high level in a foreign language springs from both the desire to imitate the language and ways of an ethnic community and a genuine interest in the ethnic community. In their writings, they replaced the term "identification" with "integrative motive"—the willingness of the learner to become a member of another ethnolinguistic community (p. 12). In their 1959 study on eleventh-grade English-speaking high school students of French in Montreal, they found that the student's attitude toward language study and toward the speakers of the target language can be more important that aptitude in determining a student's success.

Politzer (1960) found a significant positive correlation between the number of hours spent in voluntary language laboratory periods and college students' grades in course examinations; the greater the number of hours, the better the grades. Curiously, he found a significant negative correlation between time spent doing homework and grades; those who did the least homework tended to get A's.

In 1960, Carroll presented a conceptual model of the learning process, which he posited could be applied to foreign language learning in particular. According to the model, five key elements determine successful foreign language learning: (1) learner aptitude, (2) learner intelligence, (3) learner perseverance, (4) quality of instruction, (5) opportunity for learning (i.e., the time allotted for learning). In 1961, Carroll (1961a) reported that correlations between student interest in foreign languages and either aptitude or achievement were not significant. He concludes (1961b) that the uninterested but cooperative student will achieve regardless of the student's level of motivation. He points out, however, that motivation is related to achievement when it affects how well students will persevere in a learning environment in which they are relatively free not to participate.

A substantial amount of research in different aspects of motivation appeared in 1972. In 1972, Gardner and Lambert published the foremost text on motivation in foreign language learning—*Attitudes and Motivation in Second-Language Learning*. In *Attitudes*, they proposed the beginnings of a sociopsychological theory of second or foreign language learning based on the results of a series of studies over a twelve-year period. Below, their synopsis of the theory:

> This theory, in brief, maintains that the successful learner of a second language must be psychologically prepared to adopt various aspects of behavior which characterize members of another linguistic-cultural group. The learner's ethnocentric tendencies and his attitudes toward the members of the other group are believed to determine how successful he will be, relatively, in learning the new language. His motivation to learn is thought to be determined by his attitudes toward the other group in particular and toward foreign people in general and by his orientation toward the learning task itself. (p. 3)

The "orientation toward the learning task itself," which Gardner and Lambert identify as one of two determinants of motivation in second-language learning, can take one of two forms: *instrumental*, if the learner wants to learn the language because of some utilitarian reason such as satisfying foreign language requirements for graduation or making a résumé more impressive;[2] *integrative*, if the learner wants to learn the language because the learner is genuinely interested in it, to the point of wanting to be accepted eventually as a member of that other group.

In 1974, Gardner et al. proposed a model of second language acquisition (see figure 7-1) that takes three variable sets into account: (1) the social milieu in which the second language is acquired; (2) individual differences in intelligence, aptitude, and motivation; and (3) the second language learning context (classroom versus street). They also devised a classification scheme for the motivational variables associated with learning French (although the scheme could serve for other languages). The scheme includes the following categories: (1) group-specific attitudes, (2) course-related characteristics, (3) motivational indices, and (4) generalized attitudes.

Larsen and Smalley (1972) believe that a learner can become bilingual only if the learner becomes a member of the target language community. Schumann (1975) studied motivation and two other affective variables—attitude and empathy. After analyzing Gardner et al.'s model, he concluded:

> [The model] makes clear the roles of both aptitude and motivation in the second language learning process and holds out the hope that when motivational factors are better understood, we will be able to design language teaching programs which can generate the attitudes and motivation most conducive to producing bilinguals. (p. 220)

84   Creative Approaches in Foreign Language Teaching

Macnamara posits that the learner will learn the new language if the language is somehow "essential" to the learner (1973, p. 264).[3] He insists that the learner's "need to communicate has very little to do with what is commonly understood as an attitude to a people or its language" (p. 264).

Macnamara examined the language learning behavior of children and made some interesting observations about children who move to foreign countries with their families. He found that such children will try to learn the foreign language because they want to play with other children. In other words, children must fulfill a basic human need for affiliation. The child's need is urgent. Macnamara considers this "sense of urgency" in the learner an important factor in language learning. A teacher in a high school or college cannot instill a false "sense of urgency" in students because the students' most basic needs are not contingent on their learning a foreign language. However, we can do as Macnamara suggests and set up the language class so that communication in the foreign language is "essential" to the students. He encourages the teacher to turn the class hour into an activity period that focuses on some activity such as cooking. To get the job done, students will have to communicate with each other. He concludes: "Our task is to make the school more like the home and the street" (1973, p. 265).

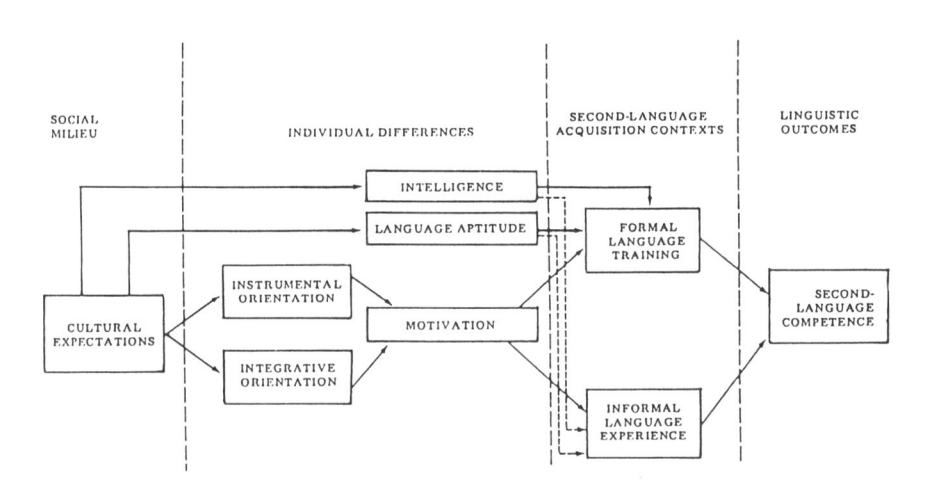

Figure 7-1. Schematic representation of the theoretical model. From Gardner et al. 1974.

From Theory to Practice:
Thirteen Strategies to Motivate Unenthusiastic Students

Keeping in mind the current theory on motivation in foreign language learning, what specific strategies might be used to energize unmotivated students? Presuming Gardner and Lambert's hypotheses on motivation are correct, how can students be helped to develop a more positive attitude toward the people of the target culture? How can teachers foster in learners a healthy balance between instrumental and integrative orientation toward a foreign language learning task? Simply put, how can motivation be enhanced in the foreign language classroom?

In search of answers to these questions, the author decided to tap the wealth of knowledge and experience of seasoned foreign language teachers. Ninety-five teachers at the K–12 and postsecondary levels were approached and asked to share one or more strategies they use to motivate their foreign language students. Some of the 95 teachers were colleagues at work; others were participants in a workshop on motivation in the foreign language classroom given by the author. The list below is a condensed version of more than one hundred different strategies submitted by the teachers. The strategies are not ranked and may overlap.

At a glance, the strategies are not especially impressive. Most foreign language teachers have used all these strategies at one time or another. If these strategies were carefully analyzed, however, it might be found that they are not used as systematically as thought. One way to use the strategies systematically is to choose one specific strategy each week and focus on it while creating lesson plans. Another way is to scan the entire list before making lesson plans for the week. The strategies are

1. Promote active, not passive, learning. Most language teachers would say that they try to engage as many students as possible in classroom activities. This author has often heard teachers proudly say "I make a real effort to call on each student at least once during a class period." Unfortunately, these teachers have not understood the difference between a teacher-centered classroom and a student-centered one. A teacher can determine whether his or her classroom is teacher- or student-centered by monitoring how many minutes the teacher habitually speaks during the class hour. After the teacher averages the number of minutes over a two-week period, the teacher can compare the number of minutes he or she speaks with the number of minutes the students speak. Except for listening comprehension exercises in which the teacher reads something to the class, the teacher should not be monopolizing precious classroom time with discourse. In the communicatively oriented classroom of today, students should be interacting with each other as they work through exercises in pairs and groups. Cooperative learning activities in pairs and groups promote proficiency. They foster active learning by encouraging the student to communicate in the foreign language instead of passively listening to teacher discourse.

2. Personalize class activities. To personalize class activities is to make class activities relevant and meaningful to the students. The teacher can personalize class activities only after finding out what topics and issues interest students. For example, the teacher can ask students at the beginning of the school year what topics are of special interest to them. Most likely, the high school students will list cars, dating, and the like. The teacher should make every attempt to find authentic materials that deal with those topics. Of course, when using authentic materials to create exercises, the teacher must be ever mindful of the proficiency level of the students involved. Students should be challenged, not frustrated.

The teacher who attempts to impose topics on students that are of interest to the teacher only will most likely meet with disaster. This author, enthralled with Spanish art, tried many years ago to force students in a fourth-semester college Spanish course to sit through presentation after presentation on art. Unfortunately, although the students *did* learn the names of one or two Spanish painters, they did *not* learn how to communicate better in the foreign language.

In addition to using authentic materials on topics of particular interest to the students, the teacher can have students keep a journal or diary, start writing a foreign pen pal, and come prepared to "show and tell" their classmates about something of *their* choosing.

3. Use authentic materials or realia. Over the past five years, many articles and conference presentations on language learning have dealt with the issue of authentic materials and the need to use them in the classroom to promote proficiency. Whereas it is often quite easy to obtain authentic materials such as newspapers and magazines for exercises of reading comprehension, it is more difficult to get conversations, interviews, and radio and television broadcasts for listening comprehension exercises.

A short-wave radio is a potential source of material. The teacher interested in using a short-wave radio can call the embassy or consulate of the country in question and request the frequencies for programs in the target language. The teacher can also call "Voice of America" in Washington, D.C., to inquire about programs in the target language.[4] A teacher could approach the head of department and propose that the college or school district pay for the broadcasting of daily news programs in the target language through SCOLA— Satellite Communications for Languages.[5] Even though it may be difficult for some teachers to access authentic materials, teachers must make the effort if they want to enhance their students' learning.

4. Use real-life situations. In *Teaching for Proficiency, the Organizing Principle* (Higgs 1984), Liskin-Gasparro defined language proficiency as "the ability to function effectively in the language in real-life contexts" (p. 12). Perhaps role-plays are the most popular way of creating "real-life contexts" in the classroom. The teacher of beginning students should try to devise simple role-plays involving several students who must perform survival tasks such as ordering food and drink, getting a hotel room, using public transportation, etc. Another type of role-play has a student acting out the role of a famous figure in the history of the target culture who answers questions posed by the class. The teacher can also create real-life contexts in the classroom by using authentic materials such as authentic radio and television broadcasts, newspapers, and magazines in the foreign language.

5. Provide students with positive reinforcement when they perform well. Most sensitive teachers know the value of positive reinforcement and do make every attempt to praise students for a job well done. Every teacher should have a system of rewards other than grades. The reward can be as simple as the candy kiss that one teacher the author knows gives to her junior high school students or as elaborate as the dollar that a bank in Cleveland donates to every student at an inner-city school who receives an "A" on his or her report card. Some high school teachers approach their first-year students with the idea of taking a trip to the target country in the third year. If the students are interested, the class spends the next two to three years saving their allowances and organizing bake sales and other fund raisers to offset trip expenses.

If every teacher should have a system of rewards other than grades, every school system and college or university should have one, too. A school system or college should have a series of awards, however modest, for the top students. Ideally, a school system or college should award a worthy foreign language student with a travel grant once a year. Rewards motivate.

6. Show enthusiasm for the subject matter. Most teachers have a genuine love of foreign languages; many, however, without even realizing it, project less and less of enthusiasm as they grow older. Although some may disagree, a conscious effort must be made to transmit some of the passion for foreign languages to students. Teachers should use whatever technique they can to rekindle in themselves the interest in foreign languages that led them to choose foreign language teaching as a career.

Fisch (1991), an educational consultant who does motivational speeches for teacher training, insists that the stage and the classroom are alike in many respects. In his article, Fisch urges teaches to improve their "performing behaviors" or to develop them if they do not already have them (p. 1). He has created a list of eighteen suggestions for the teacher—nine for improving the teacher's performing behavior and nine for designing better classroom activities. Below, one of his suggestions:

> Warm up, both physically and mentally, before entering class, if only for a few minutes. Set your mood and manner. Get into character for a particular class and material. Rehearse your activity with a rapid mental run-through. (p. 1)

7. Actively promote foreign language study. Teachers know the benefits of foreign language study, how it can broaden your horizons, sharpen your mind, sensitize you to the intricacies of your own language, make your more marketable in the new global economy, and more. The teacher should tell students about the benefits of foreign language study. The teacher may want to share excerpts from two renowned books that promote foreign language study—Pimsleur's (1980) *How to Learn a Foreign Language* and Simon's (1980) *The Tongue-Tied American.*

Writing in 1980, Pimsleur suggested that a person should *not* study a foreign language because knowledge of a foreign language will make the person more marketable. According to Pimsleur, English is now the worldwide language of business. He adds that corporations will hire a native who speaks the target language over a nonnative whom they must train to speak the language. So why, then, does he believe a person should study a foreign language?

> I think the best answer to "Why learn a foreign language?" is that it may make one's life richer. Not only after one knows it, but even during the learning. . . .

Viewed as a decision to fill a stretch of time with stimulating, purposeful activity, the undertaking of a foreign language can be a delightful voyage full of new expressions and ideas. (p. 5)

8. Supplement the predictable exercises in the book with unpredictable ones of your own. Most teachers recognize that, because each class has its own special character, a single textbook cannot possibly satisfy the demands of each and every class. Most teachers find the task of creating exercises geared to the personality of a particular class a delightful challenge. Skits, plays, songs, dances, and games can energize a class bored with routine textbook exercises. For example, a 50-minute class can revolve around planning for the celebration of an upcoming holiday in the target culture. Three books that provide a wealth of ideas on how to motivate students by using a variety of methodologies and exercises are *Caring and Sharing in the Foreign Language Classroom* by Moskowitz (1978), *Methods That Work* by Oller and Richard-Amato (1983), and *Innovative Approaches to Language Teaching* by Blair (1982).

9. Structure the class like a good speech: Begin and end with an attention-grabber. Certainly, teachers may balk at this suggestion because of the extra time required to plan two attention-grabbers. The teacher who makes the effort to do so just once, however, will see a remarkable difference in how students respond to the class. Making the two additions to each lesson plan does become easier with time. Some attention-grabbers that the teacher must set up *before* students start coming into class are an object from the target culture placed on a front desk; a slang expression or quote in the target language on the board; a thought-provoking picture on the board or overhead projector. Some teachers occasionally end their class with a "play period" for games.

10. Use nonthreatening teaching techniques. Most teachers know how important it is to create a positive learning environment in the classroom. Teachers should set realistic goals for their students and be sensitive to the needs of those students who, because of their introverted nature, do not respond well to activities in which they must speak in front of the class. According to a survey on communication administered by Toastmasters International in 1985, the organization dedicated to developing public speaking ability and leadership skills, people fear public speaking more than death. When teachers ask students to get up and speak in front of the class or even at their desks, they are actually asking them to do public speaking of a sort.

Teachers should also be aware that some students may be suffering from a form of debilitating anxiety specific to the foreign language classroom called "foreign language anxiety." Recently, researchers such as Horwitz (1986, 1991), Young (1986), Campbell and Ortiz (1988, 1991), and others have investigated "foreign language anxiety" as a construct. As Campbell and Ortiz (1991) concluded: "According to these studies (by Horwitz et al. [1986] and Campbell and Ortiz [1988]), we can estimate that anywhere from one-quarter to one-half of [foreign language] students in our institutions of higher education experience debilitating anxiety" (p. 159). Teachers should do all they can to help those students afflicted with debilitating foreign language anxiety become successful language learners.

11. Use humor in the classroom. Humor can be used to relax a particularly apprehensive group of learners or to motivate an unenthusiastic one. The comic Steve Allen (1987) believes that the ability to use humor effectively is not a talent, but a skill that can be learned. The teacher who wants to liven up classes with comic relief can bring in comic strips as an excellent warm-up exercise for the beginning of class.

12. Exploit modern technology as an aid to, but not a replacement for, the teacher. As one teacher said to the author: "We should use technology in all its forms—computers, videos, television, radio, etc. Our students are used to it, and they like it whether or not we do."

13. Encourage group competition. Competition is an inherent part of American culture. Children learn at an early age to compete to win. Although some might see competition as negative, most would agree that a bit of healthy competition can energize a group. Contests of any sort, provided that a reward of some sort goes to the winner, tend to excite students. One such contest that can be played even at the beginning levels is *"Concurso de Lengua"* (Language Contest). First, the teacher divides the class into groups of six students. Group members choose a name for the group in the foreign language. The teacher then asks all but one of the groups, which will be the jury in the contest, to spend ten minutes preparing a list of questions and answers in the foreign language such as *"¿De qué color es tu libro de español?"* (What color is your Spanish book?) or *"¿Hace frío hoy?"* (Is it cold today?). If the teacher wishes, he or she can choose a theme for the questions such as *"Información autobiográfica"* (Autobiographical Information). The teacher checks each group's questions as each group finishes and makes any necessary corrections.

The objective of the contest is to be able, as a group, to answer correctly the questions that are asked to the group. For example, Maryam Matin from Group A (El Grupo Goya—The Goya Group) asks Group B (Los Lobos—The Wolves) a question. Group B has 30 seconds to confer before one member answers the question. The jury decides whether the answer given by Group B is correct and keeps tally of the score for each team. The teacher can devise his or her own scoring scheme and offer some sort of reward to the winning group. Although the game is competitive, it fosters active, cooperative, communicatively oriented learning in groups.

Conclusion

Thirty years ago, Carroll (1961b) reported that the research literature of that period did not provide concrete information on methods for motivating foreign language students. He observed:

> It has been widely claimed that the new methods of teaching languages almost invariably stimulate students during the early stages of instruction; effective means of forestalling the tedium and fatigue that often set in at later stages have not been discovered. (p. 46)

Since Carroll made this statement, no one has invented a "magic formula" for motivating students. The thirteen strategies described above, while certainly not a panacea, can be effective tools to motivate students when used systematically.

Notes

1. Of course, one could argue that motivation and interest are two different constructs. The author found the terms used interchangeably in the literature on motivation. In this paper, the two terms are used as synonyms.
2. As Gardner and Lambert stress in *Attitudes*, they use the term "instrumental" in the same way that Skinner (1953) and Parsons (1951) used it.
3. All page numbers in the references to Macnamara's 1973 article in *The Modern Language Journal* correspond to the page numbers in the reprint of the article in *Methods That Work* (1983) by J. Oller, Jr., and P. Richard-Amato.
4. Contact U.S. Information Agency, Mr. Richard W. Carlson, Associate Director of Broadcasting and Director, Voice of America, 301 Fourth Street SW, Washington, DC 20547, at (202) 619-4700.
5. Contact SCOLA, 2500 California Street, Omaha, NE 68178-0778, at (402) 280-4063.

References

Allen, Steve. 1987. *How to Be Funny: Discovering the Comic You*. New York: McGraw-Hill.

Blair, R., ed. 1982. *Innovative Approaches to Language Teaching*. Rowley, MA: Newbury House.

Campbell, C., and J. Ortiz. 1988. "Dispelling Students' Fears and Misconceptions about Foreign Language Study: The Foreign Language Anxiety Workshop at the Defense Language Institute," pp. 29–40 in T. B. Fryer and F. Medley, Jr., eds., *New Challenges and Opportunities—Dimension—Languages '87*. Columbia, SC: Southern Conference on Language Teaching.

_____. 1991. "Helping Students Overcome Foreign Language Anxiety: A Foreign Language Anxiety Workshop," pp. 153–68 in E. Horwitz and D. Young, eds., *Language and Anxiety*. Englewood Cliffs, NJ: Prentice-Hall.

Carroll, J. 1960. "Foreign Languages for Children: What Research Says." *National Elementary Principal* 39: 12–15.

_____. 1961a. "The Predication of Success in Intensive Language Training," chapter 4 in R. Glaser, ed., *Training, Research, and Education*. Pittsburgh: Univ. of Pittsburgh Press.

_____. 1961b. *Research on Teaching Foreign Languages*. Ann Arbor: College of Literature, Science, and the Arts, The University of Michigan.

Dunkel, H. 1948. *Second-Language Learning*. Boston: Ginn.

Fisch, L. 1991. "Further Confessions of a Closet Thespian (Or, Lessons Learned from Life upon the Wicked Stage and How They Can Enhance Teaching Effectiveness." *Connexions* 4: 1–2.

Gardner, R., and W. Lambert. 1959. "Motivational Variables in Second-Language Acquisition." *Canadian Journal of Psychology* 13: 266–72.

_____. 1972. *Attitudes and Motivation in Second-Language Learning*. Rowley, MA: Newbury House.

Gardner, R., P. Smythe, D. Kirby, and J. Bramwell. 1974. *Second Language Acquisition: A Social Psychological Approach*. Final Report, Ontario Ministry of Education, Grant-in-Aid to Education. London, Ont.: Ontario Ministry of Education.

Higgs, Theodore V., ed. 1984. *Teaching for Proficiency, the Organizing Principle*. The ACTFL Foreign Language in Education Series, vol. 15. Lincolnwood, IL: National Textbook Company.

Horwitz, E., M. Horwitz, and J. Cope. 1986. "Foreign Language Classroom Anxiety." *Modern Language Journal* 70: 125–32.

Horwitz, E., and D. Young, eds. 1991. *Language and Anxiety*. Englewood Cliffs, NJ: Prentice-Hall.

Larsen, D., and W. Smalley. 1972. *Becoming Bilingual: A Guide to Language Learning*. New Canaan, CT: Practical Anthropology.

Liskin-Gasparro, Judith E. 1984. "The ACTFL Proficiency Guidelines: A Historical Perspective," pp. 11–42 in Theodore V. Higgs, ed., *Teaching for Proficiency, the Organizing Principle*. The ACTFL Foreign Language Education Series, vol. 15. Lincolnwood, IL: National Textbook Company.

Lorge, I. 1939. "Psychological Bases for Adult Learning." *Teacher's College Record* 41: 4–12.

Macnamara, J. 1973. "Nurseries, Streets, and Classrooms: Some Comparisons and Deductions." *Modern Language Journal* 57: 250–54.

Moskowitz, G. 1978. *caring and Sharing in the Foreign Language Class*. Rowley, MA: Newbury House.

Mowrer, O. 1950. *Learning Theory and Personality Dynamics*. New York: Ronald.

Oller, J., Jr., and P. Richard-Amato, eds. 1983. *Methods That Work: A Smorgasbord of Ideas for Language Teachers*. Rowley, MA: Newbury House.

Parsons, T. 1951. *The Social System*. Chicago: Free Press.

Pimsleur, P. 1980. *How to Learn a Foreign Language*. Boston: Heinle and Heinle.

Politzer, R. 1960. "Assiduity and Achievement." *Modern Language Journal* 44: 14–16.

Schumann, J. 1975. "Affective Factors and the Problem of Age in Second Language Acquisition." *Language Learning* 25: 209–35.

Simon, Paul. 1980. *The Tongue-Tied American*. New York: Continuum.

Skinner, B. 1953. *Science and Human Behavior*. New York: Macmillan.

Toastmasters International. 1985. Film on public speaking shown at a Toastmasters meeting. San Francisco.

Young, D. 1986. "The Relationship between Anxiety and Foreign Language Proficiency Ratings." *Foreign Language Annals* 12: 439–48.

8
Teaching the Working Adult and Retiree:
Considerations for the Nontraditional Classroom

Jennifer L. Knerr
Collier County Public Schools, Naples, Florida

Second language researchers have focused primarily on the "traditional" student learning languages in a "traditional" setting. To most, this implies students ranging from about five to twenty-five years of age taking a second language in school, that is, anywhere between grade school and college. But what of the "nontraditional" student? On any given evening in this country, thousands of working adults and retirees gather to learn a second language. They find themselves meeting in a number of environments, perhaps in a community center or a borrowed classroom at the local elementary school. Classes are composed of people from every age group, profession, and educational background, each attending the course for a different reason. The only element common to all these classes is their diversity.

How does one approach second language teaching in a setting where fifty years may separate the youngest and oldest learner? How does one meet the wide variety of student expectations, which often differ greatly from those a teacher has developed in a more traditional and structured environment? Is it truly possible to attain any level of language proficiency in a situation where some are hard of hearing and others refuse to speak? There is little second language literature that addresses these issues. Perhaps this is due to the belief that there is no difference between a college student and a middle-aged adult where language learning is involved, that educational practices that work well with traditional students should easily transfer to older adults. There are a whole host of factors, however, that make many second language teaching techniques unsuitable for continuing education. Frequently, it is necessary to turn to other fields for help in understanding and helping the adult learner.

The following discussion begins by identifying who these students are, that is, their motivations, general learning ability, and ability to learn a second language. Next, techniques are identified that would be most likely to succeed with this population and guidelines for developing activities. Finally, specific activities are shared that have worked well in this environment.

This paper focuses on the working adult and retiree learning a second language in a noncredit, recreational-type class. Information contained in the review of literature and suggestions for activities would also prove useful, however, for a teacher at the college level who faces older adults returning to school.

Definition of Terms

Diversity is not limited to the students and class types. Any number of terms can be found in the literature that refer to the learners and environments addressed in this paper. Some common terminology includes the adult learner/student, the continuing education student, nontraditional student, older learner, adult learning, adult education, continuing education, and lifelong learning. *Continuing education* is described by Witherell and Kersten (1983, p. 1) as "a broad term, used to cover any older student who seeks additional education of any sort after the generally accepted end of a college age—roughly around 25 years of age." Roumani (1978, p. 1) finds that the term *older learner* is "generally used in the literature to apply to persons over 60." Reiss (1982, p. 189), however, points out that these terms are generally not well defined or used with any consistency, "sometimes referring to learners or learning in an institutional setting (credit or non-credit), and other times referring simply to independent and non-directed learning."

It has been suggested that the term *pedagogy,* that is, teaching children, be replaced by *andragogy* meaning to teach adults. Vacca and Walker (1980) suggest that the two terms suggest differences in self-concept, experience, readiness, and the learning orientation of the learner. They also recommend that new methods be found to teach mature adults who (1) come to class with a greater amount of life experience that can be tapped, (2) often have a need to apply learned skills immediately, and (3) are more independent and self-directed than the traditional high school or college student.

Characteristics of the Nontraditional Student

One of the most challenging aspects of adult education is the diversity among students. The typical high school or college class consists of students similar in age and educational background attending classes on a full-time basis and whose primary concern is (or ought to be) attending classes. Most have adapted to meeting the teacher's expectations however much they may differ from their own needs.

The adult education course, in stark contrast, often brings together people who "differ greatly in age, educational level, ability, motivation and experience" (Joiner 1981, p. 3). Students whose ages differ by forty or fifty years naturally bring with them different interests and needs, both physical and psychological. Most adult learners in the second language class do have a good educational background in common—an average of 46 percent have completed schooling beyond the high school level—but there has generally been an interruption of at least a few years in their formal education (Dannerbeck 1987; Rosenthal 1978).

In contrast to the traditional student, the working adult or retiree is occupied with profession and family and civic duties. These responsibilities demand most of their attention and, understandably, take priority over the noncredit adult education course. When these students do attend class they are often tired at the end of the day and have had little time since the last session to review materials.

Older students, however, are highly motivated and generally attend the class because they have a specific and immediate use for the second language. Due to a lack of time to study and even to come to class, they are anxious to make the most of the time spent with the teacher as well as to demonstrate early and rapid progress for their efforts (Dannerbeck 1987).

The students' motivations vary as much as their ages and abilities. Many retirees come to a language class because they now have time and savings to travel whereas many working adults enroll in order to learn a second language for business-related trips and contacts abroad (Kalfus 1987). The following factors, which Dannerbeck (1987, p. 415) found to influence adults in Europe to enroll in second language courses are very similar to the reasons that motivate students in this country:

1. Job promotion
2. Short-term travel
3. Long-term residence abroad
4. Social interaction
5. Identification, because of ancestry or previous experience with the target language
6. Hobby

Among retirees the need to simply be out of the house and interact with other people is very strong. As Smith (1984, p. 4) states, the elderly person may just need company or to "do something different from what they did on the same evenings last year." This social motive can be a great advantage to teachers when making up activities, since these students are often outgoing and eager to get to know other class members.

What motivates students in any given class is far from a trivial matter. Their motivation drives the expectations they bring to class, and in a noncredit, recreational course, it is the teacher's responsibility to meet those needs and expectations. Those who do not ask why students are there and what their interests are will soon find themselves standing in front of an empty classroom. Dannerbeck (1987, p. 415) notes that in Europe, information about motivation is often gathered in the form of a survey and then used to "refine general second-language learning goals and teaching procedures, and to create materials that are compatible with the needs of adult learners." This is, certainly, very different from the traditional classroom where teachers choose a book and create a syllabus before setting foot in the classroom.

The working adult who comes to learn a second language in order to speak to business contacts abroad may come with the expectation of learning not only basic greetings but terminology specific to his or her field. A retiree who is planning a trip to Europe may expect an emphasis on "tourist" expressions, whereas another class member may only want to learn to read the second language and ask that he or she not be called upon to speak.

It is best to explain to students what they can realistically expect to accomplish by the end of the term. When students find that the class is not what they expect, the dropout rate soars. As Kalfus (1987, p. 4) notes, "The attrition rate is high among both credit and non-credit students. . . . Many adults have an unrealistic expectation of language learning." When a class meets only once per week for, perhaps, ten weeks, students must understand that quality will have to take precedence over quantity. A great deal of energy is spent reviewing material when there is such a lapse of time between sessions.

The ACTFL *Proficiency Guidelines* (1986) are useful in helping students understand the type of performance they can expect from themselves by the end of a given course. Many night courses last only ten weeks and frequently concentrate on speaking. In an average ten-session course, where each meeting lasts approximately three hours, one would most likely expect true beginners in the language to perform around the novice-high level with sporadic performance at the intermediate-low level.

At the novice-low level, a speaker can utter only isolated words and some high-frequency phrases. As a novice-mid speaker, those same words and phrases will be used with more skill to fill a true communicative need. At this point they will rarely use more than three words at a time and may still have great difficulty being understood. At the novice-high level they can still expect to rely on memorized phrases but will now be able to put together short yet original sentences. Vocabulary will center on basic objects and places, but certain vocabulary of specific interest to the class can be learned as well. They can expect errors still to be frequent but their confidence in using the language should be greatly increased as they begin to near autonomy in its use. Students generally progress at a very rapid rate through these lower levels.

Most students will be able to perform some of the tasks described at the intermediate-low level, although not consistently. The guidelines state that one should be able to perform such basic tasks as introducing oneself, ordering a meal, asking directions, and making purchases. Vocabulary at this point is only enough to sustain basic needs and there is still a great deal of linguistic inaccuracy, although, given time, they should be able to make themselves understood in a limited number of social situations.

Haycraft (1983, p. 48) suggests an extra phase be added to the beginning of a second language class for adults.

> It is argued that such students profit greatly from an introduction to the types of activity and study attitudes that will be expected of them in the language course, as their own experiences of the classroom may be radically different from what the language teacher intends.

Haycraft would suggest that the teacher also use that time to clarify student expectations and explain what language proficiency they can hope to achieve in the course. Only when both the teacher and students understand what is expected of them can the course proceed. Working adults, particularly, are giving up precious time to attend an evening course. If their needs are not being met, they will quickly abandon the second language course, unlike a traditional classroom where students frequently stay, regardless, in order to meet a prerequisite for graduation.

Age and General Learning Ability

It has been demonstrated that learning ability does not decrease with age. If older adults remain healthy, then their intellectual ability does not decline (Ostwald and Williams 1985; Roumani 1978). The older adult may, however, find certain teaching techniques more helpful than others, since they learn differently, not less well, than a younger person (Dannerbeck 1987). The following section is a discussion of the various physiological, environmental, and psychological factors that affect the working adult and retiree in the classroom.

Auditory Impairment

There is a gradual increase in hearing impairment until the age of 50, at which time it begins to increase rapidly, with an even sharper increase around age 70. In fact, impairment for speech and high frequencies is demonstrated in most individuals over the age of 50 (Bergman 1976; Joiner 1981). "Hearing loss affects more Americans that any other chronic problem" (Ostwald and Williams 1985, p. 11). Joiner (1981) notes that only 12 percent of the population over age 65 has normal hearing. Clearly, auditory impairment is an important issue for those teaching the older adult, as it affects both the speed and accuracy of learning.

Teachers in any subject area can make basic modifications in their classroom to help ease difficulties. The gradual loss of hearing that occurs due to aging interferes with a person's ability to understand speech, especially when background noise is present (Keim 1977). Therefore, it is important to choose a room that is "free from interruptions and other background noises such as a television, radio or telephone" (Ostwald and Williams 1985, p. 11). In most traditional settings this is not a problem, but adult education classes often meet in community centers, libraries, or public locales where noise can interfere. Also, students of all ages like to talk. It is important to keep personal conversations to a minimum in order to eliminate all background noise possible.

Teachers can also compensate for hearing impairment by using a combination of audio and visual presentation. Facing chairs in a semicircle, standing close to students, and directly facing them when speaking facilitate lip reading; and clear, moderately loud, and slower speech all create a more advantageous environment for the older student.

Visual Impairment

Poor vision, like hearing loss, can also affect the speed and accuracy of learning. While difficulties with vision are by no means limited to the elderly, visual impairment does increase with age. Changes begin to occur in near vision after the age of 40, requiring reading glasses for most people. Approximately 92 percent of the people over the age of 65 wear eyeglasses or contact lenses (Weale 1975). While eyeglasses can help compensate for vision loss, aging also leads to changes in the size of the visual field, difficulty distinguishing green, blue, and violet, and a sensitivity to low light, flicker, and glare (Knox 1977; Ostwald and Williams 1985).

Again, teachers can compensate fo vision loss by making simple modifications in their teaching and classroom. Both visual and auditory impairment are aided by a combination of an audiovisual presentation. In addition, print should be large and in dark colors. Older adults are less able to see subtle contrast, and therefore it is important to keep visuals on a matte surface and to avoid too much illumination, which can cause glare. Also useful is a longer exposure time to visuals and an increased time to adapt between light and dark when showing video or overhead materials, for example (Knox 1977; Ostwald and Williams 1985).

Fatigue

Roumani (1978) notes that the time of day can affect learning, especially in older students. Both working adults and retirees come to class tired after a long day. This poses an added challenge for teachers to devise ways to bring students quickly into the atmosphere of the classroom and keep content interesting and relevant. It has been suggested that classes not exceed one hour in length for the elderly—although this is not always an option. Comfortable furniture, proper lighting, breaks, and physical movement all help to combat the fatigue adults feel in evening courses (Ostwald and Williams 1985).

Fluid and Crystallized Intelligence

Horn and Cattell (Cattell 1963; Horn and Cattell 1966) propose that intelligence is formed by two interacting influences, neurophysiology, which they refer to as fluid intelligence, and acculturation, which they call crystallized intelligence. In essence these terms are used to describe groups of skills that adults frequently use in a classroom situation, such as problem solving, abstract reasoning, and knowledge of vocabulary.

It is suggested that crystallized intelligence (or acculturation) is developed throughout a person's lifetime by formal education, cultural knowledge, and the knowledge of the world that a person acquires through daily living. Naturally, this type of intelligence increases with age. The types of skills that acculturation provides a person are formal reasoning, deductive learning, vocabulary knowledge, reading comprehension, and knowledge of general information (Knox 1977).

Fluid intelligence, often associated with neurophysiology, tends to decline with age. Skills associated with this type of intelligence include abstract reasoning, forming general concepts through inductive learning, the ability to deal with complex situations, word analogies, and the ability to engage in tasks that require short-term memory, especially rote memorization (Dannerbeck 1987; Knox 1977).

Both short- and long-term memory present difficulties to adults as they age. Walsh (1983) found that older adults enter less information into long-term memory than the young because they are less likely to organize the information. Organization becomes more difficult as so-called fluid intelligence declines, since the older adult finds it harder to deal with complex materials. Physiological changes that occur with age affect the nervous system and such changes result in a reduction in the amount of information that is integrated and organized in a given period of time (Ostwald and Williams 1985).

Rate of presentation, then, is an important factor in teaching adults. When the pace is slowed, the older adult is given the extra time needed to integrate new information with previously learned concepts. As Walsh's (1983) study implies, if older adults are better able to organize information, then there is a greater chance of the information being committed to long-term memory. It has been found, too, that when the element of speed is eliminated, those in their forties and fifties are able to learn as well as those in their twenties and thirties. The older adult has the greatest difficulty with time limits and pressure (Joiner 1981; Knox 1977).

The adult education teacher can assist students with problems in organization of information and memory in the following ways (Knox 1977; Ostwald and Williams 1985):

1. Slow the rate of presentation of new material.
2. Use advanced organizers to give students time to call up background knowledge of a topic.
3. Discuss how new information relates to previously learned material throughout the presentation.
4. Summarize and review frequently.
5. Allow for personal pacing through pair or group work, which puts less pressure on the student to perform quickly and in front of the entire class.
6. Group similar material.
7. Teach students to use mnemonic devices.

Affective Variables

Until this point, only the physiological aspects of age and general learning ability have been addressed. Affective variables, too, play an important part in learning for students of all ages. Older students react differently to an environment than their younger counterparts. Adult learners seem to fear failure, for example, more than younger students (Schleppegrell 1987). Roumani (1978, p. 4) suggests that, among the elderly, the "desire for success is often outweighed by fear of failure. One may assume that the balance gradually shifts from the former to the latter during the middle years." Slowing the pace of presentation, then, is important to students not just because of the physiological aspects concerning memory and organization of information, but also because a fast-paced learning situation causes stress, and their fear of failure increases (Schleppegrell 1987).

It is also necessary for the teacher to help adult students maintain their self-esteem and confidence in the classroom. Smith (1984) finds that adults seem to suffer anxieties in the classroom more than children. They have a greater fear of looking silly or appearing stupid. In an adult education class, where such a mixture of ages is common, older students may have the added anxiety of competing with younger learners. "The older student will feel that much of his personal dignity and worth are at stake" (Roumani 1978, p. 4). Older students also seem more vulnerable to criticism (Kalfus 1987). Perhaps their fears arise, in part, because they believe the stereotype that adults are not able to learn as well as the young. Many adults must also contend with memories of difficulties in school, such as with grades or testing.

It is certainly important for the teacher to maintain a positive environment in the classroom when working with adults. The following suggestions will help teachers maximize the adult student's potential:

1. Use praise and encouragement generously (Kalfus 1987; Smith 1984).
2. Always clarify your expectations of the students. This reduces their hesitancy in class due to fear of failure and their greater need for certainty (Ostwald and Williams 1985).
3. Slow the pace of presentation and practice in order to reduce stress and anxiety.
4. Emphasize the positive and provide students with opportunities to demonstrate success (Schleppegrell 1987).
5. Recognize, wherever possible, existing knowledge and experience (Smith 1984).

Age as It Relates to Second Language Learning

"The greatest obstacle to older adult language learning is the doubt in the minds of both learner and teacher that older students can learn a new language" (Schleppegrell 1987, p. 1). Many adults seem to accept the stereotype that "younger is better" when it comes to learning. Nowhere does it seem more prevalent, however, than in the area of second language learning.

In the 1960s, Penfield and Roberts (1959, as cited in Schumann 1975) proposed a "critical period" hypothesis. It was suggested that there is a completion, at puberty, of cortical lateralization in which language functions become localized in the left cerebral cortex and the former plasticity of the brain atrophies. Lenneberg (1967) then focused attention on the relation between this brain lateralization and a point after which language learning became increasingly difficult. He posited that there were language-learning blocks that increased after puberty. In reality, the blocks are not physiological but psychological. It is the affective variables, such as anxiety and self-consciousness, that often cause adults to have difficulty with language learning.

It was noted earlier that as a person ages, he/she develops and relies on the ability to analyze and reflect on material. This skill can be a great benefit in language learning, one which was not recognized in the 1960s. In fact, cognitive maturity, which enables the adult to grasp complex ideas and concepts, allows for acquisition of the suprasegmental aspects of language more quickly than children. Adults are better able to see how ideas relate within a longer text, that is, how individual sentences fit together (Swaffar 1989). Adults also progress at a more rapid rate when it comes to the early stages of syntactic and morphological development in the language; both require the ability to acquire abstract concepts and complex ideas (Krashen et al. 1979).

Swain and Lapkin (1989) report results of the research with immersion programs in Canada. There, they have compared students who learn the curriculum primarily through a second language. Elementary school students are found to possess advantages in acquisition of phonological features and a greater confidence in using the second language. While students at the end of high school are able to perform about as well as their younger counterparts, they display a greater hesitancy in using the language. The ability to reflect and analyze that comes with age can be a detriment in this case, as speaking the language becomes more of a conscious act. It is very important to note that the older students acquired their language capability in a much shorter time than younger learners, since they did not begin their immersion experience until junior high or high school. The older student also has the ability to "abstract, generalize and classify," which makes them efficient language learners (Swain and Lapkin 1989, p. 152). The high school students also displayed a distinct advantage in the acquisition of literacy skills. Older learners are able to apply their first language reading strategies when reading the second language, whereas those who begin their immersion experience in kindergarten learn to read the second language first.

It would appear, then, that the adage "Older is better" holds true in the following areas:

1. Efficiency, that is, adults are able to acquire more language in a shorter amount of time
2. Acquisition of literacy skills
3. Development of early stages of syntax and morphology
4. Grasp of discourse features, that is, those elements that connect ideas in a text

Reiss (1982, p. 191) reveals the results of a questionnaire given to continuing education students taking, or about to take, a foreign language at a college campus:

> The level of expressed fear was quite high among these students, and words such as "scary," "lack of talent," "fear of appearing stupid," and "difficult" occurred with great frequency. One woman summed it up when she said: "To be perfectly honest, the thought of taking a foreign language makes me apprehensive."

Students who were currently enrolled in a second language course were also asked what most embarrassed them. Thirty-nine percent responded that it was being asked to perform. Taking a foreign language is a particularly good way to expose oneself to the risk of failure (Roumani 1978). As discussed earlier, adults develop an increasing fear of failure with age. Making a mistake, particularly in a public way, causes anxiety and a fear of losing face.

As Reiss's (1982) questionnaire also revealed, students express anxiety about foreign language learning because they think it is "difficult" or "scary." Frequently these ideas come from a previous (often unpleasant) experience with second language learning. They may have received poor grades, been corrected excessively, or simply been anxious because they could not understand what was being asked of them in a second language. It has been this author's experience that some students in adult education are prepared to drop out of the class if they are required to speak. Clearly, it is preferable to grant this wish and wait for them to volunteer as they become more comfortable with the class and confident about their language skills.

Not only do adults frequently suffer anxiety about having to speak the second language, but testing is another sensitive area. In a recreational adult class there really is no need to "test" formally. If the teacher is interested in diagnosing students' progress, it is best to assign something as homework or make an informal in-class project. The mere word *test* conjures up memories of frustration and failure for some. As Koehler (1984, p. 15) succinctly states, "Don't use the word 'test' in adult education classes."

Auditory impairment was discussed in the course of reviewing an adult's general learning ability above. In the second language classroom, where a brisk pace for drills and the natural speed of spoken language is revered, the adult learner, particularly the older learner, can be at a distinct disadvantage. There is difficulty both in actually hearing the language and in processing the information quickly.

> [A]ll kinds of aural-oral exercises with older learners must be conducted at an easy pace and with careful attention to acoustic conditions. The principle that the foreign language should be presented as it is really spoken, that is, as it is spoken by a native speaker in a natural situation, must of necessity be set aside in adult education, at least in the initial stages of training. (Von Elek and Oskarsson 1973, p. 49)

It has been demonstrated in numerous studies, then, that as adults age, they learn differently, not less well, than the young. The second language teacher must make modifications in the classroom and teaching techniques if he or she is to maximize the adult's potential. Success in language learning appears to be less dependent on the age of the learner than on the kind of teaching to which he or she is exposed (Von Elek and Oskarsson 1973).

Teaching Techniques and the Adult Learner

The following section is a discussion of teaching techniques that are considered commonplace in the traditional second language classroom but need to be rethought when working with adults and older learners.

Auditory Discrimination

Clearly, activities and methods that rely solely on auditory discrimination should be avoided when working with older learners. One example of such an activity might be an exercise in which students are required to listen to and distinguish sounds in the second language. Such exercises are common in conjunction with pronunciation drills. Total Physical Response (TPR) could also prove problematic with some adults. This method relies on the student demonstrating comprehension by responding with physical movement to an oral command. Although the teacher simultaneously carries out the commands, it may be difficult for the older student to hear what is being said and keep up, especially in the midst of background noise from the movement of other students. Typically, TPR relies on students responding to commands quickly and without hesitation. In using this technique with adults, it would be advisable to make certain the class is quiet when giving the commands, perhaps even giving the command twice and asking students to wait a few seconds before responding.

Performance

Given the performance anxiety that many adults and particularly older learners show, it would be wise to avoid an overreliance on oral activities and drills where a student is asked to perform individually in front of the class. Dialog recitation and fast-paced oral drills such as verb conjugation, question/answer, and sentence manipulation have been standard fare in the traditional classroom. Most of these activities would be best done chorally so that no one student is made to feel singled out in front of the class. Smith (1984, p. 7) quotes a student who summed up the feelings of many adult learners: "I began to dread going—when he picked on me I nearly died."

Total Physical Response activities would be best kept to commands that do not make adults feel self-conscious or silly. "Pick up the paper" or "close your book" would meet with more approval than "hop on one foot" or "run around your desk."

First Language Use

Exclusive use of the second language, such as the direct method requires, can be problematic for older learners. As discussed earlier, difficulties with memory are only compounded when material is not meaningful. If an adult learner is unable to comprehend all that is said, they are less likely to abstract and guess at the meaning of the words, even with visuals and props (Joiner 1981).

The audiolingual method made popular the idea of presenting dialogs exclusively in the second language and having students guess at their meanings with the help of visuals. When they are unable to do this, the decrease in meaningfulness increases both memory problems and anxiety. The adult education teacher may have to lay aside strongly held beliefs that the second language should be used at all times in class. Just as students can be taught to guess unknown words when reading, adults could also learn the skill of guessing at the spoken word, especially with the help of gestures and illustrations as clues. Adults typically need help in becoming risk takers.

Pace

A deductive method of presentation works well in that it gives the adult additional time to organize, analyze, and thus store information. Joiner (1981, p. 25) notes that "snappy, fast-paced tempo recommended for drill practice is virtually impossible for the adult learner." Fast-paced drills prove difficult, not only in terms of anxiety or hearing loss in some individuals but also because adults require more time to process and organize the material (Roumani 1978). Joiner (1981) cites Eisdorfer (1977), who found that among adults learning a second language, responses were directly related to pace. The more rapid the pace, the fewer responses offered by the students and vice-versa.

Memory

Memory becomes an increasing problem as a person ages. The teacher should avoid requiring students to memorize so-called "laundry lists," that is, lists of vocabulary words out of any meaningful context.

Things learnt recently tend to be more easily displaced from the memory by new material. Thus, the learning of sequences of short new items to be memorised becomes increasingly difficult, as each new item interferes with those previously learnt. This highlights the need for language teachers to avoid approaches relying on memorisation . . . and to develop approaches which constantly recycle material already learnt. (Smith 1984, p. 13)

Many oral drills, such as sentence manipulation, depend not only on speed but also on short-term memory. It would be best to have the drills in both written and oral form. Total Physical Response techniques would prove useful in helping a student's memory. Studies indicate that meaningfulness is enhanced by physical involvement and that, in turn, appears to produce storage in long-term memory (Joiner 1981).

Helpful Techniques for Teaching the Older Learner
The following list is a summary of techniques to keep in mind when developing activities for the adult education classroom:

1. Use audio and visual channels to enhance registration of material and aid in auditory and visual problems.
2. Develop activities that keep students involved and occasionally moving since they often come to class in the evening after a tiring day.
3. Focus on activities that enhance meaningfulness, such as using vocabulary in context in place of rote memorization.
4. Use students' first language at times to avoid anxiety and increase meaningfulness.
5. Slow the pace of presentation and practice.
6. Create a positive and friendly environment in order to reduce anxiety.
7. Use a deductive presentation.
8. Give students early opportunity to practice, orally if they wish, since they are generally taking the class for a very specific purpose and like to see rapid progress (Langran 1984).
9. Preview for organization and retention and review often with summaries.
10. Recycle material as much as possible to aid memory.
11. Allow for individuals to set the pace through pair and group work.

Curriculum and Materials
Typically, adult education courses of a recreational nature have no set curriculum. Ideally the motivations and interests of students in the class will drive the topics and forms to be covered. It cannot be overemphasized that the teacher is present to meet the needs of the students rather than coming to class with a predetermined agenda. An adult education teacher's job often depends on the ability to attract students and keep them in the class. The best way to do this is to ask first what they want and plan the curriculum later.

The traditional second language class focuses on youth-oriented topics such as parties, roommates, college majors, rock groups, and the like. That is an appropriate curriculum for the traditional second language student, but what of the adult learner? Issues of economics, politics, leisure time, retirement, and social security may be of greater value to nontraditional students (Witherell and Kersten 1983). Joiner (1981) makes the point that older students may also be more receptive to materials dealing with historical persons and eras, which allows them to bring their experience to the classroom.

Earlier in this paper, realistic expectations of performance were discussed using the *ACTFL Guidelines* as a framework. Students progress through the novice levels at a very rapid rate, but in most adult education courses it would not be unreasonable to expect that many students would reach, if only sporadically, the intermediate-low stage, which reflects moderately autonomous speech using fixed phrases and recombinations of learned material about basic topics.

Traditional courses are generally less diverse than adult education classes. In a traditional setting, school years are approximately the same in length and the available textbooks, which are not radically different from one another, tend to drive the curriculum. Recreational, noncredit adult education courses have few rules, no common textbooks, no common length of terms, and students who may or may not be able to come to class on a regular basis.

Many adult education courses meet only once per week for approximately three hours. Often classes last no more than seven to ten sessions and adults frequently miss a class or two due to business or family responsibilities. Progress, then, is slow in adult education when compared with a high school or college class, since a good deal of available time is spent reviewing what was learned the previous week and the rate of presentation is slowed. It is important that teachers in adult education, particularly those who come from a traditional setting, adjust their expectations of what can be accomplished. That is not to say that slower progress is necessarily undesirable; most adult learners are thrilled to make any visible progress.

For those teaching beginning level courses in a traditional setting, there is an ample number of books from which to choose. There are fewer students and therefore fewer books published for higher level traditional courses, but some materials are available. Second language teachers involved in adult education, particularly in a recreational course, are forced to either (1) use a textbook designed for the traditional classroom, that is, one that contains mostly youth-oriented subject matter and covers too much material, (2) use a grammar outline that is painfully dry and most likely too in-depth for their purposes, (3) work with a very tourist-oriented book, which may or may not be suitable to the needs of all students, or (4) make all the materials from scratch. Indeed it may be quite difficult to find one textbook that would suit the needs of any two adult classes, since, as it has been stressed, each class is composed of different students who come with different needs, motivations, and expectations. Unfortunately, once a book is chosen, its contents tend to drive the curriculum.

Carton-Caprio (1974) has developed a series of lessons for use with adult students. Each lesson is a self-contained unit that is beneficial in that it requires students to retain only a minimum of information from the previous week's class. Typically, in spite of the best of intentions, the previous week's lesson has been totally forgotten by the time class rolls around again. This also helps students who had to miss a class or two, since they don't feel lost when they rejoin the group. Because (1) adult students have little or no time to study during the week, (2) most material is nearly forgotten from one session to the next, and (3) the older learner's memory is declining, recycling and reviewing material becomes all-important in adult education. The idea of the self-contained unit completely takes out that crucial element except for the review and recycling of material within one class meeting. The notion of "covering" food items, clothing, numbers, or any other topic and then moving on to something new the next week would very likely meet with unsatisfactory results in this, or any other, setting.

Sample Activities

The next section outlines three activities that have worked well not only in a traditional setting but also with working adults and retirees.

1. Nationalities

This activity is particularly useful in that it gets students moving, which is very important when they are tired after a long day and tend to slump in their seats. This activity also allows them to go at their own pace and speak with individuals rather than in front of the entire class, and background noise is not usually a problem since students are speaking face to face. Basic structures and vocabulary are used so that students feel a sense of accomplishment early on as they ask and answer questions on their own yet within an organized framework.

One card is made for each student. At the top of that card the student will find information about his or her new identity, including name, country of origin, and something about his or her personality. At the bottom of the card they will be given the identity of someone they have to find. They receive that person's name, their country of origin, and something about his or her personality. This game requires an even number of "players" so that the class can eventually form pairs of people who were looking for one another. It is best to make the information fun without being too silly. Here are examples of some cards that could be used (they have been translated into English):

Card 1	Card 2
Your name is Juan Valdez.	Your name is Jacques Cousteau.
You come from Colombia.	You come from France.
You like to drink coffee.	You like to swim.
You are looking for a Frenchman.	You are looking for a Colombian.
His name is Jacques Cousteau.	His name is Juan Valdez.
He likes to swim.	He likes to drink coffee.

Card 3	Card 4
Your name is Robin Williams.	Your name is Julio Iglesias.
You come from America.	You come from Spain.
You are very funny.	You like to sing.
You are looking for a Spaniard.	You are looking for an American.
His name is Julio Iglesias.	His name is Robin Williams.
He likes to sing.	He is very funny.

Before beginning, the teacher simply reviews the names of selected countries and nationalities, how to introduce oneself and inquire about another person's name, and how to tell someone what you like to do and ask about their interests. At the end, students share aloud who they were and who they were looking for (while not requiring any student to speak who does not wish to do so).

2. Surveys

Again, this activity gets students up and moving. The questions and structures are basic, the vocabulary can be changed to fit topics recently covered, and the activity takes very little time to put together. The students enjoy it because they are able to speak to one another individually, rather than speaking under the scrutiny of the class and teacher. This activity helps students get to know one another, students are able to set their own pace, and those with hearing problems have the opportunity to speak with classmates face to face. It is best to collect personal information in the form of a short survey on the first night of class so that these activities can be personalized for each class. Before students leave their seats, the teacher can review basic vocabulary and question/answer structures.

Here are examples from two different surveys, translated into English.

A. Find at least one person who fits each category and write their name(s) in the blank.

1. He/she comes from Michigan. _____
2. He/she comes from Maine. _____
3. He/she likes to play tennis. _____
4. He/she likes classical music. _____
5. He/she has the phone number 353-2007. _____
6. He/she lives on Cambridge Street. _____

B. Find at least one person who fits each category and write their name(s) in the blank.

1. He/she has three children. _____
2. He/she has two sisters. _____
3. He/she has a relative named Mary. _____
4. He/she has a dog. Its name is Bob. _____

5. She has a husband. He works for Delta. _____
6. He has a wife. She is from Chicago. _____

3. Making Plans

This pair activity works well with adult students, since its individualization gives them the opportunity to set their own pace. It also allows them the opportunity to speak to each other, rather than the teacher, within an organized framework. They are able, in a short time, to incorporate a great deal of speaking practice using vocabulary that will likely be of use to them. Frequently, students in adult classes will be traveling abroad or entertaining guests in this country and this activity gives them the chance to practice telling time and reviewing names of places. Again, the opportunity to speak to one another face to face gives those with any hearing impairment a better chance at comprehension.

One student, the host, receives an itinerary for Saturday. The other student, presumably the guest to be shown the city, receives a list of questions concerning those plans. Here are the two sheets. Both are usually in the second language, but the questions could be kept in English for a bit of translation practice.

Questions: Ask your friend these questions about the day he or she has planned for you. Write down the answers you receive.

1. When will we eat breakfast?
2. How do we get to the city?
3. What is the first thing we will see?
4. Where will we eat lunch?
5. What will we see in the afternoon?
6. Where can I buy a gift for my son?
7. Are there any good movies playing?
8. What can we do after the film?
9. How will we get back home?

Plans for Saturday: Answer your friend's questions about the plans you have made for tomorrow.

    8:00 Breakfast
    9:30 Bus trip into the city
  10:00 City tour
  12:00 Lunch at city hall
  13:00 Cathedral tour
  14:00 Museum
  15:30 Shopping on Main Street
  16:30 Café
  18:15 Dinner at home
  20:00 Movie "Driving Miss Daisy" or "Terminator 2"
  21:30 Club for drinks
  23:30 Taxi home

Afterward, the questions and answers are discussed as a group, for those who wish to participate orally. A nice followup activity requires students to make up their own itineraries and questions regarding the specific city in which they live.

This allows for writing practice using known vocabulary and recombinations of learned phrases.

Conclusion

Those who have taught primarily in traditional settings, such as high school or college, and have worked with traditional students, those ranging from about five to twenty-five years of age, may find the transition to adult education more involved that they might anticipate. Techniques that have been so common for years in a traditional setting will need to be rethought, keeping adults and older learners in mind. There are frequently hearing and visual difficulties with which to contend, a greater anxiety and fear of failure than one might encounter with younger students, memory loss, difficulty in keeping up with a fast pace, problems with using analogy and inductive methods, competing responsibilities, fatigue after a long day, and lack of any obligation to return to class if it is not meeting their needs.

Langran (1984, p. 65) summarizes much of what is important about teaching adults and making materials for them:

> It is most important that the teaching programme retains a flexible element depending on the developing needs of the students attending the class. You are not "doing a course" with them, you are using a course to help them learn a language. What is needed from a course is a variety of authentic language materials and examples of use in an attractive format and with a reasonable structure. The way things are done will vary with each teacher and each group.

References

ACTFL. 1986. *Proficiency Guidelines*. Yonkers, NY: ACTFL.

Bergman, M. 1976. "Age Related Decrement in Hearing for Speech: Sampling and Longitudinal Studies." *Journal of Gerontology* 31: 533–38.

Carton-Caprio, Dana. 1974. "Enlivening the Adult Education Foreign Language Conversation Course." *Modern Language Journal* 58: 343–45.

Cattell, R. B. 1963. "Theory of Fluid and Crystallized Intelligence: A Critical Experiment." *Journal of Educational Psychology* 54: 1–22.

Dannerbeck, Francis J. 1987. "Adult Second-Language Learning: Toward an American Adaptation with a European Perspective." *Foreign Language Annals* 20: 413–19.

Eisdorfer, Carl. 1977. "Intellectual and Cognitive Changes in the Aged," pp. 212–27 in Ewald W. Busse and Eric Pfeiffer, eds., *Behavior and Adaptation in Late Life*. Boston: Little, Brown.

Haycraft, John. 1983. "The Pre-Beginner Phase." *ELT Journal* 37: 48–51.

Horn, J. L., and R. B. Cattell. 1966. "Age Differences in Primary Mental Ability Factors." *Journal of Gerontology* 21: 210–20.

Joiner, Elizabeth G. 1981. *The Older Foreign Language Learner: A Challenge for Colleges and Universities*. Language in Education: Theory and Practice Series, no. 34. Washington, DC: ERIC Clearinghouse on Languages and Linguistics. [EDRS: ED 208 672]

Kalfus, Richard. 1987. "An Adult Education Foreign Language Program in the Community College: An Innovative Approach." Washington, DC: ERIC Clearinghouse on Languages and Linguistics. [EDRS ED 283 579]

Keim, R. J. 1977. "How Aging Affects the Ear." *Geriatrics* 32: 97–99.

Knox, Alan B. 1977. *Adult Development and Learning.* San Francisco: Jossey-Bass.

Koehler, Russell C. 1984. *Handbook for Volunteers: Adult Education Program.* Olympia, WA: Washington Office of the State Superintendent of Public Instruction. [EDRS: ED 246 955]

Krashen, Stephen D., Michael A. Long, and Robin C. Scarcella. 1979. "Age, Rate, and Eventual Attainment in Second Language Acquisition." *TESOL Quarterly* 13: 573–82.

Langran, John. 1984. "In the Classroom," pp. 57–87 in Duncan Sidwell, ed., *Teaching Languages to Adults.* London, Eng.: Centre for Information on Language Teaching and Research.

Lenneberg, Eric. 1967. *Biological Foundations of Language.* New York: Wiley.

Ostwald, Sharon Kay, and Howard Y. Williams. 1985. "Optimizing Learning in the Elderly: A Model." *Lifelong Learning* 9: 10–13.

Penfield, Wilder, and Lamar Roberts. 1959. *Speech and Brain Mechanisms.* New York: Atheneum.

Reiss, Mary Ann. 1982. "The Continuing Education Student and the Study of Foreign Languages." *Foreign Language Annals* 15: 189–95.

Rosenthal, Edward L. 1978. "Lifelong Learning: For Some of the People." *Lifelong Learning* 2: 12–13.

Roumani, Judith. 1978. "Foreign Language Learning for Older Learners: Problems and Approaches." Washington, DC: Peace Corps. [EDRS: ED 192 627]

Schleppegrell, Mary. 1987. "The Older Language Learner." Washington, DC: ERIC Clearinghouse on Languages and Linguistics. [EDRS ED 287 313]

Schumann, John H. 1975. "Affective Factors and the Problem of Age in Second Language Acquisition." *Language Learning* 25: 209–35.

Smith, David. 1984. "Modern Languages and the Adult Student," pp. 1–15 in Duncan Sidwell, ed., *Teaching Languages to Adults.* London, Eng.: Centre for Information on Language Teaching and Research.

Swaffar, Janet K. 1989. "Competing Paradigms in Adult Language Acquisition." *Modern Language Journal* 73: 301–14.

Swain, Merrill, and Sharon Lapkin. 1989. "Canadian Immersion and Adult Second Language Teaching: What's the Connection?" *Modern Language Journal* 73: 150–59.

Vacca, Richard T., and James E. Walker. 1980. "Andragogy: The Missing Link in College Reading Programs." *Lifelong Learning* 3: 16, 24–25.

Von Elek, Tibor, and Mats Oskarsson. 1973. *Teaching Foreign Language Grammar to Adults: A Comparative Study.* Stockholm, Sweden: Almqvist and Wiksell.

Walsh, D. A. 1983. "Age Differences in Learning and Memory," pp. 149–72 in D. S. Woodruff and J. E. Birren, eds., *Aging: Scientific Perspectives and Social Issues.* Monterey, CA: Brooks/Cole.

Weale, R. A. 1975. "Senile Changes in Visual Acuity." *The Transactions of the Ophthalmological Society of the United Kingdom* 95: 36–38.

Witherell, Louise R., and Raquel Kersten. 1983. "The Adult Student in Foreign Language Classes." Paper presented at the Central States Conference on the Teaching of Foreign Languages, St. Louis, MO.

9
Learner-Initiated and Learner-Friendly:
Questions to Get Them Talking

Gregory K. Armstrong
State University of New York at Cortland

> I was having all the fun! There I was up front tap-dancing away, feeling the exhilaration of how keen my questions were—and not noticing that this was taking opportunity away from my students.
>
> Jane Schaffer (1987), English teacher

Questions have long been the mainstay of the teacher's repertoire. Whether in the foreign language classroom or in that of any other discipline, questions tend to be a teacher's primary tool of inquiry. While generations of foreign language teachers have used personalized questions, yes-no questions, and choice questions, to name a few, hosts of students were expected, sometimes unrealistically, merely to supply the answers. Unfortunately for the learner, teacher questions can often carelessly embarrass and undermine rather than build and inspire (Wolf 1987). They can also lead to dead ends or sometimes produce too much teacher talk as opposed to more meaningful two-way conversation. In recent years though, Honeycutt and Vernon (1985) and the ACTFL *Proficiency Guidelines* (1986) have suggested that learners, not just teachers, ought to be asking many of the questions in the foreign language classroom.

While approaching the subject of questions, most readers will recall the infamous query posed by the Georgia school board member who asked Professor Genelle Morain, "Why should a student who will never leave Macon, Georgia, study a foreign language?" Thoughtfully insightful in her response, Morain retorted, "That's *why* he should study another language!" (Omaggio Hadley 1986, p. 357). Like the hypothetical Georgia student cited above, this writer as a high school student held little hope of experiencing life in a culture other than his own. But as fate would have it, four short years after high school graduation he found himself on the streets of Montevideo, Uruguay. And despite accumulated language study consisting of two years of high school Latin, two of Spanish, and sixteen hours of intensive college Spanish, this new arrival felt some profound frustrations during those early days in the target culture. How vividly I recall walking down the street one morning with a companion when we were stopped by one of his

Spanish-speaking acquaintances. After exchanging greetings and introductions she glanced at me, turned to my friend, and said, "Pobrecito, no entiende nada." She was wrong! The truth is that I *did* understand their conversation. The problem was not a lack of understanding, but an inability to respond with anything more than "Comprendo sí, pero no puedo hablar." Despite feelings of frustration at not being able to join actively in the conversation, I knew what they were saying! Krashen (1983), who refers to similar experiences he and others had shared, would say that my Language Acquisition Device was not yet activated due to insufficient comprehensible input.

Perhaps that early overseas experience was not entirely unlike those of some first-year Spanish students at a large public university where the author once taught. There, not many years ago, a certain professor regularly gave his students individual oral quizzes. One by one they would file past my open door on their way to his office. The format seemed nearly always the same. Well-intentioned, but with misdirected efforts, the instructor would proceed to fire away with a series of questions (which perhaps they understood, but could not reply to), with the victims usually returning blank stares in response. While dazzling them with his questions, proving that *he* indeed knew Spanish, he failed to discover what *they* could do in the target language. Judging by their countenances, many left the interview disheartened, disappointed, and most likely determined to drop out of Spanish at their earliest opportunity. Their instructor's only apparent concern was usually expressed in terms something like, "Pobrecitos, no entienden nada."

Questions Can Be Opportunities

Much like the English teacher quoted at the beginning of this article, this former colleague was taking opportunity away from his students. He was calling all the shots. His oral exams were traps in which to catch his victims rather than opportunities for them to demonstrate what they *could* do. Anxious and intimidated, his students were reduced to a reactive mode, seldom responding except in those rare instances when conditions were just right for them both to understand and to verbalize appropriate answers. No meaningful communication was taking place. The students did not seem to have a sense of accomplishment. There had to be a better way!

Proficiency-Oriented and "Learner-Friendly"

Vowing not to repeat the colleague's error and strongly determined to make the classroom learner-friendly (Strasheim 1991), the author reviewed the ACTFL *Proficiency Guidelines* and participated in an oral proficiency interviewer's workshop, after which an approach was developed to help students move actively toward achieving the goal of real communication in Spanish. For as Strasheim (1991), Frink (1982), and Muyskens and Harlow (1991) have noted, student surveys throughout the past half century have stressed speaking as one of the primary skills foreign language students hope to develop.

Recent literature (Rivers et al. 1991; Jackson and Beaver 1991; Nyikos 1991) emphasized the importance of active student involvement and meaningful classroom interaction. In order to produce successful learners who can function orally in the target language, foreign language instruction today demands both a proficiency orientation and a conscientious awareness on the part of the teacher that learning must be more than a passive activity. Learners must also be given sufficient opportunity to be in control of the learning processes. Nyikos contrasts the need of students to organize and control their own learning processes, a strategy leading to greater success in the target language, with the teacher-dominated traditional classroom where "students are hindered by the lack of opportunity to ask each other meaningful questions through which they elicit useful information about the likes, dislikes, and lives of their fellow classmates" (pp. 31–32).

Focusing on the Learner

Turning our attention to the beginning foreign language learner and consulting the ACTFL *Guidelines* with an eye toward guiding students from Novice to Intermediate proficiency, it becomes a rather simple matter to identify some specific functions a learner will need to be able to perform in order to reach the Intermediate level. The *Guidelines* state that:

The Intermediate level is characterized by the speaker's ability to:
- create with the language by combining and recombining learned elements, though primarily in a reactive mode;
- initiate, minimally sustain, and close in a simple way basic communicative tasks; and
- ask and answer questions.

With these functions in mind, better ways of using questions were explored. Since Intermediate level speakers must be capable not only of answering questions but of *asking* them as well, why not create more opportunities for *students* to ask meaningful questions? Furthermore, knowing how to initiate discourse with questions would allow students the opportunity to guide and sustain a conversation better rather than merely react to someone else. Honeycutt and Vernon (1985) had already discussed the subject of students asking questions in the foreign language class, so the idea was not new. Moreover, with some appropriately directed effort on the part of the instructor, students could soon be asking questions and engaging in face-to-face interviews with their peers and teacher.

Brainstorming Questions

In a beginning Spanish class that was about one-third of the way through the semester, students were told they knew much more Spanish than they realized. They were asked to imagine that they were flying over central Mexico when the plane became disabled. Their only chance to survive was to parachute out. Landing successfully on the outskirts of San Luis Potosí, they were met by some people who spoke only Spanish. Based on these circumstances, what needed to be asked? To assure participation by the whole class, everybody was asked to contribute at least one question. As questions were supplied, they were written on the board. When students were no longer able to generate questions in the target language, they continued to think of questions in English, which were written on the board in Spanish. On another day class members were asked to imagine a different situation in which they were walking down the street in their neighborhood when they were approached by a Spanish-speaking person who appeared lost. Again they were asked to generate questions in order to be helpful.

The Question Inventory

After the first brainstorming session mentioned above, students were told to keep a written list or inventory of all the questions they had helped to generate. Furthermore, it was suggested that they keep it handy and update it by adding new questions they might learn throughout the course of the semester. The objective in their keeping the question inventory was to have it always available as a resource from which to select needed questions each time they would have an opportunity to interview another classmate or the instructor. The result was that they were seldom at a loss for words when the opportunity came for them to ask questions.

Early and Frequent Oral Testing

During a recent summer session, a section of beginning Spanish met two hours daily for five weeks with a quiz scheduled every fourth day. Quizzes were given during the last 50 minutes of that class day. The quizzes consisted of two major parts: (1) a pencil-and-paper section testing primarily reading, writing, vocabulary, and structure, and (2) a brief oral interview with the instructor. The written and oral portions were equally weighted. In other words, grades were based 50 percent on the written work and 50 percent on the oral interview. While class members were working on the written portion of the exam, the instructor would sit just outside the open door, permitting a full view of the class. Then, in predetermined order, individual students would step outside for a short interview with the instructor.

Students came to the interview with confidence. Having been introduced to the functions of greeting and leave-taking on the first day of class, they were already accustomed to performing those familiar functions in the target language. For the quiz they had been instructed to greet their instructor, be seated, and ask the instructor five or six personal questions about himself, his work, or his family. Topics would change from quiz to quiz just as they would in class. At all times the learners were in control of the interview situation. They, not the instructor, held the agenda, since they were asking the questions and guiding the interview. As the semester progressed it was observed that the least able students tended to stick carefully to memorized questions with which they were familiar. The risk takers and the more confident and proficient students would frequently come up with surprisingly creative queries. Oral performance was generously graded with full credit awarded whenever communication took place. Students were always given the benefit of the doubt.

On one occasion, while exceptionally busy during the next-to-last week of class, the instructor suggested omitting the oral portion of the quiz. Students wouldn't hear of it! Putting the matter to a vote yielded a unanimous consensus to have the interview! They had grown accustomed to the one-on-one, face-to-face conversation with their instructor on a regular basis and many were likely counting on the oral portion of the quiz to bolster their grades. The instructor's experience, like that of Frink (1982), indicates that oral quizzes of this type are liberating for many students. Some who perform poorly on more traditional written tests may excel in speaking. Furthermore, as Omaggio Hadley (1986) has pointed out, students frequently become more motivated after being given individual opportunities to share information about themselves and their interests with their teacher.

Conclusion

The experiences discussed in this article serve to confirm the notion that successful language learners must have opportunities to control their own learning processes. When given regular opportunities to do so, learners enjoyed reversing the traditional teacher and student roles of questioning while gleaning information from their peers and instructor. Moreover, they proved to have no difficulty with the frequency of the oral quizzes, which helped them progress toward their own goal of communicating in the language as well as meet their teacher's expectations. When learner-initiated and learner-friendly, questions are an unquestionably good way to get learners talking!

References

ACTFL. 1986. *Proficiency Guidelines*. Hastings-on-Hudson, NY: ACTFL.

Frink, Helen H. 1982. "Oral Testing for First-Year Language Classes." *Foreign Language Annals* 15: 281–87.

Honeycutt, C. Allen, and Nile D. Vernon. 1985. "Who Should Be Asking the Questions in the Second Language Classroom?" pp. 38–42 in Patricia B. Westphal, ed., *Meeting the Call for Excellence in the Foreign Language Classroom*. Proceedings of the Central States Conference on the Teaching of Foreign Languages. Lincolnwood, IL: National Textbook Company.

Jackson, Margaret, and Sharon Beaver. 1991. "Involve Me and I'll Learn: Active Participation Strategies for Foreign Language Classes," pp. 43–53 in Lorraine A. Strasheim, ed., *Focus on the Foreign Language Learner: Priorities and Strategies*. Proceedings of the Central States Conference on the Teaching of Foreign Languages. Lincolnwood, IL: National Textbook Company.

Krashen, Stephen D. 1983. "The Din in the Head, Input, and the Language Acquisition Device." *Foreign Language Annals* 16:41–44.

Muyskens, Judith A., and Linda Harlow. 1991. "Priorities for Intermediate-Level Instruction in the Nineties." Paper presented at the Central States Conference, Indianapolis, IN.

Nyikos, Martha. 1991. "Prioritizing Student Learning: A Guide for Teachers," pp. 25–39 in Lorraine A. Strasheim, ed., *Focus on the Foreign Language Learner: Priorities and Strategies*. Proceedings of the Central States Conference on the Teaching of Foreign Languages. Lincolnwood, IL: National Textbook Company.

Omaggio Hadley, Alice. 1986. *Teaching Language in Context: Proficiency-Oriented Instruction*. Boston: Heinle and Heinle.

Rivers, Wilga, et al. 1991. *Teaching Spanish: A Practical Guide*. Lincolnwood, IL: National Textbook Company.

Schaffer, Jane. 1987. "When Students Ask Questions." *Academic Connections* (Winter): 8–11.

Strasheim, Lorraine A. 1991. "Introduction: Learners and Learning Outcomes," pp. ix–xiii in Lorraine A. Strasheim, ed., *Focus on the Foreign Language Learner: Priorities and Strategies*. Proceedings of the Central States Conference on the Teaching of Foreign Languages. Lincolnwood, IL: National Textbook Company.

Wolf, Dennis Palmer. 1987. "The Art of Questioning." *Academic Connections* (Winter): 1–7.

10
High School, College, and University Articulation:
The Renewed Crisis in Foreign Language Education

Barbara Gonzalez-Pino
University of Texas at San Antonio

Need

Articulation has long been a critical issue in foreign language instruction. The elements that comprise it are complex and have been addressed by various professional groups (Gonzalez Pino 1991b) and most recently by the ACTFL Priorities Conference (1989). Articulation concerns are evident at several transition points on the education ladder. They are present between elementary school and middle school and also between the latter and senior high school. Each level has its characteristics, but because those three levels of study are generally coordinated by one person in each state and in each school district, there is greater likelihood that the teachers in those programs understand the articulation problems, and communication to resolve them is easier. On the other hand, transition between high school and higher education has traditionally been more difficult.

Definition

Colleges and universities are more autonomous. Not many states yet have uniform language requirements for university entrance, although California, Florida, Georgia, Montana, Nevada, and South Carolina do (Draper 1991). Fewer still have uniform core curricula, much less uniform approaches to teaching and evaluating language proficiency. Thus, while there is concern for the lower school transitions and articulation across programs and even across disciplines, the transition from secondary to university level in foreign languages has traditionally been the most challenging problem of articulation and the one most needing attention from language professionals. In an attempt to identify specific problems of transition and attitudes of both students and teachers who deal with these problems, the author undertook a multipronged study in Texas that focused on three perspectives:

- Of college and university foreign language departments (Gonzales Pino 1990)
- Of foreign language supervisors in public school districts (Gonzales Pino 1991a)
- Of students who had recently passed through that point of transition

In public schools, the Texas Education Agency Language Section is working toward a seamless curriculum preK–12 that contains a program of study and exit requirements to be implemented by all schools. At the college and university level, however, the Texas Higher Education Coordinating Board is not empowered to mandate curricula and may only make recommendations. The variety of requirements, offerings, and approaches used in the 200-plus colleges and universities, therefore, is great. With over 1000 school districts and over 200 colleges and universities in the state, the potential for difficulty in articulation is monumental. Added to the large number of institutions is the substantial increase in recent years of the number of languages offered, the increased enrollments in languages, and the number and type of language requirements for entrance to and exit from the university. Thus, there is an ever greater likelihood that students will go to institutions of higher education whose language offerings do not match those of their secondary school. They will compete for space and attention in placement testing and in courses with growing numbers of other students, and they will confront a variety of entrance and exit requirements in languages in the various institutions to which they apply.

The final ingredient in this mixture is one that is prevalent throughout the nation: the degree to which language departments at these respective levels do and do not embrace similar emphases in their programs. With the advent of communicative proficiency-oriented methodology, we have a possible disjunction in orientation that rivals the number of program variants we saw in the 1960s when "traditional" meant grammar-translation and audiolingual was new. Today's traditional program could combine elements of grammar-translation, audiolingual, and cognitive approaches. It may have an oral component in classes but probably not in testing. Today's proficiency-oriented program might emphasize listening and speaking as applied to real-life situations. It may emphasize these skills in teaching and testing and focus far less on grammar, reading, and writing, particularly at the lower levels. In Texas, and no doubt in some other states as well, the public school program led by state education department language specialists has been a model of communicative language teaching. At the college and university level, incorporation of this approach has been very uneven, being implemented in some institutions and not in others as well as being implemented to greater and lesser degrees and in varying combinations with other approaches. Thus, in recent years we have seen the high school student trained in a communicative approach enter the traditional college program, the traditional student enter the proficiency-based program, and every other possible combination.

Understandably, then, there is some additional frustration present on both sides of this equation: among language professionals, who need to talk to each other more about their concerns, and among students, who have been caught in a difficult situation. We have added one more powerful variable to an articulation point through which it has always been arduous to pass. For this final, significant reason, we can say that articulation is once again the crisis in foreign languages. Since our goal is hardly to make students suffer with their language studies but rather to facilitate their success, we must attend to our crisis in order to continue our growth trend and not reenter a period of program reduction.

The Study

Since the literature contains little information about articulation problems, the author created, in 1989-90, a questionnaire (Appendix 10A), which was distributed to language coordinators at colleges and universities. The purpose was to gather information about placement practices in foreign languages at those institutions. Of the 150 questionnaires sent, 50 responses were received. They came primarily from the larger universities in the state; only a few community colleges responded. In 1990, a modified version of the questionnaire (Appendix 10B) for secondary language supervisors in the state was prepared and distributed. Fifty responses (out of 70) were received. Finally, in 1991, the coordinator version of the questionnaire was given to 100 university students who had recently passed through this point of transition in order to learn how they viewed their preparation in high school to function successfully in their chosen college foreign language program.

Results on the Issue of Placement

The combined results on item 1 of the questionnaires from the three mailings showed that placement practices at the university level vary widely. Half the colleges use credits only and half use placement tests to assign students to their appropriate level of instruction. The placement tests vary in type, with roughly one-third being four-skills tests, one-third being receptive-skills tests, and one-third focusing on receptive skills plus vocabulary and grammar. Ninety percent of the coordinators and 100 percent of the students recommend a four-skills test. A broad discrepancy between their suggestion and what is practiced by universities is evident. Placement based on four-skills evaluation is actually implemented by only 7 of the 50 university respondents (15 percent). While issues of costs and numbers certainly enter into the matter and often prevent universities from implementing speaking and writing tests, the public school and the university language students clearly feel that all four skills should be tested.

Item 2 inquired about the appropriate placement for the student who took level I in the elementary school, level II in middle school, and level III in high school. Ninety percent of the coordinators and 100 percent of the students still wanted placement by test. Half the college respondents still reported placement by test, but the other half varied widely in their practices. Some would have the student start over, and some would place the student in third year; but the majority would place the student in second year. Given that the high school curriculum in Texas covers in three years what the university covers in one, the placement is too high; and once again some groups are not in agreement. In this instance, the material covered by the high school and the university in the first year is already known. Where it is not already known, this information, too, would be gathered via the questionnaire.

Item 3 inquires about the placement of a student who took level I in elementary school, level II in middle school, and level III in grade 9. In this case public school supervisors and students still preferred to determine placement but 5 percent of the university respondents unequivocally opted for first-year placement, thus requiring the student to start over. Of the universities, half would place by test score.

Item 4 asked about the student who had taken levels I and II in high school. Supervisors and students still opted for a test; 50 percent of the respondents preferred placement by testing; 16 percent required a first-year placement (start over), and 34 percent a second-year placement. The appropriate credit-based placement in Texas's 3-years-to-1-year curriculum ratio would be second semester, but the best choice would be a test. The student who has completed three levels in high school could go to second year, but again will be place best by test, especially given the time lags of the nontraditional student, who does not always enter college immediately nor take language courses immediately when he or she does enter.

Item 5 (6 in version B) referred to college transfer work. Half the supervisors and all the students thought that transfer students should be placed on the basis of credit earned at another university. Ninety-nine percent of the colleges handle this student on the basis of the transfer credit.

Item 6 (7 in version B) asked respondents to comment on the preparedness of incoming students. Forty percent of the college respondents found that students were well prepared while one-third of the coordinators and students predicted that they were. Sixty percent of the university respondents found students deficient, two-thirds in listening-speaking, and one-third in reading-writing-grammar. Forty percent of the supervisors thought their students would be perceived as deficient because of differing orientations in the public school and university programs. Sixty to sixty-seven percent of the respondents in all categories indicated problems in this area.

Item 7 (8 in version B) concerned native speakers, the one area where there was agreement among all three respondents. Ninety to ninety-five percent agreed that some sort of test or interview should be used for placing native speakers. The college respondents, however, report a variety of measures: four-skills, receptive skills, receptive skills plus add-ons, and interviews. A wide variety of measures is used with an equal variety of outcomes for placement, as harder tests are sometimes used for native speakers.

Item 8 (9 in version B) asked for more specific detail about placement tests. Again, 80 percent of the supervisors and students opted for a four-skills test, but among colleges, one-third had no test, one-third had a four-skills test, and one-third had a receptive-skills test. Ninety percent of the supervisors favored recruiting all students to take the placement test, as did 90 percent of the students, but only 40 percent of the colleges that have a test do, in fact, require students to take it. Ninety-five percent of the coordinators and 40 percent of the students favored requiring placements based on the test score, but in half the colleges such test scores are used for advising purposes only. Sixty percent of the students favored using the test only for advising.

Results on the Issue of Credit by Examination

Sixty percent of the supervisors and all the students favored credit by examination based on advanced placement test or the university's own four-skills tests. Twenty-five percent of the supervisors suggested using the College Level Examination Program (CLEP) and 23 percent the Advanced Placement Test. All the students favored these measures as well. Inasmuch as only 13 percent of the universities report using their own tests, another discrepancy emerges. Colleges are relying rather heavily on the CLEP; supervisors support using the Advanced Placement Test at twice the rate of actual use and in-house tests at five times the use rate.

All universities report that their programs are four-skills-based, but only half test four skills. All the high school programs emphasize four skills too. Sixty-seven percent of the supervisors report four-skills testing as well in their own programs. However, 45 percent of the supervisors believe college programs have little emphasis on speaking and writing, suggesting a difference or a misperception on the part of one group about how the emphasis should be defined. Quite clearly, we do not see ourselves as others see us in this regard.

Results on the Issue of Expectations

Almost all (95 percent) of the colleges and universities report emphasizing the four skills with minor emphasis on vocabulary, grammar, and culture. The public school supervisors and students report the same emphasis in their own programs. Supervisors again underline a discrepancy in the two views of college programs by indicating that colleges emphasize grammar/reading/writing just as much as they do listening and speaking. Thus, they report a view contrary to that held by the colleges about themselves. Ninety-nine percent of the respondents in all categories state that their faculty believe articulation to be important. Only fifteen percent of the supervisors report believing that college faculty think articulation is important. Clearly communication is needed between the two groups to rectify this discrepancy.

Results on the Issue of Understanding the High School and College Framework

Yet another discrepancy emerges over the nature of the secondary language program. Almost all the supervisors and students believe that the high school language curriculum emphasizes communicative competence and covers the basic language in three years. However, one-third of the university respondents think that the high school program emphasizes grammar and is completed in two years. Articulation will certainly not be accomplished effectively in those areas where such a misperception exists.

The supervisors understand that foreign language programs vary among different universities, but they do not know that language faculty do not control all aspects of student admissions, placement, and credit procedures. They do not realize that the general faculty control many aspects of such requirements, as is the case at the author's institution and many others in Texas.

Other Concerns

Supervisors would like to have feedback about student performance on placement and credit examinations. In addition, they would also like to see changes in the way language teachers are prepared by the universities. Specifically, they want more new teachers who have experienced proficiency-based models and learned proficiency-based methodology. College faculty would like more input regarding intensive language review courses (favored by students) as well as possibilities for observing the classes of other faculty in their own and other languages. Both these models are possible partial solutions to needs in the articulation area.

Conclusions

Certain problems emerge strongly. Practices vary widely; students and the teachers guiding them have a difficult time planning in the face of diverse requirements and procedures for placement. Waste of student preparation caused by asking students to start over in the language, student frustration, and general confusion are likely in all circumstances. Overall, high schools are more proficiency-oriented in teaching and testing than colleges and the two groups are not altogether clear about what the other does in either teaching or testing. To the extent that they are informed, they do not always agree on the best procedure or test or curricular emphasis. Thus, extensive opportunities for communication are needed on the topics of

- Goals for teaching/learning
- Best approaches to placement and credit procedures
- Ways to have test goals coincide with program goals
- Optional placement
- Creating in-house tests and identifying other good tests
- State and institutional restraints

At the author's institution, many of the approaches to improving articulation are being implemented. There is a four-skills proficiency-type placement testing program with data being collected for feedback to high schools. There are regular lines of communication between primary feeder high schools and the language department in the form of a newsletter, workshops and receptions on campus, and a local language professional association for teachers and professors. There is further contact through the language teacher training program as well, as the author regularly visits language programs in secondary schools with her student teachers. She and other college and university faculty join with secondary teachers and coordinators on most state-level committees working on the secondary program. In addition, there is a core curriculum project in which all area language departments (eight colleges and universities) are participating in an effort to coordinate programs, requirements, and entrance procedures. Further, these language professionals are also engaging in interdisciplinary coordination through interactions with other disciplines provided for in the project. Finally, there is articulation across and within languages, as each language group has regular meetings and the supervisors of the various languages meet as well.

Because of the investigative projects the author has conducted, the Texas Association of Departments of Foreign Languages (Chairpersons) and the Texas

Association of College and University Language Supervisors have made articulation a topic for discussion at several recent annual meetings and are slowly progressing toward the goals of understanding what one another is doing and of discussing ways to improve the overall process. They are communicating regularly by mail with all their constituent departments about articulation matters, even with those that do not participate in the meetings. Much is being accomplished through various channels.

Students at the University of Texas at San Antonio who contributed their views to the information gathering also represent an important part of such a process. We should all be finding out what our students think about what we are doing and about what we should be doing. In addition to the placement and credit testing programs and other screening tests at various levels (including exit), we presently offer them accelerated review courses at several levels. We will continue to sample their opinions and seek their advice about their needs. Their strongest point is that we should use four-skills placement tests, even though they prefer to retain decision-making rights after taking the test.

In each locale coordinators and college faculty need to talk. Further interaction is needed at the state and national level. As Phyllis Franklin (1989) said, "The key to a polyglot America is the bridge we need to build from one level to another." We have much to ascertain about ourselves, one another, and our mutual goals for a better articulated future.

References

American Council on the Teaching of Foreign Languages. 1989. Papers presented at the 1989 Priorities Conference, Boston.

Franklin, Phyllis. 1989. "Editorial." *MLA Newsletter*, Winter, p. 1.

Gonzales Pino, Barbara. 1990. "High School/College and University Articulation." *TFLA Bulletin* (January): 3–4.

———. 1991a. "High School/College and University Articulation." An unpublished paper presented at the AATSP meeting in August, Chicago.

———. 1991b. "Priorities for the 1990's from the Southwest." *SWCOLT Newsletter*, Spring, pp. 2–3.

Appendix 10A
Texas High School-College/University Articulation

Check all that apply:

I. Intake and Placement Issues
   1. We place students coming in from high school or from another college where that have taken foreign language on the basis of _____.
      _____ a. high school credits.
      _____ b. a four-skills placement test (listening, speaking, reading, writing).
      _____ c. a receptive-skills placement test (listening, reading).
      _____ d. a receptive skills plus vocabulary/grammar test.
   2. A student who took Level I FL in grades 1-6, Level II in grades 7-8, and Level III in high school would be placed in _____.
      _____ a. the level indicated by proficiency test results.
      _____ b. first year.
      _____ c. second year.
      _____ d. third year.
      _____ e. Other _____.
   3. A student who took Level I FL in grade 7 and Level II in grade 8 would be placed in _____.
      _____ a. the level indicated by proficiency test results.
      _____ b. first year.
      _____ c. second year.
      _____ d. third year.
      _____ e. Other _____.
   4. A student who took Levels I and II in high school would be placed in _____.
      _____ a. the level indicated by proficiency test results.
      _____ b. first year.
      _____ c. second year.
      _____ d. third year.
      _____ e. Other _____.
   5. We place transfer students who have taken a foreign language in college on the basis of _____.
      _____ a. proficiency test results.
      _____ b. transfer of credit equivalency tables.
   6. We find that transfer students
      _____ a. are generally well prepared to meet our program's expectations.
      _____ b. are as well prepared to meet our program's expectations as students from our own program.
      _____ c. are generally deficient in listening-speaking skills.
      _____ d. are generally deficient in reading-writing-grammar skills.
      _____ e. are generally deficient in vocabulary.

7. Native speakers of a FL who have no credits in that language are placed on the basis of _____.
    ____ a. self placement.
    ____ b. a four-skills placement test.
    ____ c. a receptive-skills placement test.
    ____ d. a receptive-skills plus test.
    ____ e. an interview.

8. Our placement test _____.
    ____ a. we don't have one.
    ____ b. is four-skills.
    ____ c. is receptive skills.
    ____ d. is receptive skills plus vocabulary and grammar.
    ____ e. is required (to take).
    ____ f. is optional (to take).
    ____ g. determines placement.
    ____ h. is advisory only.

II. Credit by Examination

9. For Credit by Examination we offer _____.
    ____ a. CLEP.
    ____ b. CLEP plus oral and written.
    ____ c. our own four-skills tests.
    ____ d. our own two-skills test.
    ____ e. advanced placement.
    ____ f. Other _____.
    ____ g. nothing.

10. The following statement(s) is/are true for our program:
    ____ a. Our foreign language program is four-skills-based, as is our examination for credit.
    ____ b. Our FL program includes little speaking and writing, and neither does our examination for credit.
    ____ c. Our foreign language program us four-skills-based, but our examination for credit is not.

III. Expectations

11. We want students entering with previous foreign language study in high school or college (as well as students progressing in our own program) to _____ at the appropriate level.
    ____ a. understand the language
    ____ b. speak the language
    ____ c. read in the language
    ____ d. write in the language
    ____ e. use extensive vocabulary
    ____ f. use accurate grammar
    ____ g. know grammar rules
    ____ h. know the target culture

12. Most of our faculty feel that high school–college FL program articulation is _____.
    _____ a. important.
    _____ b. irrelevant.
    _____ c. unimportant.
    _____ d. hopeless.
    _____ e. Other _____.

IV. Understandings of the Texas High School FL Framework

13. We understand the State secondary FL curriculum to _____.
    _____ a. emphasize grammar.
    _____ b. emphasize proficiency.
    _____ c. emphasize listening and speaking in the basic program.
    _____ d. emphasize reading and writing.
    _____ e. cover the basic language in two years.
    _____ f. cover the basic language in three years.

V. Personal Data

Name _____ Title _____ Date _____

Institution _____ Department _____

City, ZIP _____ Telephone _____

Appendix 10B
Texas High School-College/University Articulation
High School Coordination Survey

Check all that apply regarding foreign language study at the university level:

I. Intake and Placement Issues

1. Students coming into college from high school or from another college where that have taken FL should be placed on the basis of _____.
   - ____ a. high school credits.
   - ____ b. a four-skills placement test (listening, speaking, reading, writing).
   - ____ c. a receptive-skills placement test (listening, reading).
   - ____ d. a receptive skills plus vocabulary/grammar test.

2. A student who took Level I FL in grades 1–6, Level II in grades 7–8, and Level III in high school should be placed in _____.
   - ____ a. the level indicated by proficiency test results.
   - ____ b. first year.
   - ____ c. second year.
   - ____ d. third year.
   - ____ e. Other _____.

3. A student who took Level I FL in grade 7–8 Level II in grade 9 should be placed in _____.
   - ____ a. the level indicated by proficiency test results.
   - ____ b. first year.
   - ____ c. second year.
   - ____ d. third year.
   - ____ e. Other _____.

4. A student who took Levels I and II in high school should be placed in _____.
   - ____ a. the level indicated by proficiency test results.
   - ____ b. first year.
   - ____ c. second year.
   - ____ d. third year.
   - ____ e. Other _____.

5. A student who took Levels I, II, and III in high school should be placed in _____.
   - ____ a. the level indicated by proficiency test results.
   - ____ b. first year.
   - ____ c. second year.
   - ____ d. third year.
   - ____ e. Other _____.

6. Transfer students who have taken a FL in college should be placed on the basis of _____.
   - ____ a. proficiency test results.
   - ____ b. transfer of credit equivalency tables.

7. We find that students who undertake college FL study _____.
   ____ a. are generally well prepared to meet the program's expectations.
   ____ b. are well prepared but improperly placed.
   ____ c. are generally deficient in listening-speaking skills.
   ____ d. are generally deficient in reading-writing-grammar skills.
   ____ e. are generally deficient in vocabulary.
   ____ f. are sometimes viewed as deficient because high schools focus on proficiency more than colleges do.
8. Native speakers of a FL who have no credits in that language should be placed on the basis of _____.
   ____ a. self placement.
   ____ b. a four-skills placement test.
   ____ c. a receptive-skills placement test.
   ____ d. a receptive-skills plus test.
   ____ e. an interview.
9. A placement test _____.
   ____ a. should be used in every program.
   ____ b. should comprise four skills.
   ____ c. should comprise receptive skills.
   ____ d. should include receptive skills plus vocabulary and grammar.
   ____ e. should be required (to take).
   ____ f. should be optional (to take).
   ____ g. should determine placement.
   ____ h. should be advisory only.

II. Credit by Examination

10. For Credit by Examination colleges should offer _____.
    ____ a. CLEP.
    ____ b. CLEP plus oral and written.
    ____ c. their own four-skills tests.
    ____ d. their own two-skills test.
    ____ e. advanced placement.
    ____ f. Other _____.
    ____ g. nothing.
11. The following statement(s) is/are true for my/our FL program:
    ____ a. The FL program is four-skills-based, as is the examination for credit.
    ____ b. The FL program includes little speaking and writing, and neither does the examination for credit.
    ____ c. The FL program us four-skills-based, but the examination for credit is not.

High School, College, and University Articulation 127

III. Expectations
   12. The following statement(s) are true for many college FL programs:
      _____ a. The FL program is four-skills-based, as is the examination for credit.
      _____ b. The FL program includes little speaking and writing, and neither does the examination for credit.
      _____ c. The FL program us four-skills-based, but the examination for credit is not.
   13. We want students entering college with previous FL study in high school (as well as students progressing in our own program) to _____ at the appropriate level.
      _____ a. understand the language.
      _____ b. speak the language.
      _____ c. read in the language.
      _____ d. write in the language.
      _____ e. use extensive vocabulary.
      _____ f. use accurate grammar.
      _____ g. know grammar rules.
      _____ h. know the target culture.
   14. College FL departments want students with prior FL study in high school to _____ at the appropriate level.
      _____ a. understand the language.
      _____ b. speak the language.
      _____ c. read in the language.
      _____ d. write in the language.
      _____ e. use extensive vocabulary.
      _____ f. use accurate grammar.
      _____ g. know grammar rules.
      _____ h. know the target culture.
   15. Most of our faculty feel that high school–college FL program articulation is _____.
      _____ a. important.
      _____ b. irrelevant.
      _____ c. unimportant.
      _____ d. hopeless.
      _____ e. neglected and in need of attention.
      _____ f. Other _____.
   16. Most university FL faculty feel that high school–college program articulation is _____.
      _____ a. important.
      _____ b. irrelevant.
      _____ c. unimportant.
      _____ d. hopeless.
      _____ e. neglected and in need of attention.
      _____ f. Other _____.

IV. Understandings of the Texas High School FL Framework
   17. We understand the State secondary FL curriculum to _____.
       ____ a. emphasize grammar.
       ____ b. emphasize proficiency.
       ____ c. emphasize listening and speaking in the basic program.
       ____ d. emphasize reading and writing.
       ____ e. cover the basic language in two years.
       ____ f. cover the basic language in three years.
   18. We understand the college and university FL curriculum and requirements in the state to be _____.
       ____ a. mandated by a state entity.
       ____ b. varied from one system to another.
       ____ c. different at each campus.
       ____ d. controlled by FL faculty.
       ____ e. controlled by the general faculty at each institution.
       ____ f. controlled by both FL faculty and general faculty at each institution.

V. Personal Data
   Name _____ Title _____
   Date _____ Institution _____
   Address _____
   City, ZIP _____ Telephone _____

11
The Impact of Site-Based Management and School-Based Teacher Training on Foreign Language Education

Audrey L. Heining-Boynton
University of North Carolina at Chapel Hill

As foreign language educators, we tend to focus most of our energy on the improvement of instruction at our schools. Teachers work hard to deliver creative, interesting, proficiency-oriented classes. Some professionals become involved with foreign language organizations at the state and national levels to ensure quality programs for a broader audience. What is often missing, though, is an involvement of foreign language teachers with general education issues and policies. Many of these local, state, and national policies and trends directly affect foreign language instruction from kindergarten through the university. Foreign language educators not only need to be aware of the current trends in education, but they must also take an active leadership role in order to protect foreign language interests.

Presently, there are several strong waves of educational reform. These come in response to a deluge of negative reports since 1983 concerning the state of education in the United States.[1] *A Nation at Risk* (National Commission 1983) began the flood of reports criticizing seemingly every aspect of our schools. Since then, books like Bloom's (1987) *Closing of the American Mind* or headlines like "Johnny's Miserable SATs" (Cohen 1990) frequently remind us something is wrong with our schools.

Ideas on how to reform our schools abound. Recently, President George Bush (1991) outlined a reform plan "America 2000: The President's Education Strategy." Among his ideas for improving education, he states that national standards must be set in five core subjects: English, mathematics, science, history, and geography. The president also encourages states and communities to provide alternative routes of certification for additional teachers.

Two solutions to our education problems repeatedly mentioned in numerous publications are site-based management and school-based teacher training. These two concurrent movements have gathered momentum over the past five years, causing a direct and major impact on foreign language education in the United States. To disregard these issues would be as imprudent as ignoring a tornado in line for a direct hit on your home. The purpose of this article is first to define and briefly examine site-based management and school-based teacher training. Next, a description will follow of how one district created a school-based foreign language teacher-training program. Finally, the implications of site-based management and school-based teacher training on foreign language programs nationwide will be discussed.

Site-Based Management

Site-based (or school-based) management (SBM) restructures schools and their governance with a bottom-up approach (Prasch 1990). Many define site-based management in broad terms to afford schools the flexibility to regulate themselves within the parameters that individual states, districts, and schools allow. For example, schools may not be able to choose textbooks where there are statewide adoptions. Besides, other state regulatory controls such as minimum salary and curriculum mandates may limit decision making at the local level.

A recent survey published by the American Association of School Administrators (1990) reported that almost one-fourth of all school districts represented utilize SBM. Potential advantages of SBM are

1. Better programs for students
2. Full use of human resources
3. Higher quality decisions
4. Increased staff loyalty and commitment
5. Development of staff leadership skills
6. Clear organizational goals
7. Improved communication
8. Improved staff morale
9. Support for staff creativity and innovation
10. Greater public confidence
11. Enhanced fiscal accountability
12. Restructuring due to changing roles and responsibilities of teachers and administrators (see Prasch 1990)

Although SBM continues to gain in popularity, the concept has disadvantages. For example:

1. There is more work for teachers and administrators.
2. Less efficiency occurs when there are more people involved in the decision-making process.
3. Decisions are made by generalists rather than specialists.
4. Weak schools will not automatically improve.
5. A greater need for staff development occurs.
6. Confusion about new roles and responsibilities may result.

Site-Based Management and School-Based Teacher Training 131

7. In-district coordination is difficult.
8. Authority to act may not be paired with the necessary resources.
9. Once begun, it is difficult to disengage school-based management (Prasch 1990).

Additionally, blockades that impede site-based management implementation are

1. Staff and administrative resistance to change
2. Unstable school leadership
3. Budget increases
4. Existing federal, state, and local governance structures
5. Misinterpretation of control
6. An attitude of "quick-fix"
7. Inappropriately reduced staffing

What ramifications does site-based management have for foreign language education in the United States? In states such as Michigan, site-based management usually signifies input in the budgeting process for individual schools and districts. With foreign language teachers involved in the resource allocation, this may ensure that their departments are considered for staff increases or that their acquisitions budget is made comparable to that of other departments.

Other states or localities use a more all-encompassing definition of site-based management. In North Carolina, for example, Senate Bill 2 in 1989 permitted all school districts to submit plans to the State Department of Public Instruction in order to be approved for self-governance. The state attached merit pay monies to the bill, and every district is currently involved in the process. Foreign language programs, especially foreign language in the elementary school (FLES) programs, were unprepared for what transpired during the first year (1990–91) of implementation. For example, if the local SBM committee decided that there were not enough resources to go around, foreign language programs were often cut. Even though the K–6 North Carolina state law mandating that all children will study a foreign language still exists, FLES programs experienced particularly deep cuts. Not all administrators and site-based management teams understand or choose to understand what state rules and regulations supersede local decision-making power.

Many districts that elected to keep foreign language offerings now have a different school calendar for each school, thanks to SBM. This yields enormous consequences for the larger districts that could potentially have more than 50 different school calendars a year. Additionally—and this is even more complex—not all schools within a district offer foreign language instruction for the same amount of time. For example, one elementary school may decide to provide instruction three times a week for 30 minutes a class. Another elementary school in the same district may choose to offer FLES five times a week in 30-minute sessions. Districtwide articulation becomes extremely challenging. Also with site-based management, resources spent for foreign language instruction differ at each school within a district, meaning that some students may have books and materials while others may not.

During initial implementation, school administrators placed teachers untrained in interpersonal relations and decision making on committees to make important choices on the restructuring of their school. Some proved uninterested in the process, others lacked the necessary tact to deal with colleagues. This split teachers into distinct competing groups, vying for power and limited resources. Obviously, divisiveness works counterproductively, and all disciplines, including foreign languages, suffer.

School-Based Teacher Training

What happens when school systems are unable to fill teaching positions due to a lack of qualified, certified candidates? States and organizations look for alternative ways to certify individuals other than requiring them to go through traditional teacher-training programs at colleges and universities. For example, "Teach America" is a program created from a model described in an undergraduate Harvard thesis that called for top graduates from colleges and universities nationwide to receive training during the summer and begin teaching in the fall in inner-city or rural schools across the country.

Connecticut and New Jersey offer nontraditional teacher-training programs. Connecticut formulated its program to improve the quality of teachers in eight areas, with foreign language being one of them. New Jersey created its alternative certification route not only to improve the quality of teachers but also to address shortages at both the elementary and secondary levels. In both of these programs, the candidates, who already have bachelor's degrees in a content area such as a foreign language, receive 200 hours or more of pedagogy instruction, taught mostly by experienced teachers with some university teacher-training involvement (Zumwalt 1991).

School-based teacher training derives from the SBM movement. When schools acquire the right to restructure and govern themselves, the next step is to train the teachers they need. Site-based management opens the door for schools to formulate creative ways to satisfy staffing needs when universities cannot. The Los Angeles Unified School District (LAUSD) accounts for over one-half of the teacher shortages in the West, and one-fourth in the United States (Stoddart and Floden 1989). Faced with a severe need for teachers, the district created a certification route for already-hired teachers for elementary, secondary, and bilingual-education programs. The employed noncertified teachers receive nearly 300 hours of training delivered by experienced teachers and LAUSD staff (Zumwalt (1991).

Another alternative teacher training route is available in North Carolina. Beginning in 1990, a K–12 school district may become a teacher-training, certifying institution. This option evolved, in part, as a response to a severe foreign language teacher shortage created by the state mandate.[2] The Basic Education Plan of 1985 states that all elementary school children in North Carolina will study a foreign language, and that foreign language must be offered as an elective in the middle and high schools. Implementation of the foreign language mandate began in 1988, and the teacher demand quickly exceeded the supply. What follows is a step-by-step recounting of school-based foreign language teacher education in North Carolina.

Site-Based Management and School-Based Teacher Training 133

Circumstances Leading to School-Based Teacher Education

It is imperative to begin by saying that no school district willingly set out to become involved in the teacher-education business. Nevertheless, a set of circumstances necessitated that districts move in that direction.

North Carolina Senate Bill 1 of 1985 required implementation of foreign language in the elementary school programs for all children by 1993 (Heining-Boynton 1991). The state provided monies to assist elementary schools with the implementation of FLES programs, and most school districts commenced in the 1988–89 school year. Universities and colleges across the state received notification of the changes in the K–12 curriculum and of the implications for the teacher-education programs. They were required to have state-approved programs in place no later than July 1, 1989. What follows is a list of circumstances that led the state to approve a modified certification plan.

Lack of Approved Teacher Training Programs

As implementation began, the State Department of Public Instruction (SDPI), Division of Second Languages, projected the need for approximately 1500 new foreign language teachers at the elementary school level by 1993. At the time, less than 100 students per year graduated from North Carolina institutions of higher education (IHE) with foreign language teaching certificates. Also, these initially certified teachers received a secondary (9–12) permit. Their credentials did not include teaching at the elementary level.

The SDPI informed the colleges and universities that all curricular changes for offering a K–12 foreign language certification program had to be in place and approved by the SDPI by July 1, 1989. No IHE met the deadline. The SDPI then extended the deadline to July 1, 1990.

Lack of a Pool of Qualified Applicants

In the meantime, school districts began the implementation process of FLES, employing teachers without the K–12 credentials, granting the newly hired teachers provisional certificates. School districts recruited not only within the state, but also nationally and internationally. National recruitment was not successful, since few colleges and universities offered training and ultimately a certificate to teach FLES. International recruitment was too expensive and complex to satisfy the staffing needs of the state.

During the first years of implementation, personnel directors statewide found fewer than five individuals with clear credentials to teach a foreign language at the elementary level. Districts therefore hired teachers with a variety of backgrounds. Some had 9–12 and middle-grade (6–8) certificates with majors or minors in a foreign language. Other teachers held elementary certificates and possessed a knowledge of a foreign language. Yet another group of FLES teachers possessed liberal arts degrees in a foreign language, or college degrees in disciplines other than foreign language. These individuals demonstrated either a native or near-native ability in a language other than English. The teachers who already held certificates in areas other than FLES obtained provisional certificates. Clear certificates could be acquired by demonstrating the foreign language competencies dictated by the SDPI (North Carolina SDPI 1988). Those who had college degrees but were not certified teachers received lateral-entry certificates. In North Carolina, a lateral-entry certificate is issued to an individual with a college degree in a discipline other than education. With these certificates came the requirement that the teacher must affiliate with an IHE and successfully complete at least six semester hours per year toward certification. Becoming affiliated with an approved institution posed a problem.

Difficulties Faced by Lateral-Entry Teachers

In the 1989-90 school year, only one IHE in North Carolina had an approved K-12 foreign language education program. Even if IHE programs had not received total confirmation, though, lateral-entry teachers were eligible to take classes, workshops, or summer institutes offered by the colleges and universities that would count toward meeting the SDPI's foreign language teacher competencies and the six-hour-per-year requirement (North Carolina SDPI 1988; 1985). Yet the following circumstances occurred either in isolation or in combination: (1) universities had enrollment limits and were unable to admit more students; (2) IHEs offered the needed courses at hours during which working teachers could not attend; (3) campuses were located too far to commute; (4) universities were not interested in serving the lateral-entry individual. All the above circumstances inhibited the lateral-entry FLES teachers and their districts from complying with state regulations.

Difficulties Faced by IHEs

Most IHEs wanted to cooperate but were unable to deliver services adequately for the following reasons. First, districts usually hired their FLES teachers in August when state monies became available to them. By then, some universities had closed their once-a-year admissions.

Also, before affiliating with a university, the uncertified FLES teacher "shopped around," looking for the program that was the most efficient in time and cost. The lateral-entry teachers took their credentials to the area colleges and universities to be reviewed. They received from each IHE an individualized program of study based on the requirements of each institution. Reviewing the transcripts and supporting evidence of each potential candidate and then writing an individualized certification program required, on the average, fifty minutes per student. This placed an extra burden on the workload of the IHE certification officer.

Many institutions have long, complicated procedures for changing and approving curricula. Therefore, some institutions offered FLES teacher-training courses and seminars as independent studies while the programs moved through the formal confirmation process of the university. Most faculty usually taught the independent studies as an unpaid overload.

Finally, some education departments were unable to communicate with foreign language departments concerning the need for cooperation when scheduling language classes. Foreign language departments offered needed courses at hours when the lateral-entry candidate was teaching.

First Steps toward School-Based Teacher Education

After several years of attempting to follow traditional routes with IHEs, one region in North Carolina developed a consortium. School districts contracted directly with the universities to offer courses required by the provisionally certified teacher. In 1989, the state granted yet another option to school districts. The North Carolina School Improvement and Accountability Act, also known as Senate Bill 2, allowed schools to propose site-based management plans with wide-reaching parameters. Senate Bill 2 permits school districts to propose to the state a course of study leading to clear certification for lateral-entry teachers.

Development of a School-Based Teacher-Education Program

District Demographics

The Wake County School System (Raleigh, NC) was the first district in the state to write an alternative teacher-education plan for foreign languages. The district, second-largest in the state, comprises 40 nonmagnet and 2 magnet elementary schools serving over 25,000 children. During the 1991–92 school year, the district employed 27 FLES teachers, only 14 of whom had clear certification. Inservice education furnished by the district made the clear certificates possible for the fourteen (Heining-Boynton 1990).

The academic background of those with lateral-entry certificates is diverse. For example, one FLES teacher with a strong background in Spanish has a bachelor's degree in science. Another teacher who is a native speaker of the language has a degree in food and nutrition.

Foreign language is not the only discipline requiring lateral-entry teachers in Wake County Schools. The district employs a full-time certification specialist who works closely with the approximately 30 provisionally certified teachers. Due to the difficulties met by the lateral-entry teachers, the district took the first steps to create an alternative teacher-training model.

Preparing for the Project

In the fall of 1989 Wake County Schools and the SDPI called a meeting, inviting representatives from the five teacher-training institutions serving the area. Members of the school district and the state department presented to the university representatives the challenges facing the district and its provisionally certified teachers. Wake County Schools requested that the universities make available educational psychology, child psychology, and/or foundations of education in the late afternoon or evening. In spring of 1990, one university offered specifically for Wake County teachers an educational psychology course. The district paid the difference between the students' tuition and the university's cost to offer the course.

A solution was underway, yet the district desired a more thorough, articulated, expeditious answer to the problem. The SDPI suggested that the district write a grant proposal to the U.S. state department. The funds would provide support for the development of an alternative professional-studies-program delivery system that would be designed to meet the needs of lateral-entry teachers employed by Wake County Schools.

136   Creative Approaches in Foreign Language Teaching

The SDPI funded the grant. The district invited three foreign language teacher trainers, two district foreign language teachers, and three members of the district's central office to form a design team. The group met for five days, led by the staff development coordinator for the Wake County Schools. She charged the team with the goal of creating an alternative approach to foreign language teacher education that could lead to participant certification within two years. Besides writing a curriculum, she asked for recommendations on the delivery of the program.

Preliminary Steps to the Curriculum Writing
Before beginning to write, the design team leader presented a list of seven assumptions under which the district was operating:

1. The focus of the school-based teacher-education program would be on K–12 professional knowledge and skills, not on knowledge and skills in the foreign language.
2. The program should be well-conceptualized, relevant, concentrated, and accessible.
3. The curriculum might be designed in three components: planning to teach, a summer institute for methodology, and foundations.
4. The teachers should complete the program in two years or less.
5. The major goal would be to ensure that teachers are capable of providing highly successful instruction to students.
6. The teachers may need additional work in the foreign language.
7. The teachers may be able to enroll in this professional studies program while simultaneously working on the sixteen North Carolina foreign language teacher competencies. This would be determined at the point of admission to the program.

After becoming familiar with the assumptions, the committee examined other alternative certification programs. For example, one was a twelve-month experience for mathematics and science lateral-entry teachers developed and delivered at East Carolina University.

Another preliminary step was to make a list of issues that concerned members of the design team. The seven issues expressed were

1. Who and how will assessment of an individual's competencies and needs be conducted prior to "admission" into the professional studies program?
2. Will others who are not lateral-entry second language teachers be able to participate in the program, that is, can lateral-entry teachers in fields other than foreign language participate?
3. Can people participate who are not lateral-entry, but who want to add foreign language to their already existing certificates?
4. Will lateral-entry teachers in other systems be able to enroll?
5. Who will recommend the lateral-entry teacher for certification?
6. What will be the costs and how will resources be obtained to sustain the program?
7. Will IHEs continue to support and be involved?

The next step required a decision on the components of the program. The group chose three: methodology, psychology (including educational psychology and child/adolescent psychology), and foundations of education. These three components encompassed all the necessary competencies and guidelines dictated by North Carolina for accrediting certification programs at colleges and universities (North Carolina SDPI 1988; 1985).

The Curriculum Writing

The design team planned the curriculum based on the North Carolina foreign language teacher competencies as well as the professional competencies and the guidelines required of all education programs (North Carolina SDPI 1988; 1985). The team set about listing under each of the three components (methodology, psychology, and foundations) where each competency would be addressed. Once the group was satisfied that the three components encompassed all the competencies and guidelines, the committee began the writing process. The format used was to (1) list the component, (2) state the competency or guideline, (3) state the major topics to be covered, (4) name the major outcomes, and (5) set forth any significant activities or clinical experiences.

The end result of the weeklong retreat was a curriculum detailing how the three components would meet all the state professional competencies and guidelines. Also included was a program description that restated and elaborated on the original assumptions, addressed some of the original issues, and described special features of the program.

Program Delivery

The planning committee discussed program delivery. The Wake County Schools' participants stated that the best time to begin the program would be in November, once the school year had begun and all teachers had been hired. Also decided was that evenings, weekends, and the summer would be the most convenient times for the teachers to take courses and seminars. The planning committee agreed that the experience should begin with the psychology and methodology components, and that they should be offered simultaneously. The first topics from those two components would be ones the lateral-entry teacher would benefit from immediately, such as developmental stages of children and foreign language teaching methods that incorporate the cognitive, physical, and emotional characteristics of the child.

The committee concurred that Wake County Schools should allow only their employees to participate. The committee members from the school district stated they were interested only in meeting the needs of their employees, and not in becoming a teacher-certification institution.

The modified certification plan was approved by the state, and upon successful completion, the lateral-entry teacher receives a North Carolina K–12 foreign language teaching certificate issued by Wake County Schools. Since the Wake County Schools' proposal, the state received ten others. As mentioned earlier, school-based teacher training is tied closely to site-based management. Because of North Carolina Senate Bill 2, another 1500 requests for waivers from a wide variety of state requirements (e.g., class size, teachers' aides, and offering

FLES) have been received. As of fall 1991, the Second Language Division of the SDPI has no data regarding how many school districts have requested foreign language school-based teacher-training status, nor do they know how many schools have requested a waiver to drop foreign language from the curriculum.[3]

National Foreign Language Implications for Site-Based Management and Alternative Teacher Certification Routes

Some foreign language educators will read this report and maintain that site-based management and school-based teacher education will never occur in their district or state. Others will continue to concern themselves only with the foreign language world that exists behind their classroom door. Still others who are in the general field of education, possessing little vision or commitment to excellence in education, will point to this paper saying that all the time and energy spent on site-based management and school-based foreign language teacher training would have been better spent on the 3 Rs.

Site-based management and school-based teacher training promise numerous challenges in the decade to come. They can deliver needed services to make schools run more smoothly and provide an excellent education for all students from kindergarten through the university. They also can, through lack of care, concern, or participation on our part, have a damaging effect on foreign language programs. It is up to us to participate in all steps of these movements to ensure high-quality foreign language programs at all educational levels.

Conclusion

This paper defined and described site-based management and school-based teacher-training programs. It traced thoroughly the evolution of one alternative approach to foreign language teacher education. The district was able to create a modified certification plan due to a site-based management law under which the state currently operates. School-based teacher-training models develop when the staffing needs of school districts are not met by the teacher-training institutions.

The goal of the Wake County school-based teacher-training project was to develop and deliver a high-quality, accessible, and efficient teacher-education model to meet the needs of the lateral-entry teachers of the district. A collaboration of university, school system, and state department personnel created the model curriculum that would focus on the professional knowledge base of the provisionally certified teachers.

It will be several years before a complete evaluation can be made of the effectiveness of the Wake County Schools' alternative teacher-training model. Due to the care taken during the planning process, the curriculum design team hypothesizes that the outcomes will be comparable to the positive results of similar studies (e.g., Boser et al. 1986; Brown et al. 1989).

Notes

1. Although reports critical of our educational system surfaced before 1983, the outpouring of writings began with *A Nation at Risk* (National Commission 1983).
2. Other content areas such as art, healthful living, drama, science, and math are experiencing shortages and are utilizing alternative certification routes.

3. Each request for a waiver is handled in the State Superintendent's office. The information regarding those requests has not been disseminated to the division level.

References

American Association of School Administrators. 1990. *Leadership News* 61: 3.

Bloom, A. 1987. *Closing of the American Mind.* New York: Simon and Schuster.

Boser, J., et al. 1986. "A Comparison of Participants in Traditional and Alternative Teacher Preparation Programs." Paper presented at the meeting of the Mid-South Educational Research Association, Memphis, TN, November.

Brown, D., et al. 1989. "A Comparison of Alternative Certification, Traditionally Trained, and Emergency Permit Teachers." *Teacher Education and Practice* 5,2: 21–23.

Bush, George. 1991. "America 2000: The President's Education Strategy." Washington, DC: Office of the Press Secretary.

Cohen, R. 1990. "Johnny's Miserable SATs." *Washington Post*, September 4.

Heining-Boynton, Audrey L. 1990. "Staff Development for the FLES Teacher: Networking to Make It Happen," pp. 63–73 in Gerard Ervin, ed., *Realizing the Potential of Foreign Language Instruction.* Proceedings of the Central States Conference on the Teaching of Foreign Languages. Lincolnwood, IL: National Textbook Company.

―――. 1991. "Implementation of State Mandated FLES in North Carolina: An Update." *Hispania* 73,3: 430–32.

National Commission on Excellence in Education. 1983. *A Nation at Risk: The Imperative for Educational Reform.* Washington, DC: U.S. Government Printing Office.

North Carolina Department of Public Instruction. 1985. *North Carolina Professional Competencies and Guidelines.* Raleigh, NC: North Carolina SDPI.

―――. 1988. *North Carolina Teacher Competencies: Second Languages.* Raleigh, NC: North Carolina SDPI.

Prasch, John. 1990. *How to Organize for School-Based Management.* Alexandria, VA: Association for Supervision and Curriculum Development.

Stoddart, T., and R. E. Floden. 1989. "School District–Based Teacher Training: An Alternate Route to Teacher Certification." Paper presented at the meeting of the American Educational Research Association, San Francisco, April.

Zumwalt, K. 1991. "Alternate Routes to Teaching: Three Alternative Approaches." *Journal of Teacher Education* 42,2: 83–92.

12
The Cooperative Curriculum Development Project*

Dave McAlpine
The University of Arkansas at Little Rock
Gayle Yeska
The Sioux City (Iowa) Community Schools

The Cooperative Curriculum Development Project was a multiyear plan designed to bring together foreign language educators from a geographic area and to facilitate their collaboration in the process of curriculum development. The shared curriculum work sought to produce the best possible curriculum documents, to develop leadership in the educators involved, and to encourage ongoing professional development through the networking of foreign language teachers growing out of their shared work. The project supported and supplemented local curriculum work. Local curriculum committees would need to adapt and customize the products developed to fit local needs and philosophies.

In 1988, the Iowa legislature passed the Standards for Accredited Schools, which were concerned with curriculum review and development. As a result, each school district in the state was mandated to establish and implement a process for conducting an ongoing needs assessment to develop a statement of philosophy and a five-year plan for the achievement of educational goals. Furthermore, the law required each curriculum area to have goals, suggested activities, materials, content, and expected outcomes for each level of instruction. Assessment procedures and the monitoring of student progress were also required. A way to share the energy and the expertise of foreign language educators from many districts was developed in order to give direction to local districts as they developed a core curriculum that would meet the new state standards, that would reflect current professional thinking, and that would lead to successful learning experiences for all students.

How was this curriculum project developed to assist 26 school districts? First, local school superintendents authorized the formation of the project. In all cases this meant funding commitments on the part of each district. For year one, the cost

The Cooperative Curriculum Development Project 141

to each district was $650 plus 15¢ per student and in the second year these costs were changed to $200 plus 55¢ per student to participate in the project, a relatively inexpensive way for districts to have curriculum written. The superintendents appointed a curriculum development committee (CDC) to develop and manage the project. The committee established the schedule for completion of the curriculum guide, identified the school districts interested in participating, developed the plan to supply clerical and administrative support, and established a budget to fund the project. This group also identified and secured the services of a team leader and selected a three-member foreign language steering committee, which planned and directed the curriculum project on a daily basis. The remaining members of the foreign language curriculum team were selected by the participating school districts. The members of the foreign language curriculum team met for two-week periods for two consecutive summers and then returned to their respective districts to share ideas and implement the new curriculum.

The curriculum review cycle developed by the CDC consisted of seven steps, each step designed to be completed in a one-year period. The Cooperative Curriculum Development Project was instituted to help districts accomplish steps 1 and 2, with the remaining five steps to be finished at the district level. The seven-step format is reproduced below.

Step 1
Study Trends, Research, Assess Local Needs

A. Write/revise a philosophy or statement of purpose designed to guide all development/revision work. This should relate to the general district philosophy or mission statement.
B. Study the research and survey parents, business and industry persons, students, and staff for curriculum strengths, needs, problems, and concerns.
C. Examine and map the current curriculum as well as the instructional materials for
   1. Relevancy
   2. Sequence and articulation
   3. Scope and balance
   4. Appropriate level of difficulty
   5. At-risk students
   6. Technology
   7. Communication
   8. Learning skills
   9. Talented and gifted students
   10. Career education
   11. Global education
   12. Special education
   13. Human growth and development
   14. Multicultural nonsexist qualities
   15. Higher-order thinking skills
   16. Appropriate instructional approach

D. Identify priority needs, gaps, and problems. Will the staff, administration, school board, or parents need orientation/inservice to explain the committee's rationale for recommending any major changes?
E. Establish priorities for the second year of the cycle.
F. Report results of the above year's work to the board of education.

Step 2
Develop Philosophy, Student Outcomes, Scope and Sequence

A. Review present program of courses and consider revisions, additions, or deletions in light of needs in step 1.
B. Revise program of course goals.
C. Revise student learning outcomes for each goal.
D. Develop the program guide in light of Cooperative Curriculum program guide and local needs.
E. Examine, discuss, and select alternative instructional materials and methods under review.
F. Visit other schools or programs using the materials and methods under review.
G. Plan meetings with appropriate staff to explain and provide staff development about any proposed new approaches.
H. Establish priorities for the third year of the cycle.
I. Report results of the above year's work to the local board of education.

Step 3
Design, Pilot, Adapt, Adopt

A. Institute one or more pilot programs of instructional materials if and where appropriate.
B. Evaluate alternatives.
C. Consider and recommend inservice and staff-development activities for staff if needed.
D. Prepare appropriate recommendations to district curriculum council about the proposed curriculum.
E. Revise or develop local curriculum guides for all levels and courses by adapting and applying Cooperative Curriculum guide to fit local needs.
F. Carry out textbook-adoption study to fit local curriculum needs.
G. Establish priorities for the fourth year of the cycle.
H. Report results of the above year's work to the board of education.

Step 4
Adapt and Implement Curriculum in Local Districts

A. Plan and conduct inservice and staff-development activities.
B. Implement the program as approved.
C. Monitor and recommend adjustments as needed.
D. Establish priorities for the fifth year of the cycle.
E. Report results of the above year's work to the local board of education.

Step 5
Monitor and Evaluate Adapted Curriculum in Local Districts

A. Monitor the overall implementation process.
B. Assist with the conducting of continuing inservice and staff-development activities.
C. Continue to assess the effectiveness of new materials and methods.
D. Establish priorities for the sixth year of the cycle.
E. Report results of the above year's work to the local board of education.

Steps 6-7
Monitor and Evaluate Adapted Curriculum in Local Districts

A. Monitor the overall implementation process.
B. Assist with the conducting of continuing inservice and staff-development activities.
C. Modify goals and outcomes if appropriate.
D. Continue to assess the effectiveness of new materials and methods.
E. Establish priorities for the first year of the cycle.
F. Report results of the above year's work to the local board of education.

Responsibilities for First Session

To accomplish step 1 of the curriculum review cycle, foreign language team members were assigned seven responsibilities or tasks.

Responsibility One
Leadership/Communication Skills

Tips on leadership skills for foreign language teachers were presented because teachers are often called upon to communicate with people outside their immediate departments, such as administrators, curriculum councils and committees, school board members, parents, and students. Various reasons for the study of foreign language were discussed and listed as global education outcomes, practical outcomes, and self-improvement outcomes. Teachers brainstormed anticipated questions and possible answers that might be asked of foreign language teachers in their role as curriculum leaders.

Responsibility Two
Research and Communication

Realizing that all areas of foreign language education could not be researched in a period of two weeks, the team formulated research questions in the following areas: the increasing societal need for foreign language study, trends and recommended practices in methodology, teaching all students, student achievement, articulation, and staff development. The team divided into small groups to conduct the research in a limited time and returned to the full team to share their findings. All articles were abstracted and provided to each team member.

Responsibility Three
Standards

The team reviewed the legal references and state standards for foreign languages. Copies of the Iowa Code pertaining to curriculum review and development and to the specific laws concerning foreign language instruction were discussed.

Responsibility Four
Horizontal Articulation

The team explained fourteen areas of horizontal articulation (career education, communication, global education, higher-order thinking skills, learning skills, multicultural nonsexist education, technology, special education, talented and gifted, students at risk, guidance, information/media, activity program, and human growth and development), as well as the integration of special skills, students, and special considerations. The team defined the application of each horizontal articulation area for foreign languages. Resource material for each of the fourteen horizontal articulation areas was suggested and the team formulated staff-development ideas for them.

Responsibility Five
Needs Assessment

A needs assessment was undertaken by each district represented in the Cooperative Curriculum project in order to analyze past, present, and future practices in foreign language instruction. The process helped districts define the strengths and weaknesses of the foreign language program. Team members conducted a teacher self-study, a survey of student perceptions of the foreign language courses, and a study of the staff-development opportunities and the foreign language budget. Community opinion was also solicited and recommendations of the profession were investigated via articles in professional journals, reports of national professional organizations, and department of education reports.

Responsibility Six
Program Philosophy

Team members studied other philosophy statements from districts across the country and a statement of philosophy was developed cooperatively by the team.

Responsibility Seven
Program Goals

The final responsibility for year one was the writing of foreign language program goals that would reflect the philosophy statement developed in responsibility 6. Goals were divided into three major areas: language acquisition and learning goals, cultural awareness goals, and social and personal goals. At the end of the first summer session, all materials generated by the team were compiled into a notebook and given to each team member for use during the academic year to provide inservice to other foreign language teachers, administrators, or board of education members in their home districts.

Responsibilities for Second Session

Team members gathered again the following summer for another two-week session and carried out nine more assigned responsibilities.

Responsibility One
Program Strands

Team members determined the program strands, the large subdivisions of the subject that continue over several years, to make the writing of curriculum more manageable. The curriculum team decided upon five strands: listening, speaking, reading, writing, and culture. The strands were then related to the program goals developed in year one.

Responsibility Two
Student Outcomes

Team members developed objectives stated in terms of student outcomes. These objectives were derived from the program goals and strands developed in responsibility 1. Team members created the following objectives: (1) the student will respond to basic commands, (2) the student will identify items, (3) the student will express likes and dislikes, wants and needs, (4) the student will react to social situations, (5) the student will describe, (6) the student will ask and answer questions, (7) the student will initiate, sustain, and end a conversation, (8) the student will narrate, (9) the student will support opinion in simple situations, (10) the student will hypothesize in simple situations. Objectives 1 through 6 served as the foundation for the level 1 curriculum; objectives 1, 2, 5, 6, 7 for level 2. Level 3 objectives were 6, 7, and 8; level 4 objectives were 6, 7, 8, 9, and 10.

Responsibility Three
Horizontal Articulation

Project team members related the horizontal infusion area goals and considerations studied in year one to the appropriate student outcome objectives written in responsibility 2 of the current year. The purpose of this activity was to show more concretely how the horizontal areas connect with the foreign language curriculum. Teachers came to realize that there was considerable overlap of the infusion area goals. One program objective thus connected with several different infusion areas that have similar goals.

Responsibility Four
Sequencing

Team members assigned the strands and the objectives to a sequence appropriate to foreign languages. A suitable format was developed to depict the sequence of the curriculum. Team members had access to computers, printers, word processing and spreadsheet software, and secretarial support in order to accomplish the curriculum writing in a short time. Costs for this support came from the districts' contributions to the project.

Responsibility Five
Assessment

Ideas on how to monitor student progress and how to assess student achievement were discussed. The curriculum specialist for the project discussed the oral proficiency movement and demonstrated the process of conducting an oral proficiency examination. Of all the responsibilities covered in the four-week period, this assessment responsibility was the least well developed. The authors suggested that carrying out this responsibility be continued in another two-week session during a third summer.

Responsibility Six
Instructional Strategies

Once again small groups were used to provide suggested instructional strategies, approaches, and sample activities that embodied the outcomes, infusion goals, and assessment methods. Participants left the workshop with sample leveled activities for listening, speaking, reading, writing, and culture (see Appendix 12B for a sample).

Responsibility Seven
Written Products Format

There was much discussion among participants on the format to be used to display the curriculum guide. Part of this responsibility was to prepare a sample format that all participants agreed to and could use in their home districts. The final product was typed and copied by the clerical staff hired for the project. A sample from the level 1 product is found in Appendix 12A.

Responsibility Eight
Leveled Program Guides

The leveled program guides pulled together the work of the foreign language curriculum team in a program guide to be used by curriculum committees of local districts. In the local district the guide was customized to fit local decisions about goals, materials, and format of working local curriculum guides. This responsibility brought everything previously described together into one document. Each team member received a copy of the completed guide by the beginning of the fall semester.

Responsibility Nine
Recommended District Staff Development

The final responsibility was to develop a plan for the necessary staff development, which would create an awareness within the district of the recommended curriculum and also create an understanding and commitment to the curriculum as the district customized it. A sample letter to administrators was provided in the guide that explained current recommendations for foreign language instruction. The team chose to address the area of elementary school foreign language instruction. The team chose to address the area of elementary school foreign language instruction and included information on key definitions (immersion, FLEX, FLES), a rationale for elementary foreign language study, considerations when planning an elementary program, recommendations, and resource information.

Conclusion

Important side effects occurred as a result of the Cooperative Curriculum Development Project (CCDP). A strong camaraderie developed among the participants. Language-specific "get-togethers" were held during the project and even during the two academic years. Ten participants enrolled in graduate courses in foreign language methods, curriculum design, and textbook selection as an additional incentive to participate in the project. A core of workers, brought together by the curriculum project, formed the local committees to host the successful state foreign language teachers' conference. An Academic Alliance was established to continue the networking begun as a result of the CCDP. Some were so inspired by the project that they have shared the concept at national, regional, and state foreign language teachers' meetings.

In essence the Cooperative Curriculum Development Project benefited all who were involved and improved the foreign language instruction of the students in the classrooms—which, after all, was the ultimate goal.

Note

* The authors wish to acknowledge the Western Hills Area Education Agency, Sioux City, IA 51106, and Ms. Nancy Lawrence, Educational Services Consultant, for their leadership in this project. Copies of the complete guide may be obtained from the Western Hills AEA. Further information on replicating the project can be obtained from the authors, Dr. Dave McAlpine, Foreign Languages Department, The University of Arkansas at Little Rock, 2801 S. University Ave., Little Rock, AR 72204, and Ms. Gayle Yeska, Foreign Languages Consultant, The Sioux City Community Schools, 1221 Pierce St., Sioux City, IA 51105.

Appendix 12A
Sample Guide Format

Contexts	A. The student will respond to basic commands . . .					B. The student will identify items . . .					A. B.
	Listen	Speak	Read	Write	Culture	Listen	Speak	Read	Write	Culture	Text Key
Abbreviations								✓	✓		
Animals						✓	✓	✓	✓		
Art											
Body parts	✓					✓	✓	✓	✓		
Classroom	✓					✓	✓	✓	✓		
Clothes						✓	✓	✓	✓		
Colors						✓	✓	✓	✓		
Contemporary culture						✓	✓			✓	
Courtesies						✓	✓			✓	
Current events											
Daily routines/respons.											
Directions	✓										
Environment/nature											
Expressions of time						✓	✓	✓	✓	✓	
Family members						✓	✓	✓	✓		
Food						✓	✓	✓	✓		
Forms of communication											
Geography											
History											
House						✓	✓	✓	✓		
Introductions											
Leisure activities						✓	✓	✓	✓		
Literature											
Mass media											
Moods/feelings						✓	✓	✓	✓		
Nationalities/languages											
Numbers						✓	✓	✓	✓		
Personal experiences											
Personal information						✓	✓	✓	✓		
Physical characteristics						✓	✓	✓	✓		
Places						✓	✓	✓	✓	✓	
Professions/occupations											
Quantity						✓	✓	✓	✓		
School subjects						✓	✓	✓	✓	✓	
Services											
Shopping											
Social events											
Transportation						✓	✓	✓	✓	✓	
Travel											
Weather						✓	✓	✓	✓		

✓ indicates mastery

Level 1—Contexts, Objectives, Strands

Contexts	C. The student will express likes/dislikes, wants/needs...					D. The student will react to social situations...					C. D.
	Listen	Speak	Read	Write	Culture	Listen	Speak	Read	Write	Culture	Text Key
Abbreviations											
Animals	✓	✓									
Art											
Body parts											
Classroom						✓	✓				
Clothes	✓	✓									
Colors	✓	✓									
Contemporary culture											
Courtesies						✓	✓				
Current events											
Daily routines/respons.											
Directions											
Environment/nature											
Expressions of time											
Family members	✓	✓									
Food	✓	✓	✓	✓							
Forms of communication											
Geography											
History											
House											
Introductions											
Leisure activities	✓	✓	✓	✓							
Literature											
Mass media											
Moods/feelings											
Nationalities/languages											
Numbers											
Personal experiences											
Personal information						✓	✓				
Physical characteristics	✓	✓									
Places											
Professions/occupations											
Quantity											
School subjects	✓	✓	✓	✓							
Services											
Shopping											
Social events											
Transportation	✓	✓									
Travel											
Weather											

✓ indicates mastery

Level 1—Contexts, Objectives, Strands

Contexts	E. The student will describe . . .					F. The student will ask and answer questions . . .					E. F.
	Listen	Speak	Read	Write	Culture	Listen	Speak	Read	Write	Culture	Text Key
Abbreviations											
Animals						✓	✓				
Art											
Body parts						✓	✓				
Classroom											
Clothes		✓		✓	✓	✓	✓				
Colors						✓	✓				
Contemporary culture					✓						
Courtesies						✓	✓			✓	
Current events											
Daily routines/respons.											
Directions											
Environment/nature											
Expressions of time						✓	✓				
Family members		✓		✓	✓	✓	✓				
Food		✓		✓		✓	✓				
Forms of communication											
Geography											
History											
House		✓		✓	✓	✓	✓				
Introductions											
Leisure activities					✓	✓	✓				
Literature											
Mass media											
Moods/feelings		✓				✓	✓				
Nationalities/languages											
Numbers						✓	✓				
Personal experiences											
Personal information		✓		✓		✓	✓				
Physical characteristics		✓		✓		✓	✓				
Places						✓	✓				
Professions/occupations											
Quantity						✓	✓				
School subjects		✓		✓	✓	✓	✓				
Services											
Shopping											
Social events											
Transportation						✓	✓				
Travel											
Weather		✓				✓	✓				

✓ indicates mastery

The Cooperative Curriculum Development Project

Level 1—Grammar

	Level 1	Level 2	Level 3	Level 4	Text Key
Adverbs of quality and quantity	✓				
Conjunctions	✓				
Subject pronouns	✓				
Immediate future	✓				
Indefinite articles	✓				
Infinitives	✓				
Contractions	✓				
Definite articles	✓				
Formal/informal	✓				
Demonstrative adjectives					
Interrogatives					
Intonation					
Ordinal numbers					
Possession with "of"					
Present tense					
Word order					
Superlatives					
Demonstrative pronouns					
Nominalizations					
Possessive adjectives					
Comparison					
Adverbs					
Past tense					
Pronunciation					
Punctuation					
Reflexives					
Gender					
Negation					
Noun/adjective agreement					
Number					
Future tense					
Imperatives					
Reciprocals					
Possessive pronouns					
Capitalization					
Passive voice					
Prepositions					
Present subjunctive					
Past subjunctive					
Relative pronouns					
Object pronouns					
Perfect tenses					
Conditional tense					

✓ indicates mastery

Creative Approaches in Foreign Language Teaching

Level 1—Culture					
	Level 1	Level 2	Level 3	Level 4	Text Key
Appropriate dress					
Art					
Bartering					
Calendar					
Celebrities					
Climate					
Currency					
Dates					
Dialects					
Dining					
Education for occupations					
Extended family					
Family responsibilities					
Folk dress					
Gender roles					
Geography					
Gestures					
History					
Hobbies					
Holidays					
Housing/architecture					
Hygiene/health					
Insults					
Interjections					
Literature					
Maps					
Marital/civil status					
Metrics					
Movies					
Music					
Names/titles					
Pets/animals					
Phone numbers					
Polite register					
Politicians					
Privileges of age					
Regulations and procedures					
Religion					
Report cards					
Schedules					
School/facilities					
School structure					
Shopping					
Sizes					
Social etiquette					
Socializing					

The Cooperative Curriculum Development Project

Level 1—Culture, continued					
	Level 1	Level 2	Level 3	Level 4	Text Key
Specialized stores					
Status of occupations					
Superstitions					
Televisions					
Terms of endearment					
Transportation					
Twenty-four hour clock					
Un/lucky numbers					
Work/rest schedules					

Team members stopped short of indicating when mastery of the culture topics would occur. The cultural topics were decided upon collectively, allowing each district to decide when mastery would occur, thus no ✓ appears here.

154   Creative Approaches in Foreign Language Teaching

Appendix 12B
Culture Activity: Insulting the Teacher!

Program Objective: The students will react to social situations.

Contexts: Courtesies; forms of communication

Materials: Dialog found here is either in print for students to read or read aloud by the teacher. If native speakers are available to read the parts, so much the better. Sheet with four possible answers.

Procedures:
1. Teacher and students discuss the cultural implications of addressing someone with **familiar** or **formal.**
2. Students are given the dialog to read or hear the dialog read to them (twice only).
3. After the reading, students are given the four-question cultural check given below.

Assessment:

María: Sra. López, ¿Tienes tú otro libro?
Profesora López: Por favor, María, no me . . .
María: Pero señora, necesito un lápiz y probablemente tú me das otro.
Profesora López: María, soy la profesora y tienes que . . .
María: ¿Sabes que José es . . .
Profesora: María, ¡Basta! ¡No lo aguanto más!
María: Pero, Sra. López, no te entiendo.

Why are Sra. López and María failing to get along?
A. Sra. López hates students and treats every child like she treats María.
B. María is an especially obnoxious child.
C. María addresses Sra. López incorrectly.
D. Sra. López is angry because she is "Señorita López."

Alternatives: Tell students to whom they are speaking and ask them to indicate whether they would use formal or familiar.

You are talking to:
1. your brother   tú   Ud.
2. your teacher   tú   Ud.
3. President Bush   tú   Ud.

4. your grandmother	tú	Ud.
5. the school principal	tú	Ud.
6. a classmate	tú	Ud.

Level: Levels One, Two, Three, Four

Horizontal Articulation: SPED, TAG, COMM, GLO, MCNS, RISK, HGD, HOTS

13
Evaluating Communicative Risk and Achievements for Students Abroad

Philippa B. Yin
Cleveland State University

The purpose of this paper is to present practical ideas and techniques for teachers whose aim is to build student confidence in their speaking ability during a study-abroad period. The discussion will examine realistic goal setting, associated risks for students at various levels of speaking ability, and practical achievement assessment for the teacher involved in study-abroad programs. Several preparatory and on-site activities will be discussed.

Background

Many articles have been written on the teaching of foreign languages in the context of a proficiency orientation. Elements of the proficiency orientation and of the proficiency interview process have gradually been incorporated into our summer study program. This paper brings together several of these elements in a systematic way. To better understand the ideas associated with this approach, we may look at Alice Omaggio Hadley's discussion of proficiency in her work *Teaching Language in Context* (1986). Here she distinguishes the term *proficiency* from *competence* and *performance* (p. 2). *Competence* concerns primarily knowledge of the language's system, including grammar, vocabulary, and so forth. *Performance* refers to the actual production and comprehension of specific linguistic events. *Proficiency*, then, includes elements of both competence and performance; as Hadley says, it "refers to a somewhat idealized level of competence and performance attainable by experts through extensive instruction" (p. 2).

The notion of levels is implicit in the concept of proficiency, as Higgs and Clifford (1981) noted: "A student cannot merely be declared competent in communication. The functions that s/he is competent to express must be specified" (pp. 60–61). The ACTFL Oral Proficiency project (1986) and the Educational Testing Service Project (1982) further developed the scales by which we now commonly refer to oral proficiency. Of particular interest here is what is known as the *functional trisection* (ETS, p. 22) of oral proficiency levels, which specifies what typical speakers of teacher language can express in terms of linguistic function, speech context, and levels of accuracy. It is not the purpose of this discussion to espouse the oral proficiency testing method exclusively, but the materials have much to offer in the way of food for thought for the language teacher and for the enterprising student. For the purposes of this discussion the simpler terms of beginning, intermediate, and advanced student will be used to refer to general linguistic competence. Those teachers who have worked with the oral proficiency scales may, of course, prefer to use its more precise terms for level of competence.

Confidence is also an important key to the second language learner's progress and is related both to the student's acquisition of the foreign language and to his or her performance in it. "The willingness to take risks," says Patricia Westphal (1976), "is no doubt a function of the student's self-confidence." She explains further, "The student has to have some expectation that all the effort to produce or understand a message is going to pay off" (p. 41). While few high school or college students of a foreign language will become proficient at the highest level, that of "educated native speaker," regardless of the amount of time spent in the environment and the competence of our linguistic structures, most students can be made to feel confident of their ability to function and progress at various stages of their learning. This discussion proposes that the student and the teacher together can determine which strategies are most likely to enable the student to achieve a higher level of speaking proficiency.

Evaluating Students and Setting Goals

It almost goes without saying that setting goals must be related, in good pedagogy, to prior evaluation of the student's performance. Nevertheless, it is often assumed that a foreign study experience will work the analogous equivalent of the old army saying, "It'll make a man of him." That is, that the student will return showing enthusiasm and speaking like a native speaker. Yet we know this is not true, and for some excellent and some unfortunate reasons. The good reasons have to do with the fact that there are too many factors involved to assume that all of them can be altered by any single experience or controlled by the student within the process. In the other instance, it is unfortunate that too often both the student and the teacher have a very incomplete sense of where the student is at the beginning in terms of proficiency and where the student wants to be at the end of the foreign study experience.

For effective assessment, the student's social behavior, the student's language competence, and the student's general communication patterns should be evaluated. Both the student's and the teacher's input to the process are valuable. The student should learn and practice self-assessment, a metacognitive strategy, i.e., one in which students exercise some control over their learning (Nyikos 1991, p. 32); and only the teacher knows where the student is in terms of command of the basic subject matter taught through the curriculum. Additionally, the teacher often has a good sense of the student's social personality. A relatively simple interview process can elicit this information. This interview should include questions on the student's social stance, such as "How outgoing do you think you are in general?" and "How much do you like mixing in new or strange situations?" It also includes an assessment of the target language grammar and fluency, with questions such as "Do you feel you have a good sense of the past and future tenses?" and, conversely, "Do you feel a need to review frequently what you consider to be basic grammar?" The oral proficiency interview will, of course, yield precise data and may be used. In this case, the teacher will need to interpret the results for the student. The communicative skill orientation of the student can be gauged on the basis of questions such as "Do you feel comfortable contributing to general conversation in your foreign language?" and "Do you listen to the other students in your class?" or "Do you initiate conversation with them?" When both the student and the teacher have participated, a graphic representation such as that in figure 13-1 will emerge.

While unique tools have not been developed among my colleagues and myself to elicit the information discussed above, the questions many foreign study advisers normally ask of a student inquiring about the study-abroad process fit into the categories shown above and can be used in the initial assessment and as the basis of goal development. The student can be characterized as a low-level or beginning student, an intermediate student, or an advanced student according to the preponderance of evidence in the student and teacher's language competence assessment. The medium levels in the social orientation and communicative skill orientation will indicate a student who is a "people type of person" and who is at least willing to take the risks associated with oral skill development. The student who shows low levels in both of these areas is not so likely to benefit from the study-abroad program without a considerable change of attitude and habits of communication.

The results of the interview should be followed by a discussion of the student's capabilities to capitalize on the strengths indicated in the interview and

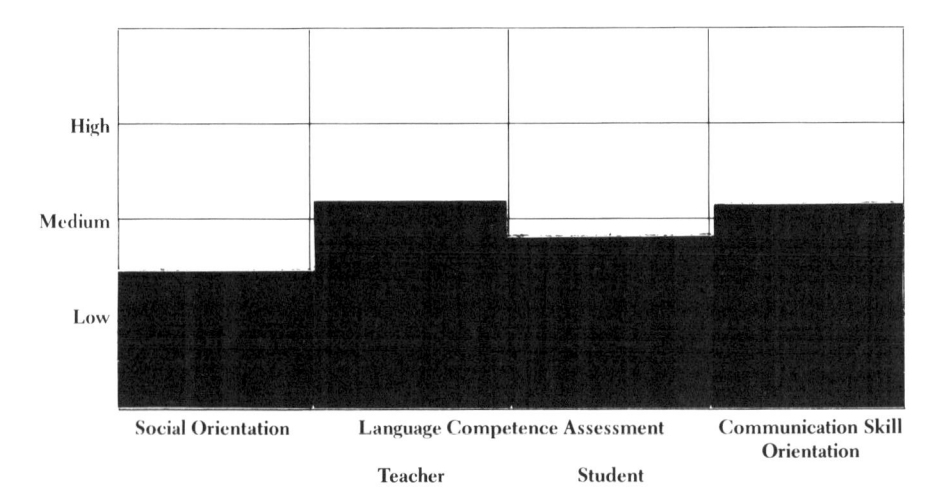

Figure 13-1. Typical student profile.

to develop or augment skills in those areas where the student does not indicate at least moderate interest or ability. Achievement assessment after the study-abroad term should follow the same course as the initial evaluation, with the difference that questions and answers may reflect particular experiences the student had, both in class and beyond. The student and the instructor will then be able to discuss which aspects were particularly beneficial and evaluate the student's future directions for study and growth.

After the initial analysis is completed, the student and teacher can set reasonable goals. These will depend on the length of time the student will be studying abroad and the context of the student's work. Variables here include the structure of language study classes, the living situation, and the extra-curricular experiences the student is likely to have available. Caution should be exercised so that goals are attainable; the student can be encouraged to work in the present level and then gradually extend his or her work toward the next level. On the ACTFL/ETS scale, the distance between levels is not linear; i.e., geometrically increasing skill in terms of linguistic function, social context, and accuracy is required to demonstrate a higher level of proficiency.

In simple terms, a lower-level learner can count on acquisition of vocabulary and skill in using grammatical structures to become effective at a higher level of speaking ability. This seems to be the case because vocabulary and skill acquired will let the speaker participate in increasingly varied and complex discussions. At higher levels, however, the ability to participate in discussions of professional or abstract topics, the ability to tailor language to formal or informal situations, and other considerations necessarily call for prolonged study of the language features, considerable practice, and increasingly acute perception of the social and cultural environment in which the student is working.

In general, the focus of study should expand outward from the individual, his or her personal life, and the present time to descriptive fluency, more abstract topics, and professional and abstract concerns and hypotheses. These, it may be noted, follow the progression of all human psychological growth, from the self-centered to the more comprehensive and abstract. Ralph Carter (1981) refers to the difference between the student's native language and ability and that in the second language as follows: "Picture now, if you will, a high school junior or college sophomore, dressed as a six-year-old. This is the dichotomy faced by the mature student striving to bring his second language skills up to the level of his chronological age" (p. 55). The foreign language learner, in fact, regardless of the age of the participant, may be thought of as emerging from another childhood into a mature sociolinguistic environment.

Risks Associated with the Study-Abroad Experience

The term *risk* is used here to indicate the gamble or chance that students may undergo when turned loose from the text and encouraged to utilize their own resources. Remembering the role that confidence plays in the acquisition of a foreign language, at the same time there can be dangers associated with taking risks. The dangers associated with study abroad are often of three kinds: underdoing, overdoing, and doing things incorrectly. The student who underachieves often is approaching the study situation as another class experience and does not derive

160 Creative Approaches in Foreign Language Teaching

the direct and often intangible benefits of the experience of being immersed in the culture. This experience can occur with students at any level, but is, naturally, more obvious among those students who are less outgoing and more unsure of their linguistic ability.

The student who has considerable confidence in meeting people and new situations may, at the same time, fail to integrate the very real benefits of classes, grammar books, and dictionaries. This student goes resolutely forth into the foreign culture and decides for himself or herself that if one can order food and drink and catch the right bus, achieve understanding with gestures and infinitives, then he or she has arrived at a high level of proficiency. The ETS Oral Proficiency Testing Manual (1982) refers to this problem in its discussion of people who have learned their language through use alone. Their grammar flaws often become permanent, or "fossilized" (p. 19). This pattern is especially evident among outgoing students and those who tend to overrate their grammatical level. Figure 13-2 indicates a typical profile for this "overdoer" student; the social factors are relatively high and the language competence levels are considerably lower. Especially noteworthy is a difference between the student's and the teacher's estimate of the language competence.

The student who does not give due attention to all parts of the program—either for lack of information, oversight, or inattention or intentionally—fails to benefit from some aspect of the planned experience because of getting sidetracked or undue influence from a particular aspect of the experience. Taking the experience as a whole is the most desirable approach. A student can get sidetracked by making a good friend in the target culture with whom he or she spends a great deal of time, thereby losing sight of his or her own language learning while enjoying the undeniable benefits of close friendship. Similar effects may occur when a student

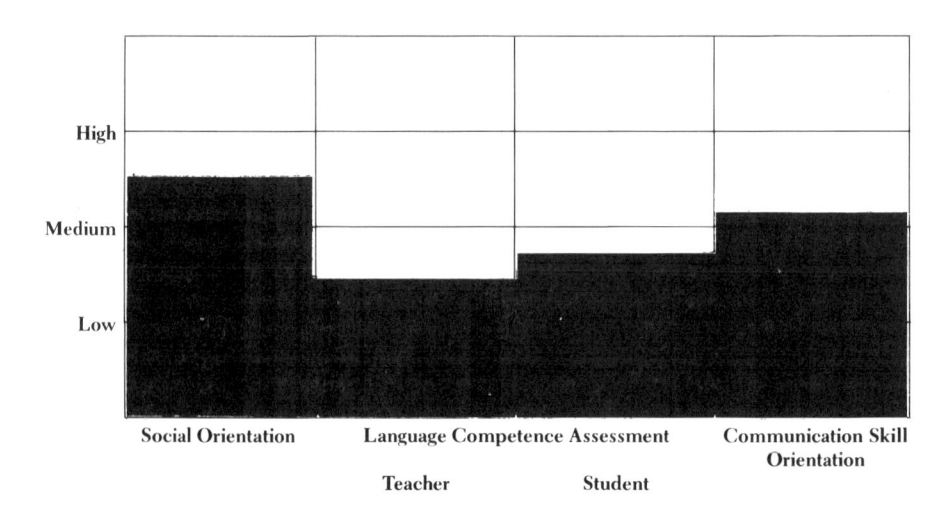

Figure 13-2. "Overdoer" profile.

becomes involved with a political issue or even a cultural aspect of the experience that takes up so much time and energy that other "tasks" are neglected. The on-site director can often correct this in discussion with the student, basing the discussion on careful attention to the students' checklists and journals as discussed below.

This brings us to the student who truly benefits from a foreign language study program. The ideal student (1) works in a constant cycle of systematic grammatical learning through some kind of class schedule; (2) is provided with or seeks out contexts (homestay, conversation groups) in which to try out the newly learned material; and (3) utilizes the whole city as his or her personal laboratory for language development. This last activity is relatively low-risk and, when frequently and carefully engaged in, contributes to overall language proficiency as do other low-risk large-quantity activities (Krashen 1989, p. 450).

Pretrip Activities

The teacher can shape the students' approach to the study-abroad experience in several ways that minimize some of the dangers associated with the experience. In addition to the assessment and goal orientation discussed above, pretrip activities can acquaint the students with the salient features of the foreign culture, the physically meaningful points, and how the key points of the process of learning the language in the foreign setting will differ from the process of learning in the class.

Prior knowledge and discussion of the foreign culture specific to the area of study will allow the student to relieve herself or himself from anxiety-inducing misconceptions and to be as "correct" as possible. For example, not inviting a guest of the opposite sex into the student's bedroom in Mexico will avoid a difficult or even offensive scene that could bias negatively the empathy of the host family toward the student and affect negatively the student's benefits of the homestay. The trip director has an obligation to smooth the way as much as possible for students in this aspect of their experience for them to have a comprehensive learning process.

As with cultural awareness, the teacher should provide concrete knowledge of what the student can expect with regard to daily class schedule, local transportation, eating customs and schedules, telephone usage, and whom to contact in case of questions or problems with the above or other quasi-emergency situations (medical questions, for example). This is not "coddling" the students; past experience, confirmed by many others, has demonstrated that the student abroad is normally insecure for several days after arriving at the destination. The student who is further preoccupied by any other problems such as those described above is not able to benefit from the experience in a positive and progressive way.

The student should understand the differences between the largely independent and holistic learning situation that is the greatest asset of study-abroad programs and the typical teacher-directed classroom or school situation. Discussion of the kinds of activities the student may benefit from, the ways in which the student should record his or her progress, and some metacognitive strategies are all useful in this regard. Further, each student should be provided with materials appropriate to his or her work. Then the student can approach the study experience with confidence and the knowledge that she or he can work toward specific goals. In a recent study (Yin et al. 1989), it was determined that the highest probability for grammatical correction and growth occurs in the classes themselves; that a family (homestay) experience provides the opportunity to express oneself more freely, that is, to experiment with new tenses and situations, and to receive gentle encouragement and correction; and that extracurricular experiences provide many situations in which the student can absorb and try out sociolinguistic experiments such as asking directions and ordering food.

At the lower levels, structured activities will help the student to feel more confident and will stimulate interest. There are some interesting and novel differences between the structured activities that are useful to the student abroad and those used in textbook-oriented learning. This is true even when a proficiency orientation is utilized in the classroom. The student is still normally accountable for a fixed amount of text-based material, which is tested in terms of activities based on these materials.[1] Structured activities for the beginning-level study-abroad program should include questions and answers the student will need to know in the particular study environment. Then the student should be taught basic survival vocabulary and should practice these situations with other students. While still not authentic in terms of the situation to come, these simulations will give the student practice in working to be understood and in communicating information. Questions should be formulated around tasks such as those given in the lists below, on the topics of bus routes, food ingredients and preparation, inventory, price, and use. They all provide the kind of practice lower-level students can benefit from.

One factor not yet discussed in the consideration of the growth of foreign language communicative competence is what might be termed "inaction for communicative competence." In our native language we generally use informational questions to provide data on which we can act. An *inactive* task may be asking if Bus A goes to the center of town via the aqueduct (but not getting on the bus). Repeating the same inquiry four times during the week will allow the student to rephrase and perfect the question; at the same time the student will receive several variations on the answer. Asking information for proficiency practice is an unfamiliar activity. Once students are aware of the potential, however, they become enthusiastic practitioners of this technique. At the intermediate level, the student can pose questions about past and future events. At the advanced level, the student might elicit opinions on a topic from different people. Both posing questions and eliciting opinions lend themselves to rephrasing and rebutting.

On-Site Activities

The purpose of *task lists, skill lists, checklists, journal* reports, and *evaluations* is to provide the student a structure for undertaking and evaluating the varied experiences of the study-abroad period. It is assumed, for the purposes of this discussion, that these tools are being used in tandem with a structured grammar experience for the student. Even where they are not, however, they provide useful tools for the experience.

The *task lists* are as varied as the contents and the language levels of the students involved.[2] The student should begin working on the list for the initial assessment level. The students should have tasks that confirm their abilities to work at their initial level, that expand the quantity of activities at this level, and

Evaluating Risk and Achievements for Students Abroad

that encourage movement to a slightly higher level of performance. Where tasks are found at more than one level, the response will vary according to the skills used and the student's language accuracy. The following are samples from a task list, a skill list, and a checklist.

Task List

Discuss the following with a friend or family member each day.

A. Lower level: General/personal topics (examples)

1. How you feel today
2. Your family in the United States
3. The weather
4. How your classes are—what you are learning

B. Intermediate level: General/survival topics (examples):

1. Your classes—what you are learning
2. A current event
3. An activity with your class/friends/family
4. Food, recipes, customs, pastimes, etc.

C. Advanced level: Practical/professional topics (examples)

1. A current event
2. A topic of local/regional/national importance
3. Theoretical discussion of a professional or abstract topic

Skill List

As you go about your daily routine, try to develop the following skills.

A. Lower level: Try to practice what you already know and to create new sentences.

1. Acquire new vocabulary in context.
2. Describe the world around you in as much detail as possible; use colors, part names, functions.

Advanced lower level: Begin to use the past tense to describe yesterday's actions and then the future tense to state future actions.

B. Intermediate level: Try to describe in greater detail and narrate more fully.

1. Restate and paraphrase your own descriptions and ideas and those of others.
2. Relate descriptions of events to causes and begin to state outcomes.

Advanced intermediate level: Use the perfect tenses to relate events in chronological sequence.

C. Advanced level: Try to describe concretely, hypothesize, support ideas.

1. Use hypothetical considerations to bring additional factors into your discussions.
2. Restate discussants' considerations in terms of outcomes. ("You are saying, then, that if they had done X, then Y would have occurred.")
3. Question others and volunteer topics of exploration and discussion.

Checklist

Complete each item daily or more frequently as appropriate.

A. Beginning level

1. I talked to _____ about _____.
2. I learned about _____ from _____ (class, newspaper, radio, etc.).
3. I met _____.
4. I asked about _____.
5. Other:

B. Intermediate level

1. I talked to _____ about _____.
2. I learned about _____.
3. I inquired about _____.
4. What's new? _____.

C. Advanced level

1. I read and thought about _____ or learned and thought about _____.
2. I discussed topic #1 with _____.
3. I encountered or created an unfamiliar situation.
 (Describe:)

For use in the program abroad, of course, separate lists are compiled for the students at each level. A sample intermediate sheet is given as figure 13-3.

The lists and journal activities provide for both structured and experimental open-ended activities. They are both geared to the student's initial proficiency level. They can serve to remind the students of their expanding cultural awareness and be especially helpful to the student who is less self-assured about functioning independently in the foreign society. They are also important for developing variety of contexts in language use exploration. The checklist should be written up daily by the student.

The personal journals students keep provide for a fuller recording of the events that are important to the student. They will be written in English at the lower level, in the target language at the intermediate level, and with paragraphs in the target language as much as possible at the intermediate level. Advanced students may be expected to keep their journals completely in the target language.

Intermediate Level

TASKS: Discuss the following with a friend or family member each day. General/survival topics (examples):

1. Your classes—what you are learning
2. A current event
3. An activity with your class/friends/family
4. Food, recipes, customs, pastimes, etc.

SKILLS: Try to describe in greater detail and narrate more fully.

1. Restate and paraphrase your own descriptions and ideas and those of others.
2. Relate descriptions of events to causes and begin to state outcomes.

CHECKLIST:

1. I talked to _____ about _____.
2. I learned about _____.
3. I inquired about _____.
4. What's new? _____.

Figure 13-3. Sample compilation of lists for intermediate level.

For grading purposes, extra points are granted for extra student attention to this aspect of the journal. The development of descriptive skills and thoughtful consideration of the foreign culture will benefit the student's writing ability and provide many memories for the student after returning home. They also permit the student to work through emotions and ideas that may be important but inappropriate to share with friends or the homestay family. Committing these thoughts to paper in private (and often to the trip director) frees the student to progress more rapidly. The journals also provide the basis of discussions with the trip director and provide ideas for further development.

The checklists and journals should be evaluated weekly with the student. Evaluative comments may be written with periodic conferences for student participation. The student's involvement in the process here, as in the initial assessment, is relevant and useful. Nyikos (1991) states that "the critical difference between successful learners and their less successful peers may lie in the finding that successful language learners make more frequent use of metacognitive strategies" (p. 33). The supervisor's comments should confirm the student's level of proficiency and serve as the basis for encouraging further development. When the teacher sees that the student is working so well in terms of quality and quantity at one level that expansion to the next is warranted, then the next level's checklists should be discussed and implemented—without, however, abandoning the lower-level lists, so that the student can make a gradual and natural progression. Sutton's (1981) discussion of this gradual transition provides a good description of the art of encouraging growth in students at the boundary between levels of language competence (p. 30).

Conclusion:
The Student Abroad Is a Competent Learner

The student is reassured by the typically quick accumulation of experiences and skills within the foreign study environment. Further, the student sees that she or he can seek out people who are helpful and situations from which she or he can benefit. As success breeds success, the student is motivated to continue and even increase his or her efforts, becoming a competent learner and a more proficient speaker of the foreign language.

It is hoped that the above suggestions will provide a context useful to those who believe it is important to combine the undeniably important study-abroad experience with a tangible increase in the student' language proficiency. This makes the experience richer and more satisfying to the student and will carry back to the students' coursework in valuable measure.

Notes

1. The discussion of Snyder, Long, Kealey, and Marckel (1987) makes the point that a variety of materials for real-world situations is included in a proficiency-oriented classroom. At the same time, activities are related to the skills being taught (p. 62) and have observable outcomes (p. 63), strategies that cannot be predicted in the student-directed environment, which plays a large role in the study-abroad program.
2. See also Omaggio Hadley's (1986, pp. 177ff.) strategies for teaching oral proficiency according to the ACTFL/ETS scale for many additional topics and ideas.

References

ACTFL. 1986. *Proficiency Guidelines*. Hastings-on-Hudson, NY: ACTFL.

Carter, Ralph M. 1981. "A Situational Approach to Advanced Conversation," pp. 55–67 in Donna E. Sutton and John M. Purcell, eds., *Filling and Fulfilling the Advanced Foreign Language Class*. Boston: Heinle and Heinle.

ETS. 1982. Oral Proficiency Testing Manual. Princeton, NJ: Educational Testing Service.

Higgs, Theodore V., and Ray Clifford. 1981. "The Push toward Communication," pp. 57–79 in Theodore V. Higgs, ed., *Curriculum, Competence, and the Foreign Language Teacher*. The ACTFL Foreign Language in Education Series, vol. 13. Lincolnwood, IL: National Textbook Company.

Krashen, Stephen D. 1989. "We Acquire Vocabulary and Spelling by Reading: Additional Evidence for the Input Hypothesis." *Modern Language Journal* 73: 440–64.

Nyikos, Martha. 1991. "Prioritizing Student Learning: A Guide for Teachers," pp. 25–42 in Lorraine A. Strasheim, ed., *Focus on the Foreign Language Learner: Priorities and Strategies*. Proceedings of the Central States Conference on the Teaching of Foreign Languages. Lincolnwood, IL: National Textbook Company.

Omaggio Hadley, Alice C. 1986. *Teaching Language in Context: Proficiency-Oriented Instruction*. Boston: Heinle and Heinle.

Snyder, Barbara, Donna R. Long, James R. Kealey, and Beverly Marckel. 1987. "Building Proficiency: Activities for the Four Skills," pp. 43–64 in Diane W. Birckbichler, ed., *Proficiency, Policy, and Professionalism in Foreign Language Education*. Proceedings of the Central States Conference on the Teaching of Foreign Languages. Lincolnwood, IL: National Textbook Company.

Sutton, Donna E. 1981. "Coping with Choices," pp. 15–35 in Donna E. Sutton and John M. Purcell, eds., *Filling and Fulfilling the Advanced Foreign Language Class*. Boston: Heinle and Heinle.

Westphal, Patricia. 1976. "Communicative Competence: Even for the Non-Major," pp. 33–44 in Renate A. Schulz, ed., *Teaching for Communication in the Foreign Language Classroom*. Proceedings of the Central States Conference on the Teaching of Foreign Languages. Lincolnwood, IL: National Textbook Company.

Yin, Philippa, Patricia Stolzenburg, and Catherine Tedeschi. 1989. "Study Abroad and Oral Skills: Context and Competence." Paper presented at the Ohio Foreign Language Association Convention, Dayton, Ohio, March.

14
The Popular Song:
An Authentic Tool for Enriching the Foreign Language Classroom

Jayne Abrate
University of Missouri, Rolla

The proficiency orientation of current foreign language methodologies underscores very clearly the need for cultural knowledge in mastering a second language. Culturally based assumptions regulate communication and determine the many underlying meanings of the spoken and written word. Unfortunately, although teachers try to incorporate cultural contexts in the classroom, they cannot transport the foreign environment to their students. Practical applications of the popular song offer one way to bring an element of living culture to foreign language instruction. As a contemporary medium, popular music reflects the social and ideological preoccupations of the artists and their audiences, and variety in musical styles contribute to the atmosphere of the classroom. Besides introducing authentic culture to the learning process, popular songs provide contextual models of natives speaking "real" language. Recordings, supplemented by the written texts, encourage language practice, increase cultural awareness, and provide a sensory dimension absent from printed materials or imagined situations.

Popular music constitutes a separate art form that combines poetry, music, and theatricality, and both scholars and performers view text, music, and rendition as integral components of a whole. These descendants of ancient lyric traditions have successfully served as the focus of advanced academic courses. If the musical background of the instructor allows, melody and accompaniment may occupy a significant place in song analysis. For the purpose of this article, however, discussion of musicality, except in a superficial sense, will be overlooked in order to concentrate on the potential of the words as a language-learning device. Nevertheless, song is communication with words representing only one part of the message, and students will react to that message whether or not they grasp the words. Popular songs, by example and as a stimulus for further language use, demonstrate for students the complexity and diversity of factors influencing communication.

Popular music offers an effective means of illustrating culture, especially when two cultures appear outwardly similar. Musical styles help students distinguish between countries where people speak the same language. The music of France differs from that of Quebec or francophone African countries, and Spanish tastes do not mirror those of Argentina, Columbia, or Mexico. Many countries actively promote popular music through subsidies to individuals and sponsorship of contests and festivals, because they respect songwriting and performing as serious art forms and want to preserve this reflection of the national culture. Traditional local styles such as the French-Canadian two-step or Cajun zydeco, the Spanish flamenco or Argentine tango, highlight this variation between countries and their diverse heritages. Comparisons might also extend to traditional American music—jazz, blues, rock and roll, or country and western—as students try to envision the unique cultural forces at work in evolving musical trends.

Selecting and Preparing a Song Text

There are songs appropriate to all levels of study. They cover an immense variety of topics and are replete with linguistic, cultural, and historical information from which teachers can derive a multitude of material. Although nearly every song can serve some pedagogical objective, certain texts prove richer than others. Making notations of specific benefits a song might provide allows teachers to incorporate works easily into a syllabus. The notations might include the following:

1. Illustrates the use of the past tenses
2. Reviews numerous irregular verbs
3. Shows many instances of adjective agreement
4. Gives clear examples of pronunciation
5. Provides vocabulary relating to vacation, school, meals, etc.
6. Contains many idioms and puns
7. Discusses family or social interaction
8. Refers to natural surroundings or environmental concerns
9. Draws clearly defined characters
10. Presents historical figures or events
11. Shows a well-defined poetic form
12. Is especially moving or entertaining

Most songs fit in several categories. In selecting a piece, teachers should consider whether the song is merely to enhance atmosphere, to serve as enrichment, to form an integral part of a lesson presentation, or to be the foundation of a minilesson. The clarity of the voice and accompaniment as well as the availability of the printed text constitute other criteria that affect the extent to which a work can be utilized.

Lyrics to many recordings are printed on album jackets or are enclosed with cassette tapes. Unfortunately, there are frequent errors in the printed words. Often, on the other hand—particularly for major French artists—texts have been published in collections or biographies,[1] and occasionally sheet music is available. If the text cannot be obtained, transcribing the lyrics generally is not a viable option even for native speakers; it is not only time-consuming but extremely difficult to produce an error-free text because of interference from the music and imperfect or exaggerated articulation in the artist's interpretation. At the same time, accuracy is paramount, especially if students will be tested on the material. Teachers should carefully verify published texts to ensure agreement with the recording, since performers sometimes transpose verses or lines or improvise as they sing. Once the lyrics are complete, handouts, either with a complete version or with blanks inserted, can be prepared for students. The quantity and placement of blanks and the inclusion of notes or glossed vocabulary determine presentation. Too many blanks, particularly in a fast song, frustrate students as they frantically attempt to keep pace with the singer. Furthermore, this moves the emphasis away from comprehension to the act of transcription. If discussion follows immediately, glossing is usually unnecessary, and instructors can handle explanations orally. Homework assignments, on the other hand, may require additional information for students to understand the text on their own. Finally, leaving the page as free of markings as possible, including most punctuation, permits students to use it as they wish. Some like a clean copy to keep; others scribble copious notes. Supplementary materials such as a biographical sketch of the artist or comprehension exercises and discussion questions may also be devised.

Possibilities for exercises and activities based on a song are numerous and can address all language skills, listening comprehension and pronunciation, speaking, vocabulary acquisition, grammar usage, cultural proficiency, reading and writing. Obviously, an individual song may serve several pedagogical purposes; those that illustrate the above-mentioned skills are no exception. Additional suggestions are marked with an asterisk below. Since musical appreciation relies heavily on personal experience and preferences, students will react more strongly to certain works, and several authors have analyzed the affective factors involved (Chamberlain 1974; Thompson 1986). It is important not to overuse a selection nor to forget that the implementation of songs succeeds to the extent that it remains enjoyable.

Listening Comprehension and Pronunciation

Listening comprehension exercises range from students simply filling in blanks to listening for meaning prior to seeing a text. Songs function well in training the ear to discriminate rhythms and sounds in the target language. As they listen, students can indicate pronunciation characteristics such as *liaison* or the pronunciation of the mute *e* in French or the Castilian use of [θ] or the pronunciation of the letter *v* in Spanish. They may also locate examples of rhyme, alliteration, and assonance. "Prisonnier d'un souvenir" by Pierre Bachelet (Polydor 813078-1) offers several types of listening exercises:

> Toi qui l'as recontré dis-moi donc
> Ses yeux son cœur sa vie son prénom
> Dis-moi ses mains ses cheveux son adresse
> Et sais-tu où se cache une déesse
> Raconte-moi son rire de cristal
> Et son odeur de bois de santale
> Et cette médaille d'or de Padoue
> Que j'ai cru voir briller à son cou.

Exercises:

1. Underline the nasal vowels.
2. Indicate rhyming words, both final and interior (i.e., *adresse/déesse, yeux/cheveux*).

3. Find examples of alliteration (i.e., *dis-moi donc*).
4. Mark examples of *liaison*.
*5. Consider also the use of possessive adjectives.

Thompson (1986, pp. 23-24) suggests consciously inserting errors, not grammatical mistakes but words slightly different from those sung, which students must find through careful listening to the text. In an advanced class, pairs or groups of students might attempt to transcribe a complete song. This activity requires access to several tape recorders or a language laboratory so groups can start and stop the tape as necessary. It is highly unlikely that they will arrive at a perfect transcription. Therefore, the teacher should choose a song with complete lyrics in order to respond to students' queries and settle disputes. Transcription encourages group communication and problem solving with regard to possible meanings and unfamiliar words, but when students' interest is genuinely engaged in the activity, disagreements about the "correct" answer can grow heated.

Vocabulary

Songs offer an inexhaustible source of vocabulary, individual terms as well as idiomatic expressions and slang. These are often related to a specific topic as songwriters, like poets, develop images in their works. The contextual presentation of these items aids in retention of meaning, genders, use of prepositions, and even spelling. "Recuerdo un tren" by José Luis Perales (CBS S 86342) includes vocabulary referring to train travel—*el equipaje, la maleta, la estación, el reloj en la pared, la parada, el tren, el camino, la despedida,* and *el andén*. Similarly, Pierre Perret regales the listener with terms and puns about eggs in "Quoi de plus sympa qu'un œuf" (Adèle AD 39 532)—*une omelette, une coquille, à cheval, un œuf à la coque, pondre, un œuf gobé, l'œuf de Colomb, un œuf en gelée, un œuf couvé, étouffer l'affaire dans l'œuf,* and *aller vous faire cuire un œuf*. Vocabulary-based exercises for such songs can involve listing synonyms and antonyms, matching terms with given definitions, creating definitions, or exploring word families or idioms (Abrate 1983).

Grammar

As examples of authentic language, song texts illustrate acceptable grammatical usage, and many have a particular, predominant stylistic feature that the teacher can exploit in the classroom. Verb tenses, adjective agreement, and the use of articles, prepositions, and pronouns—among many other topics—occur frequently in song texts and in sufficient quantity to merit examination. In "Nos Quinze Ans" by Georges Moustaki (Polydor 247301 9) one finds examples of definite and indefinite articles whose usage can be identified, explained, and practiced:

La guerre était finie racontaient **les** journaux
Mais **les** armes en secret réglaient notre destin
Comme nous n'étions pas tout à fait **des** gamins
Chacun choisissait **la** couleur de son drapeau
Boris était Tarzan et moi j'étais Zorro
Pour sortir **une** fille on vendait nos bouquins

On se prenait pour **des** voleurs de grand chemin
Lorsqu'on fauchait **des** billes **des** briquets **des** stylos.

Exercises:

1. Underline and identify all articles.
2. Explain why each is used.
3. Transform from singular to plural or vice-versa.
4. Modify expressions to cause changes (e.g., *de gentils gamins*).
*5. Consider also past tense usage, slang, and references to war.

It often proves helpful when inserting blanks to replace with blanks the grammatical feature under study in order to focus students' attention on the missing forms.

"Me Iré Calladamente" by José Luis Perales (CBS S 86324) uses the future tense extensively:

Mañana *buscaré* esa cometa de papel en el desván
Y *arreglaré* la vieja bicicleta con que ayer jugué
Arrancaré la hierba del jardín
Y *plantaré* un cerezo y un rosal
Mañana cuando **vuelva** si vuelvo
Mañana *borraré* cada minuto de la esfera del reloj
Mañana *colgaré* en alguna percha lo que fue disfraz
Mañana *alegrará* mi corazón
La risa de unos niños al jugar.

Exercises:

1. Fill in the future forms [shown in italic here].
2. Change the subject to *tú, él, nosotros, ustedes.*
3. Rewrite the song in the past tense, making any necessary changes.
4. Rewrite the song from the point of view of *los niños.*
5. Indicate and explain the use of the subjunctive (in bold).
*6. Consider also the use of articles and explore the singer's state of mind.

Transposing the song to the past would force students to differentiate between the preterite and imperfect as well as the pluperfect tenses and necessitate other changes such as *mañana* to *ayer*, for instance (Herman 1987; see also Herman 1986, 1988). By examining the living language of songs, students can observe how grammar rules apply when native speakers actually use the language rather than in contrived textbook sentences, however realistic.

Speaking

The ideas or themes presented in songs create a context for discussion that can be limited to basic comprehension or encompass debates about a social or political issue. Informational questions to test understanding as well as to elicit initial reactions to a song serve as a springboard for more in-depth consideration of ideas. Teachers may require students to formulate their own questions about content or give oral reports based on the song. Beyond the general meaning, students can identify the social or political bias of the singer and indicate agreement or disagreement with his or her point of view. Michel Sardou's "Le Rire du sergent" (Impact 6995 500) and Maxime Le Forestier's once-banned "Le Parachutiste" (Polydor 2393 040) present two sides of a debate on the military. The lively accompaniment of Sardou's song underlines its comic intent:

> Je me suis présenté tout nu devant un infirmier
> Moyennant dix sacs il dit moi je peux vous aider
> Je me voyais déjà
> Retournant chez moi
> Mais quand ils m'ont dit
> Que j'étais bon pour dix-huit mois
> À ce moment-là juste derrière moi
> J'ai entendu rire un type que je ne connaissais pas.

*Consider also military vocabulary, clear pronunciation, use of past tenses, and humor.

He treats military service as a rite of passage for young French males, while Le Forestier scathingly criticizes the elite forces:

> Puis on t'a donné des galons
> Héros de toutes les défaites
> Toutes les bonnes actions
> Que tu as faites
> Tu torturais en spécialiste
> Parachutiste
>
> Alors sont venus les honneurs
> Les décorations les médailles
> Pour chaque balle au fond d'un cœur
> Pour chaque entaille
> Pour chaque croix noire sur ta liste
> Parachutiste

*Consider also vocabulary, use of past tenses, poetic structure, rhyme, and reference to French military defeats.

In light of the recent war against Iraq, these two songs provoke animated discussion among students regarding the nature of and need for the military. In addition, students might research France's participation in the Persian Gulf and the role of the French Foreign Legion. Students may also compare a song to other songs or texts previously studied.

A creative exercise might have students adapt content into the form of a skit, particularly if the song presents interesting characters. Robert Charlebois sings of "Madame Bertrand" (Gamma 9.8501/2), a matchmaker, and the prospective spouses' descriptions of themselves inspire lively re-enactments and digressions in the same spirit:

> Madame Bertrand je suis un jeune veuf de 54 ans
> Catholique et bon pratiquant
> Dans mon tourment je cherche une maman pour mes enfants
> Claude et Armand de 11 et 12 ans

Madame Bertrand je suis une brunette de 45 ans
Un peu grassette j'adore les enfants
J'aimerais bien connaître un veuf ou un célibataire
Distingué avec des bonnes manières.

*Consider also personal description vocabulary, French-Canadian accent, use of articles, use of verb tenses, and the importance of religion in Quebec.

Students cannot only invent dialogs but imagine other traits such as clothing, hairstyle, accent, and physical characteristics.

In a darker, ironic vein, "Veneno en el piel" by Radio Futura (BMG 410638) offers a similar context with only two characters but places them in different circumstances, a restaurant, bar, and discotheque:

Pero primero quieres ir a cenar
Y me sugieres que te lleve a un sitio caro
A ver si aceptan la cartilla del paro
Porque si no lo tenemos que robar
Yo voy haciéndome la cuenta de cabeza
Y tú prodigas tu sonrisa con esmero
Y te dedicas a insultar al camarero
Y me salpicas con espuma de cerveza

*Consider also the use of the subjunctive, object pronouns, and prepositions and the problem of unemployment.

Re-enactment gives the students the opportunity to imagine the characters' conversation, appropriate behavior in these places, and whether they conform. The scenes described in both these songs can be staged by students using dialog, props, and even a simple setting.[2] Teachers should watch for songs of this type, since they present scenarios upon which students enthusiastically build.

Cultural Proficiency

Popular songs reflect contemporary phenomena, referring to people, places, events, celebrations, food, relationships, and behavior. Often teachers must explain these before students understand the whole meaning of the text.[3] Thus, songs provide a valuable stimulus for cultural discussion and comparison. Works do not have to be about a cultural topic per se; even love songs may contain relevant images. In this verse from "La Culpa fue del cha-cha-cha" by Gabinete Caligari (EMI 793356-4), the association of the cha-cha and the couple's relationship with *el arte torero* could introduce a discussion of bullfighting:

Salimos por la puerta del night club
Cogidos de la mano para celebrar
El triúnfo verdadero
Del arte torero y del cha-cha-cha
Que nos unió para siempre
Sentimentalemente por casualidad.

*Consider also the use of past tenses, *por* and *para*, adjective agreement, and other types of Hispanic dances.

The Popular Song   175

The use of bullfighting as a symbol along with dance to refer to a love relationship gives rise to interesting comparisons of bullfighting as dance or the man and woman as the matador and the bull.

Still another song, Joan Manuel Serrat's "Manuel" (EMI 17979), paints a vivid portrait of rural life far removed from an American student's frame of reference:

Le llamaban Manuel
Nació en España
Su casa era de barro
De barro y caña
Las tierras del señor
Humedecían
Su surro y su llanto
Día tras día
Mendigo a jornal fijo
Como él no hubo
Entre olivos y trigo
Por un mendrugo.

*Consider also the use of past tenses, vocabulary, pronunciation, geography, possessive adjectives, and aspects of peasant life.

The cultural impact of a song may lie in terminology for things and in situations that do not exist in America, in references to actions typical of a culture, or in descriptions of life-style or historical events with which Americans are unfamiliar. Therefore, songs offer referential as well as contextual applications to culture.

History plays a prominent role in French music as shown in this song by Francis Cabrel entitled "Les Chevaliers cathares" (CBS 25639):

La fumée des voitures
Les cailloux des enfants
Les yeux sur les champs de torture
Et les poubelles devant
C'est quelqu'un du dessus de la Loire
Qui a dû dessiner les plans
Il a oublié sur la robe
Les tâches de sang.

*Consider also the possessive construction with *de*, articles, geography, and vocabulary.

The song alludes not only to the real Cathares of the Middle Ages but also to a recently constructed rest area along highway A-61 near the Lézignan-Corbières exit. These stone figures have openings at the top resembling the visor of a helmet; tourists can climb to this point and survey the surrounding countryside through telescopes. The site gives the impression of being a child's playground rather than a serious commemoration of history. An amusing exercise, if one has access to pictures of the statues, is to ask students to draw what they think the *chevaliers* look like from the description in the song and then compare their efforts to the picture. The variety of possible activities underlines the significant cultural content offered by popular music with the added benefit that explanation and discussion of culture involve language practice. Cultural references can combine with linguistic examples to produce a thought-provoking yet practical package.

Reading

Typical reading activities applicable to any passage can highlight a song text. Given the words to study before listening to the recording, students might attempt to guess musical style from the rhythm and subject matter. Reading exercises such as inferring meaning from context, comprehending colloquial usages or unusual syntax, or deciphering image-laden texts can combine with biographical or current-events materials relevant to the singer or content to offer valuable reading practice.

Numerous authors have dealt with the subject of popular songs as literature (Brown 1975; Chamberlain 1974; Cruz-Sáenz 1990). They can often serve as models of versification; Georges Brassens, often admired for his poetic use of French, recounts the story of a rural wedding in "La Marche nuptiale" (Phillips 9 101 046) using classical *alexandrins* in rhyming couplets:

C'est dans un char à bœufs s'il faut parler bien franc
Tiré par les amis poussé par les parents
Que les vieux amoureux firent leurs épousailles
Après longtemps d'amour longtemps de fiançailles.

°Consider also accent and pronunciation, imagery, use of past tenses, and the description of a wedding.

The counting of the mute *e* before a consonant is respected throughout. Rhymes, the balanced structure of each line, and the suggestive value of sound all contribute to the effect created by the words and reinforced by voice and music.

Writing

As a corollary to reading activities, writing can also be inspired by songs. Students can summarize content, retell a narrative song, or simply offer their reactions in journal form. Also, value-judgment questions can be posed to which students must compose a logical argument supporting or disagreeing with the performer's stance. In fact, several of the conversation and culture-related activities may double as writing exercises. Students can employ the *explication de texte* to analyze songs as literature. Many represent beautifully constructed poetry, and composers have frequently set traditional poems to music. Out of class, students can write essays based on research of related subjects or on the artist himself.

Activities

Participatory exercises inspired by a song text might take the form of individual or group projects. Some ideas are (1) a singalong or live performance of a work, (2) a "radio" broadcast spotlighting French or Spanish singers, and (3) skits based on the plot of a song. In a French culture course organized around popular songs (Abrate 1988), one student who knew sign language interpreted a song for the class along with the recording; no one present will ever forget the moving rendition of "Compiègne" by Marie-Paule Belle (Carrère 67.927). In addition, food preparation and tasting of dishes mentioned in song further reinforce the internalization of foreign cultural traditions.

Presentation

There is no one best way to present a text. The most straightforward method consists of a brief oral summary by the teacher of the content or theme, perhaps accompanied by a written biographical sketch of the artist, followed by a first playing of the recording. This might be a passive listening comprehension exercise, or students might be required to jot down words or phrases they hear. Copies of the text are then distributed before a second playing, during which students fill in blanks or perform some other activity based on listening comprehension or sound discrimination. The song may be replayed a third or fourth time, if necessary.[4] Fill-in exercises, especially for beginning students, should be corrected immediately with an overhead projector or by handing out a full copy of the lyrics. In an advanced class, students may check their own responses against a key.

The class can complete exercises right away or be assigned to read the text and finish a series of questions as homework. At some point, teachers may wish to spot-check for comprehension and then proceed to discussion of content and analysis of corresponding vocabulary or grammar exercises. Finally, the instructor can play the song another time for fun or for the class to sing along.

Conclusion

All types of songs are available for use at all levels of instruction. Children's songs and folk songs can be used in FLES classes (Braehm 1977; Caré 1984; Garcia-Saez 1984). At higher levels, folk songs, Christmas carols, marching or drinking songs, historical songs, even hymns or operas (Vialet 1992) can serve pedagogical purposes. Furthermore, the texts of these works, often free of copyright restrictions, have frequently been published. It is popular songs, however, that reflect the current state of a society and provide the additional advantage of up-to-date examples of language and references to culture. Therefore, although texts and recordings may be somewhat more difficult to obtain, the result is definitely worth the effort.[5] Copyright laws on recent music make the collection and preparation of song texts an individual task to be pursued by dedicated teachers much as they gather and utilize other realia. Especially rich songs can serve as the basis of minilessons to supplement or enrich instruction in dual-level classrooms or advanced placement classes or to provide language activities that a substitute teacher can direct. Nevertheless, variety remains crucial to success in the classroom use of songs. In addition to offering a wider vision of the culture, such works can appeal to different musical tastes and offer contrasting images, attitudes, and registers of language. Students do not have to like all they hear, but they should learn to understand the content and appreciate the artistry.

The advantages if using popular music in the classroom are many and the drawbacks are few. The inclusion of songs in foreign language instruction brings an added dimension to language study that calls upon the senses as well as the intellect. Beyond the sounds and rhythms, songs exemplify real-life use of language and references to culture in a native context, providing students with elements of cultural knowledge possessed by native speakers. The richness of many texts furnishes an endless variety of illustrations, exercises, and activities that permit frequent use of songs without repetitiveness, yet with depth and some complexity. As contemporary works of art songs call upon students' imaginations and the necessarily brief expressions leave room for them to invent and discuss language, meaning, and behavior. The concepts presented here can apply to any language, while at the same time, each culture's popular songs remain unique. Thompson (1986, p. 39) cites the following observation from Angèle Guller:

> La chanson est le mode d'expression qui reproduit de la manière la plus spectaculaire et avec le plus d'exactitude le langage quotidien des hommes d'une génération et jusqu'au rythme, au souffle, à la respiration organique, aux tics, aux malformations, aux néologismes de ce langage.
>
> *The song is the mode of expression that reproduces, in the most striking manner and with the greatest precision, the daily language of the people of a generation, even to the rhythm, breath, organic respiration, tics, malformations, neologisms of that language.*

Teachers who have experimented with songs in the classroom can attest to their effectiveness in enlivening language instruction and encouraging student participation in a way no other medium can.

Notes

1. Seghers in Paris has devoted volumes in its collection *Poésie et Chansons* to many of the major French singer-songwriters. A list of current titles can be obtained from Éditions Seghers, 6, place Saint-Sulpice, 75279 Paris Cedex 06.
2. Videotaping such efforts offers students feedback on their pronunciation, and appropriate behavior patterns and body language can be analyzed. The song may even serve as background music.
3. I have observed that French songwriters, both of France and Quebec, deal more frequently with the particularities of their culture and language and write many songs specifically about cultural phenomena. The French appear very conscious of their culture in their work. On the other hand, while my collection of Spanish songs is much more limited, cultural references seem more subtle. Performers tend to illustrate cultural patterns rather than talk directly about them.
4. Thompson suggests a more lengthy presentation stretching over several days and allowing students to absorb meaning more gradually (pp. 17–18).
5. Both Muñoz (1970) and Thompson (1986) list numerous addresses and sources for obtaining printed and recorded materials.

References

Abrate, Jayne. 1983. "Pedagogical Applications of the Popular Song in the Foreign Language Classroom." *Modern Language Journal* 65,1: 8–12.

———. 1988. "Popular Music as a Foundation for a French Culture Course." *French Review* 62,2: 217–28.

Braehm, B. 1977. "L'Enseignement du français par le chant au jardin d'enfants." *Le Français dans le monde* 131: 23–27.

Brown, James W. 1975. "For a Pedagogy of the Song-poem." *French Review* 49: 23–31.

Caré, Jean-Marc, et al. 1984. "Manipulation de textes de chanson: illustrations de quelques principes." *Le Français dans le monde* 184: 57–60.

Chamberlain, Alan. 1974. "Modern French Music and Language Teaching." *Babel: Journal of the Australian Federation of Modern Language Teachers Association* 19,3: 15–18.

Cruz-Sáenz, Michèle S. de. 1990. "Hispanic Balladry in the Foreign Language Classroom." *ADFL Bulletin* 21,2: 30–33.

Garcia-Saez, Santiago. 1984. "The Use of Song in Class as an Important Stimulus in the Learning of a Language." [EDRS ED 240 872]

Herman, Gerald. 1986. "How to Make (French) Composition Challenging and Productive." *French Review* 60,1: 56–64.

———. 1987. "Pedagogical Techniques for Advanced Writing Classes: Verb Modification." *French Review* 60,4: 466–73.

———. 1988. "Developing Logical Thinking and Sharpening Writing Skills in Advanced Composition Classes." *French Review* 62,1: 59–66.

Muñoz, Olivia. 1970. "Songs in the Foreign Language Classroom." *ERIC Focus Report on Teaching Foreign Languages* 12: 1–10.

Thompson, Brian. 1986. *Le Clef des chants: La Chanson dans la classe de français*. Cambridge, MA: Polyglot.

Vialet, Michèle E. 1992. "L'Opéra en classe de français: du rock au baroque." *French Review* 65,4: 589–601.

Central States Conference Proceedings

Published annually in conjunction with the
Central States Conference on the Teaching of Foreign Languages

CREATIVE APPROACHES IN FOREIGN LANGUAGE TEACHING
                  ed. Hatfield (1992)

FOCUS ON THE FOREIGN LANGUAGE LEARNER: PRIORITIES AND
 STRATEGIES   ed. Strasheim (1991)

REALIZING THE POTENTIAL OF FOREIGN LANGUAGE INSTRUCTION
                    ed. Ervin (1990)

DEFINING THE ESSENTIALS FOR THE FOREIGN LANGUAGE CLASSROOM
                  ed. McAlpine (1989)

SHAPING THE FUTURE OF FOREIGN LANGUAGE EDUCATION
                   ed. Lalande (1988)

PROFICIENCY, POLICY, AND PROFESSIONALISM IN FOREIGN LANGUAGE
 EDUCATION   ed. Birckbichler (1987)

SECOND LANGUAGE ACQUISITION: PREPARING FOR TOMORROW
                   ed. Snyder (1986)

MEETING THE CALL FOR EXCELLENCE IN THE FOREIGN LANGUAGE
 CLASSROOM   ed. Westphal (1985)

STRATEGIES FOR FOREIGN LANGUAGE TEACHING:
 COMMUNICATION • TECHNOLOGY • CULTURE ed. Westphal (1984)

THE FOREIGN LANGUAGE CLASSROOM: NEW TECHNIQUES
                  ed. Garfinkel (1983)

ESL AND THE FOREIGN LANGUAGE TEACHER ed. Garfinkel (1982)

A GLOBAL APPROACH TO FOREIGN LANGUAGE EDUCATION
                    ed. Conner (1981)

NEW FRONTIERS IN FOREIGN LANGUAGE EDUCATION
                    ed. Conner (1980)

TEACHING THE BASICS IN THE FOREIGN LANGUAGE CLASSROOM
                  ed. Benseler (1979)

TEACHING FOR TOMORROW IN THE FOREIGN LANGUAGE CLASSROOM
                   ed. Baker (1978)

PERSONALIZING FOREIGN LANGUAGE INSTRUCTION:
 LEARNING STYLES AND TEACHING OPTIONS ed. Schulz (1977)

TEACHING FOR COMMUNICATION IN THE FOREIGN LANGUAGE
 CLASSROOM   ed. Schulz (1976)

THE CULTURE REVOLUTION IN FOREIGN LANGUAGE TEACHING
                  ed. Lafayette (1975)

CAREERS, COMMUNICATION & CULTURE   ed Grittner (1974)

For further information or a current catalog, write:
National Textbook Company
a division of *NTC Publishing Group*
4255 West Touhy Avenue
Lincolnwood, Illinois 60646-1975 U.S.A.